ON FOOT TO
THE GOLDEN HORN

Jason Goodwin was born in 1964 and studied History at Trinity College, Cambridge. He was the joint winner of the *Spectator/Sunday Telegraph* Young Writer of the Year Award in 1987, and has travelled extensively in the Far East and India. His first book, *The Gunpowder Gardens: Travels Through India and China in Search of Tea*, was published in 1990, and was shortlisted for the Thomas Cook Travel Book Awards in 1991. *On Foot To The Golden Horn* was winner of the Mail on Sunday/ John Llewellyn Rhys Prize 1993. He lives in London.

BY JASON GOODWIN

The Gunpowder Gardens:
Travels Through India and China in Search of Tea

On Foot To The Golden Horn
A Walk To Istanbul

Jason Goodwin

ON FOOT TO
THE GOLDEN HORN

A Walk To Istanbul

V

VINTAGE

Published by Vintage 1994

2 4 6 8 10 9 7 5 3 1

First published in Great Britain
by Chatto & Windus Ltd, 1993

Vintage
Random House, 20 Vauxhall Bridge Road,
London SW1V 2SA

Random House Australia (Pty) Limited
20 Alfred Street, Milsons Point, Sydney
New South Wales 2061, Australia

Random House New Zealand Limited
18 Poland Road, Glenfield, Auckland 10,
New Zealand

Random House South Africa (Pty) Limited
PO Box 337, Bergvlei, South Africa

Random House UK Limited Reg. No. 954009

A CIP catalogue record for this book
is available from the British Library

ISBN 0 09 999390 2

Printed and bound in Great Britain by
Cox & Wyman, Reading, Berkshire

J 2/09/94

Contents

Departure

From a long way off a traveller would see the city's massive walls; rooftops, domes and minarets mounting seven egg-shaped hills, and a forest of masts where sails unfurled like the tents of a crusading army. In the city (as it seemed) lay half the treasure of the world, and treasures that weren't of this world at all: the remnants of the feast of loaves and fishes, for instance, the True Cross discovered by St Helena in Jerusalem, a memento of Troy rescued by Aeneas, Noah's hatchet, and a single hair from the beard of the Prophet. The city was old and wealthy, tough and snooty. When Europe plunged into its Dark Ages, and hapless knights went questing for the lost Grail, Byzantium was bathed in light.

The city was old from its beginning. Constantine dreamed of a withered crone transfigured into a young woman, and founded the city, in 330 AD, to be Rome all over again, on those seven hills like Rome's, filling it with relics brought from every corner of his empire, so that its stones and statues bore witness to ancient history. The presence of these survivals from the past would perhaps ensure the city's future. The Arabs called it Rum, and the Vikings, high in the Baltic, wove it into their sagas as Mickelgard, Big City; but chippy German prelates called it every name under the sun, like Babylon, and were duly overawed if they had the honour of paying a visit.

An honour it was. The Byzantines believed it was the greatest gift a barbarian could ever know, to be invited into the city and to be involved, for a moment, in the perpetual ceremony by which it functioned, an order that reflected the order of Heaven itself. From where it stood, on the turnstile between Asia and the West, moated on three sides by the sea, the city ruled an empire, east and west; sent out armies and missionaries, gifts and retribution, and watched the barbarians, wheeling like stars upon its borders in their search for settlement: Goths in Italy, Magyars in Pannonia, Vikings on the Dnieper and the Don, Slavs in the cold north, Bulgars in Thrace, Armenians and Jews and Indians, even, who played music in the palace when the empire was most exalted – and scattered when it declined. They said the Greeks were soft, and weak; but the city was tough.

After a thousand years the city took fresh blood. The corpse of the last Roman emperor was identified by his red boots in a pile of bodies at the gate. The Conqueror styled himself Lord of the Two Seas, and was heir to another vision of the city, vouchsafed to his forefather Othman, of a tree with seven branches giving shade: the seven holy cities of Islam, all sprung from Istanbul. Once again the city ruled an empire east and west, sending out armies and missionaries, rumour and alarm; but slowly it grew dark under the chant of the muezzin and the threat of the silken bowstring. Its rulers fled; the panoply of state withdrew, and the city was dispossessed from afar, by men still wary of its influence.

Which is how it reached me, as a story slipping in and out of myth.

I learned that the city was in Europe, but I knew from the first that it wasn't in mine. I could point it out on a map: it made no difference. Europe had nothing to do with this distant city, piled on a city, built on a village called Byzantium, that rose so splendidly over its gong-tormented sea.

Nothing around it was perfectly real. That mirror to Rome stood at the back of a mirror Europe, too – a funfair mirror that distorted reflections, producing weird, implausible shapes. This other 'Eastern' Europe had concerned itself with orthodoxy and Islam and great land empires; its people sometimes fought them, sometimes succumbed to them, at different times and in different degrees. For forty years they had been embroiled in an empire controlled by a city which had, oddly enough, once claimed to be the third Rome: an imposture which hadn't lasted.

As I got older the myth of the city only grew. I studied Byzantine history. Everyone was tutored by a Byzantinist; they read scholarly monographs published in Dumbarton Oaks, where a man who grew rich in children's laxatives had bequeathed his house and fortune to further Byzantine studies. But I was side-tracked by a Magyar who wore thigh-high riding boots and her hair in a wild flaming mane. We drank Georgian tea, black with honey. She could take herself blindfold around the dome of St Sophia. She treated Leo the Armenian, last and most terrible of the iconoclasts, as a personal enemy. We looked at photographs of mosaics in Ravenna; her red hair tumbled across the page. We did not study 'my period'. We didn't discuss feudatories, manorial rolls, or tenurial reforms – she was not a tax inspector, as she pointed out. She spoke Chinese, Russian, Hungarian, French, German and English. She was born in Peking. She went to school in Moscow. But if she had been to Istanbul she never let on.

Some people care so much about the moon that they say the Apollo landings were faked. They want to preserve a mystery from men driving buggies and playing rounds of golf, so they point to the grainy texture of the film and the curious similarity between alleged moonscape and the country around Houston. I approved of their lunacy. Friends sent me postcards with Hagia Sophia on the front and biro arrows to show where they were staying, and once or twice on a plane the pilot had announced that we were crossing the Bosporus; but when I met the friends later I was astonished to find them unchanged – and then suspicious; and when I peered greenly through the airplane windows all I ever saw were clouds.

I didn't quite believe in Istanbul.

Then one cold, sunny November I cut my finger. The bright snap weathered over. At Christmas I bore a scar where the cut had mended, so slowly I knew I wasn't growing any more. It was a shock, something I had never considered – if anything, I thought I'd stopped growing years before. I hadn't noticed, and hadn't cared. I wasn't immortal any more, I was healing more slowly, dropping brain cells by the minute, waiting to need less sleep and false teeth. I touched the crown of my head. I was grown-up.

I wasn't ready. I wouldn't be any good at it. The flat was rented. I'd proposed to Kate so often it had become a bit of a joke. I didn't have what concerned relatives called a job, let alone a steady one. The bank took a dim view. Even the face that peered at me from the mirror last thing at night wasn't mine. I looked like a roué after a week of early nights and cocoa. I always appeared to have spent the night in my clothes. On the floor. In somebody else's house.

That night, while Kate was asleep, I ruefully picked over childish things; Father Christmas, and the crock of gold, and my sister's assurance that I would die before I was eight because once my pee had smelled of Sugar Puffs. I'd rumbled all these impositions and the myths of childhood exploded one by one. And it came to me sadly that my vision of Istanbul wouldn't last forever.

It was the last unexploded mine. Sooner or later it was bound to go off. One day I'd be stepping off a plane and Boom! That would be the end of it. But I didn't want it to go off by surprise. I wanted to nudge it myself, very gently. I wanted to keep my barbarian awe, earn the right to enter the city. I would run off into the wide open spaces. Forget buses and trains: it would be a pilgrimage. I'd travel on foot to Istanbul. I'd wield a staff and carry a knapsack and have the feeling of the open road underfoot. It was an electrifying image to spring from the gloom of a London winter. Under huge skies trod a figure with wild hair, great pockets stuffed with crusts and a gourd slung over his back. He was grown-up, but it didn't matter. He was a vagabond.

He strode around my head and after a while he complained that he was lonely.

'Would you like to walk to Istanbul? Over Eastern Europe?'

Kate was asleep. She suddenly opened her eyes and said with clarity:

'I can think of nothing more grim.'

'What, walking?'

'It would be terrifying.'

'What if we found someone to come with us?'

Kate pulled the bedclothes round her head, and made a sleepy noise that sounded like disbelief.

Mark liked to meet us in a pub when he came to London – a good smelly one round the corner done up like an ostler's buttery with barrels and sawdust – and then come home to eat and spend the night. He always did this, coming crabwise at our hospitality. Now he swirled his beer and talked slowly, as ever, about Istanbul. From him it sounded plausible. He'd eaten there. He described cauldrons bubbling at the restaurant door; he gauged the world by its second helpings, and Istanbul was his favourite place. He had stayed to paint, and learnt Turkish.

He was raised in Yorkshire on plain old-fashioned cooking, cowpie and pudding. As a child he built things, graduating from model planes and kits to devices of his own like a mechanical bear which drank real tea from a cup and returned it to its saucer. He had stacks of prewar Annuals for Boys and built whatever they suggested, scouring York for a chemist shady or old-fashioned enough to supply him with all the toxins and explosives, like saltpetre, barred from open sale, which he needed to make them. He once made a realistic spider that exploded when 'the house-maid' touched it with a duster. By the time he went up to Oxford to read Egyptology he stood well over six foot tall and 15 stone in socks, and resembled all his childhood heroes: bear-wrestling, viper-charming, maverick Foreign Office Arabists known through the bazaars from Alexandra to Lucknow simply as The Eng-lishman.

It was hardly surprising that he took to the idea. He had visions of crawling into haystacks, following railway lines over Europe by moonlight and accepting the odd crust or jug of ale from a surprised villager at dusk. We half knew it was make-believe; but we went through the motions. And Kate would see me poring over maps, or mooning in the windows of Adventure Shops, and she'd frown, with a kind of baffled scorn.

Pilgrims journeyed to improve their chances and to steal a march on death; pilgrimage was a firm act in a fleeting life, storing up such benefit in the afterlife that it seemed to open a tiny window into eternity. And pilgrims, like Chaucer's, set out to liven them-selves up, tickled by Spring.

Winter in England was giving ground. In Eastern Europe, as the papers said, it had been Spring all year.

Eastern Europe was like a rackety attic from which spies, writers and defectors were occasionally heaved out and paraded with a mixture of nostalgia and delight. In the attic gloom you could make out rows of winking medals, grey citizens in concrete blocks, anti-semites in the villages and thin intellectuals, chainsmoking. Then the Wall had fallen and sober commentators reached for seismic metaphors: upheaval, tremor, landslide. The pale faces of exiles, nurtured on dim reunions and moonlighting, bounced light into our sitting rooms on the evening news. Soon they'd slide off home, slide eastwards again.

For so long the tilt had been the other way. Eastern Europe had been turning out exiles for as long as anyone could remember, as some conquering power of man or nature drove refugees west, from all but the last Byzantine emperors, making his desperate tour of Lombard Street and the Bourse in 1400 to raise help against the menacing Turks, to the Czechs in flight after 1968. In between had come Jews from the Pale, and rebels now and then, nationalists after 1848 or the Polish uprising of 1868; white Russians and persecuted Jews; and of course the great tide of peasants emigrating to America in the late nineteenth century. My own godfather left Russia on a Lithuanian passport in 1924; my step-grandmother left Danzig for Paris between the wars.

I'd visited the Polish Government in Exile, when Poland was under martial law. For the old men and women in Eaton Square this was just another usurpation, like installing that first illegal regime in Poland on the back of the Red Army. The Polish Government had protested then and waved the text of Yalta. The British let them keep their grand building, and accorded them shadowy diplomatic status, but the Government in Exile became merely a nuisance, an unhappy reminder of bad faith and power-lessness, best ignored. They belonged to the wrong time, resting their grey heads on the antimacassars, ankles crossed, polished brogues gleaming in the weak electric light. The president lay in bed with a nasty cold. They signed treaties with wraith-like institutions sharing the same limbo as themselves: the Lithuanian Government in Exile, the Estonian consul-general.

The German Walter Benjamin once described the Jews in words that suited these elderly Poles as well: 'We know that the Jews were prohibited from investigating the future. The Torah and prayers instruct them in remembrance, however. This does not imply that the future turned into empty time. For every second of time was the strait gate through which the Messiah might enter.'

And now for these Poles, quite suddenly, the Messiah had leaped in.

At home I grew furtive, tracing routes across the atlas when Kate wasn't about. Before long I could pick out a line of march. It touched none of the capitals we'd seen on TV; my route lay through the provinces, always lagging behind: the small towns and villages where differences are more pronounced, where events move more slowly, away from the flashbulbs and the TV lights and the corridors of power, and all the pundits propping up bars in international hotels.

Our route was quiet, geographical. From Gdansk on the Polish Baltic it crossed lowland as far south as Cracow – all green on the atlas. It left Warsaw far to the east: Warsaw belonged to a political axis, on a line with Berlin and Moscow, and it didn't fall across the old trade route to the south. The route came up over the brown freckled Tatra mountains, and sank as the colours paled again to green on the Great Hungarian Plain. From there it could either drop south into Yugoslavia, to wheel east, near Nis, along the Maritsa valley through Bulgaria, or slant across the spotted amphitheatre of Transylvania, bordered by the high Carpathians. I liked this version much the best: my blood was up for Transylvania, though it meant – after crossing the Danube – tackling the double ranged oblong of Bulgaria from top to toe, against the grain: for mountains and rivers in Bulgaria tend from left to right, towards the Black Sea. And down there, but for a small tag of Turkey which I considered insignificant, Istanbul digs Asia in the ribs. There it seemed you could stand with the whole of Europe at your back.

It didn't look far. I worked it out, adding up numbers from a German road atlas. Three thousand kilometres, or thereabouts; 2000 miles. I slunk round the flat, hugging the figure like an atomic secret. Kate felt there were better ways of bridging the gap between traveller and indigene: grubbing about in mud and boots struck her as dim.

One night she sat up in bed and switched on the light.

'Where are you going to sleep?'

'In haystacks and places, I suppose.'

She said (again) that it sounded grim. She said she couldn't see why any farmer would want us on his haystack.

I tried to reassure her. She made me uneasy. There might, I supposed, be dangers. Kate sighed, frowned, and bit her lip: for she realised then that she would have to come along, to ward them off like a mine canary.

The protractor made the trip with ease, vaulting the mountain ranges as lightly as it bestrode the plains. But I got blisters popping out for cigarettes. I had no idea if a day's walking meant five miles, or twenty-five, and I read that if the beginner tried too hard his heels would split like ripe tomatoes. We ought, I knew, to go into training; it was more fun to go into shops, looking for boots.

Or so I thought. I had a pair in mind. They were brown leather, snub-ended and high-laced; they were built like tanks, discreetly; waterproof, immensely comfortable; twin arks for sailing over Europe.

But they were not for sale. We were offered instead the boot equivalents of firecrackers and disco queens. No-one else seemed to mind. Elderly ramblers became Malvolios without demur; vigorous hill-walkers took them in their stride; rangy loners and shy bird-watchers brushed past us to the boot-racks and sprang off with their feet stuck into distress flares. Jungle explorers wore boots that risked being raped by African parrots. Suddenly I noticed that everyone on the street seemed to be wearing screaming 100 per cent Mambo Hike-Teks or Laser Hillmasters. There was even a rugged purple boot apparently *de rigueur* on the Acid House scene.

Slowly we pieced together all the jargon. Our boots would have Vibram soles to last forever; double-stitched leather uppers with a cambrelle lining to 'wick away' sweat, as the trade revoltingly puts it; eyes and hooks of cadmium-nickel and padded bellows tongues to keep pond-water out. They'd have shock-absorbing insoles to protect our spines, and tailored heels to protect the turf.

We learned all this from the brightly lit, scientific outdoors shops which made, I felt, a cheery, bustling ring around London;

nature lovers sprang from them and out of the city into the Great Outdoors; their salesmen were earnest and concerned. There existed, though, an infernal inner ring of shops that were quite different. They sold webbing and machetes and stuff to dye your teeth black at night; cheap rubber boots that laced to the knee, kukris and assegais and Chinese army vests. They sold replica handguns, steel helmets, balaclavas. From these shops we learned to adopt an expression of geeky vacancy to meet the stares of all the survivalists and psychopaths who went shopping with us.

Some people said we might just as well walk in gym shoes. Kate and I had tea with the author of a book about walking, who recommended shoes and an umbrella, which he called a gamp. He thought we should travel south to north and take the good weather with us. We listened respectfully, and ignored everything he said. After all south to north, Istanbul to Poland, was plainly uphill. And anyway I needed boots: apart from collecting visas and booking our passage, the 'right gear' was all I had to bring me closer to the feeling of a Polish road. I looked at lines on maps, made lists of potential postes restantes, and bathed my feet, whenever I remembered, in surgical spirit to toughen them up.

We skeltered around London collecting visas. The Czechs diverted the crowds at the consulate with a video of two silent clowns capering through a dollar shop, smacking their lips at a stream of Western goodies. Everyone queue-dodged as much as possible. The Poles refused to handle Mark's passport. I was not entirely surprised. It seemed to have been stonewashed, and a rust-stained hole obscured the middle letters of his surname; we were forced to wait while he applied for another. The Hungarians were cheap and quick, the Romanians were expensive and slow but became quick in return for more money. The Bulgarians were unbelievably slow, but they didn't keep your passport so you could go round to everyone else while they drafted letters to Sofia.

Mark phoned from Yorkshire now and then to say he'd bought a thornproof waistcoat or a military haversack at a jumble sale. He had to be gently dissuaded from wearing a pair of ancient firemen's boots made of a dozen layers of oiled leather, and eventually he rang to say that he'd booted up on a brand available nowhere else but York, which he'd softened up by stepping off a ladder into a bucket of Nitromors. To round off his kit he bought a 1911 Primus in a tin box for 35p.

I surveyed a pair of boots and fingered my cheque book hesitantly.

'Superb boots, sir. The best, for any money,' urged the salesman, a wispy youth who was about to cycle to Australia.

I studied them again. They were certainly quiet. Depressingly so. There was a colour fashionable in the last days of the *ancien régime* known piquantly as *caca de dauphin*.

'I am going to polish them dark,' I said wildly, exceeding in that instant the bounds of the guarantee.

Standing heroically by the front door the boots looked right. I had polished them like ripe chestnuts. Their Vibram rubber soles curled slightly upwards at the toe in a sneer at the Way Ahead. They looked friendly about the ankles, padded in bulging rings like Michelin man or a fat labrador. The lace-hooks, the slightly bulging lowers, and the padded tongue gave them the robust, rollicking air of young Falstaffs.

They needed breaking in. I took dogs for walks, and wore the boots rather self-consciously in the street, stealing glances to see that they were creasing properly. The mild arc of the sole tilted my feet forward. They walked me up the Charing Cross Road where I found a book about walking and studied its training programme very thoroughly, lying on the sofa with my boots on.

It was a very good book. The author wore a beard and flared jeans but his advice sounded up to date. He was slightly hysterical on the subject of load-weight, I thought; he referred often and ominously to the kitchen sink. To my mind, the spirit of ho-for-the-open-road meant a toothbrush, an apple and a pair of socks slung in a satchel over one's back. It was the sort of stuff our predecessors claimed to have carried – Patrick Leigh Fermor, or Laurie Lee, or Leslie Stephens, or the gypsy-trailing violinist professor Walter Starkie – when they set out on foot in the bright days before the war.

The war, it seems, changed everything. We assembled our requirements on a spare bed and watched in horror as it spilled from the bed to the floor.

The sleeping bag rolled to the size of a large cat. We'd been persuaded to carry bright orange plastic sacks for climbing into and for attracting someone's attention in an emergency, which folded quite small but were rather heavy. We had heaps of socks: we'd have to wear two pairs at once to reduce friction, which causes blisters; the outer socks were thick and made of loop-stitched wool. Against the Baltic Spring I had underwear (silk and thermal), three shirts and two jumpers. I was carrying the first aid pack, and a radio my father thought we should carry, hand-sized wizardry of black enamelled steel with minuscule buttons and a comprehensive dial (it was also startlingly heavy and completely useless). The maps we'd gathered made a five-inch stack. I took a *History of the Jews* in paperback and a Victorian history of the Ottoman Empire bound in cloth. To these I added a give-away camera from the chemist and half a dozen rolls of film.

A knife. Boot-food in a tube. Half a dozen spare straps for strapping things. Two mess tins which I'd agreed to carry if Mark took his primus. A little sack of water-purifying pills, aspirin, pills for constipation and diarrhoea. A thick envelope containing travellers' cheques, serial numbers, photocopies of relevant bits of our passports, visa forms, spare photographs. A notebook, gummed envelopes, pens. Five packets of Bendick's Sporting & Military chocolate, very dark. A horrid water bottle made of rough pigskin which flavoured the water with pork. A pair of Chinese slippers. A loo roll. Needles, thread, two candles and a torch. Our only concessions to luxury, I thought, were the sleeping mats of foam rubber which rolled up and hung off the bottom of the pack. We used them once.

There was something deranged about the claims manufacturers made for their plastic hoods and cerulean tri-ply dripless underwear. Kate took me off to markets and jumble sales. She bought herself a black waistcoat with a big inside pocket for passports and money, a black cotton skirt, a big silk shirt and a wonderful woollen undersuit. I bought a thick black riding jacket that buttoned to the chin, cheating all winds and rain; it weighed a lot, and a glad Hungarian wears it now. She bought herself a green jacket, very light, and finally succumbed to a stack of eleven elderly cashmere sweaters, shrunk tight by innumerable washes.

'You can take two of those,' I said, authoritatively, aghast at the sight of so much kit. She discarded the one with tiny arms, but then put it back because she liked the colour. She put aside the sky-blue roll neck that might strangle a small child. Then she changed her mind. She took the lot.

To carry it all we had scrounged a couple of elderly canvas packs, which felt fine – but my father, who had been in the SAS, was so scornful that the day before we sailed Kate and I were panicked into making a trawl of the rucksack shops of London. Rootling in an army surplus store in Victoria I found a serious looking Swedish army pack with a flexible leather frame. I was trying it on when a voice at the counter growled:

'See vis? Gotta holster for it?'

There was a metallic clunk. I backed away from the pack and out of the door.

Nice salesmen were much against green packs; people could get into trouble wearing military gear. But the alternatives came in the same disco colours as the boots and we ran the gamut through a psychedelic rainbow all over again, dithering between internal or external frames, tall thin packs like crop spraying tanks, or squat ones with side pockets. We got our packs by five o'clock. Mine was voluminously military, and Kate's a neat bright baby blue. We both hated it on sight. I assured her that over the months it would tone down.

I was wrong. It remained electric to the very end.

Mark arrived, walking like a Cyberman under his load. He wore a black hat and moleskin trousers and a thornproof waistcoat and a red bandana. My Russian godfather was in London that evening; he took a dim view of Eastern Europe. There would be all sorts of unexpected trouble, he said: he'd experienced revolutions there before. He advised us to check in with our embassies, never to allow our passports out of our sight, always to sound out the country ahead, and not to walk at night. He wanted us to sew Union flags to our packs, so that we wouldn't be mistaken for the wrong side.

We didn't sleep much that night. Our packs at the foot of the bed made thoughtful shapes in the gloom. On a soft mattress the sheets felt sensible and warm, not like the glossy nylon of the sleeping bag. My passport and money lay in a leather wallet which I could touch for reassurance beside the bed. Soon the alarm would go off in the dark, and we would be off.

A car drove by, feeling the ceiling with its lights, and in the pre-dawn silence the alarm tensed itself, ready to burst.

Arrival

Purfleet-on-Thames looked half adrift, a straggle of houses perched on the bank of the estuary like migrant birds resting in the reeds. At their back stretched the marshes, a boggy place for infilling rubbish as if the bedrock of the island proper stopped a few miles short, and Purfleet rose squelchily on dustbin bags.

The houses ended in a grocery selling articles that housewives and sailors might want, mostly packet soups and pipe tobacco, and I went in for twenty boxes of matches, relieved to have remembered them and immediately anxious that I might have forgotten something else. The shopkeeper held the corner of her sari firmly to her shoulder as she bent down under the counter. I paid her and ran back to where Kate and Mark were waiting on the quay and staring at the SS *Inowrocław*.

I was proud of our ship, *Inowrocław*, of the Gdynia-Amerika Shipping Line Co Ltd. At first her existence had been shrouded in mystery, a name overheard by chance; even when I'd tracked her down it was so difficult to arrange berths that I felt sure I'd stumbled on a well-kept Polish secret. She was not, at a glance, a ship for quoits and deck chairs. She carried cargo – eighty containers, bound for Gdynia on the Baltic coast – and just twelve passengers in two-berth cabins. She was reasonably cheap – £136 a berth – but the journey to Poland took five days. Her chief appeal, I suspected, lay in her galley, in the meats and wines that would cover the captain's table. I'd told Mark we would feast. She even looked like a well-cooked *île flottante*, lightly caramelised where streaks of rust were coming through the white paint.

I gave Mark a knowing smile when, on finding our cabins, a steward appeared wearing a tiny bow tie and announced lunch. We assembled in the mess downstairs, smiling shyly at the other passengers and finding places to sit at a large table. The cook had the ketchup-red hair of a Parisian concierge and an expression of such ferocity that we instinctively ducked when she emerged from the galley, delivering plates for the steward to pass around. My eyes were riveted on a small side table laid for two, as if they expected lovers, and for a moment I didn't notice the glutinous paste on my plate. It was following the ship's list, to ooze around a grey promontory of meat and clasp a boiled potato in a floury hug. I sawed at the meat, added a lump of potato to the fork, and put it in my mouth. It was freezing cold.

At once I felt homesick and anxious. Purfleet was squared off in the window, soundless and thin like a photo in a frame. There were the cranes, the containers, and further back a solid row of council houses. I could have opened the window and shouted to the woman hanging out laundry on her rotary washing line, and she could have thrown me packet soups and pipe tobacco; but I couldn't get back. Purfleet wasn't adrift at all: we were, close to home and already abroad.

The other passengers murmured in Polish. The ship was caught in a time-lock rather like the house in Eaton Square where the Government in Exile had lived, only here it was 1974 rather than 1944: not antimacassars and standard lamps but squishy sofas in orange plastic, vinyl wood veneer, and swirly carpets that wouldn't bear looking at when the ship heaved in an estuarial swell.

The floor gave a low hum; cutlery tinkled and the goo on our plates began to shake gently. The shore wheeled slowly back and the woman looked up from her washing and then slid from view while the sunlight curved across the tables.

'Shall we go and have a look on deck?' Kate asked.

Mark shook his head.

'Finish my feed,' he said, happily. Kate slipped something formless from her plate onto his.

'Finish mine too,' she said.

After lunch we were all taken to a common room to watch a sailor demonstrate the emergency procedure. The man shook out a large orange bag, stepped into it, drew it up to his head, pulled a cord and disappeared. For a while we stared at the bag. Then there was a slight movement, and one of the Poles giggled. Straining our ears over the crackling plastic we could hear the faint squeak of a pea in a whistle.

Everyone laughed, but sadly: and I felt I liked the Poles very much for the sound we had heard was really the peep of a man overboard, trapped in a bag, going down at sea for the third time.

Ours was a ship of Rip van Winkles, for the Poles were returning home after months, if not years, away. They had collected so much luggage that they had to return by ship to carry it: boxes of equipment for the scientist who shared Mark's cabin, suitcases full of clothes and electronics for the rest. They brought old bicycles and new computers, jars of Nescafé and pairs of shoes. But they also chose the ship because it was a little Poland, easing them back like divers in an air lock, returning them to a country they weren't sure of recognising any more.

Andrjez struggled to explain what Poland was like. For a while all he could think of was that Polish had five different words for potato, rather as eskimos are supposed to have a hundred different words for snow. Most of the things he associated with being Polish were bound up with communism: the low and easy pay, the shortage of sugar, or truth, or convertible currency. He discarded them impatiently, one by one. History wouldn't help: when he peered into the country's past he grew confused. Before the communists there had been the Nazis; before the Nazis two brief, tumultuous decades of statehood and dictatorship in what sounded like a different country altogether. It had existed for twenty-one years, from its restitution after World War I to its collapse in 1939, not even occupying the territory it possessed now, shunted 70 miles further west, its eastern flank absorbed into the Soviet Union, its western regions incorporating land that had once been Germany. Then he had to go back more than a century to find Poland at all: for over a hundred years it had been governed as part of Russia, or Prussia, or Austria. Polish history went in fits and starts.

'Before Second World War, fifteen per cents of Polish people is Jews,' he said. 'But in Polish cultural life, they are many per cents.' This reminded him that he had seen a Jew with corkscrew curls and a black hat in London a few weeks earlier. 'Incredible! For me, a Pole, he is the first Jew I see.'

Being Polish had meant private resistance, and learning to read between the lines, and possessing a sense of the absurd. Sometimes it had meant getting away, as Andrjez had done.

Being Polish wasn't even an ethnic thing. His grandmother was German. His mother's family came from the Ukraine. He had a Tartar uncle and a brother in law in Cracow was Czech. 'Even the captain of this ship is a Pole,' he said.

The captain sat at the table I'd reserved for lovers: vast, Mongol-eyed, with eyebrows winged like Brezhnev's, he would nod across at us over a plate piled with meat and potatoes. In the terrible October storms, they said, he contentedly ate in here, alone. Mark loathed him, with a jealous passion, resenting his double helpings. He never spoke or smiled; he inspired respect. Sometimes we peeped at him on the bridge, where we could stand in the teeth of the wind near an area of deck marked out by red lines where the radar would cook your insides.

'So that he can eat them,' said Mark, cautiously pointing at the captain.

We tried to second-guess Gdynia, attempting to picture our arrival; and the possibility that it might be rather like reaching Middlesbrough (where the ship docked on the second day), gave me a sleepless night. We had stood on deck to watch the sea subsiding into oily whorls and threads where it met the descending river; the soft drumming of the engines as we glided in caused a gleam to widen at the edge of the mud flats, while the wind on deck remained brisk, smelling of salt and burning oil, blowing for miles over a clinker waste carved by straight black roads. A block of flats, marooned on its edge, shimmered in a haze of soot that spread from a tubular refinery nearby.

When we moored the rubber screeched. Beside us a Soviet freighter was taking on grain. Our own drab containers were being manoeuvred into place on the upper cargo deck and a boxy little vehicle from the port authority was shunting them into line. Some-one had painted a swastika, neat and black, on the driver's door.

We watched the crew beetle off in a minibus across the scorched waste to do some shopping, and felt forlorn.

But in the evening we pitched into the North Sea, stern first, on a course that would carry us east, over the Skagerrak, through the Baltic's mouth, and down to the bights and sandy spits that bristled from the Polish coast. Beyond that, we had no idea: no plans, no timetables, just packs and boots and maps.

R. L. Stevenson said maps bored only fools. When he went to the United States on an emigrant ship he wrote excitedly of the empty spaces that echoed across the sheet maps of America. It was called a new world, still to be made; the millions who followed from Poland and Hungary and beyond must have hoped it was true.

Eastern Europe looked snarled up. We spread our maps across the bunks, where they lay like wiring diagrams to a particularly fiendish computer. There are no straight lines on European maps: they lack that kind of innocence. Wily, crabbed, they surround you with persuasion like a barrage of touts at an Eastern port. They slip innuendo into place names, skip inconvenient details, and play odd games against each other with scale, with borders, and with politics.

Names carry unexpected resonance. Gdynia-Amerika, for instance, was an unlikely name for a company that for forty years had been the state shipping line. In 1936, when it was first created, it must have sounded very go-ahead and modern, very hands-across-the-ocean. America was mechanised farms and skyscrapers, but Gdynia was spanking new as well. It had just been built where the famous Polish Corridor met the sea: a new port for the fledgling Polish republic, avoiding the Prussian coast and the 'free' port of Danzig, a Nazi stronghold. The Poles were fantastically proud of their port. They built it in record time. Two years after it was opened the Germans seized control and the Second World War began.

Gdynia-Amerika now sounded less like a partnership and more like a line of flight, a route from all the choked-up, battle-torn Gdynias of the Old World towards the open continent of the new.

I looked down at the maps and gave a short gasp like a potholer lowering himself down the bore.

Even the trickiest maps were better than none: maps had been the biggest headache in our preparations. Eastern European cartographers were niggardly with information, tending to show a few fast roads that led from scheduled hotels to notable sights, and then away. The US Air Force produced charts of the entire region to a fairly large scale, but the charts themselves were far too big, awkward to wield in a windy field. They focused on geographical relief, power stations, 'works', and bore the sinister legend: AIRCRAFT MAY BE FIRED ON. Large cities were shaded grey and given names in minuscule print; towns and villages weren't even marked. It was a curious view, of a *Top Gun* Europe as empty and simple as Stevenson's America.

On other maps, wars and politics had bled over borders, leaving a slight impression like a slow dissolve.

Our route to Istanbul was covered by Bartholomew's *Eastern Europe* and Berndt's *Ost Europa*. They were both the same size, but Berndt could show more detail because of his *Ost Europa* was a smaller place. It took me a while to realise this. Bartholomew, the bluff Churchillian, showed you all those countries that ever lay behind the Iron Curtain, from the DDR to Bulgaria. Berndt, on the other hand, revealing an ambition to see the two Germanies reunited, left out the DDR. The blood then rushed to his head and he left out half of Poland, too.

The edge of Berndt's *Ost Europa* was a line which dropped south from Gdansk, excluding all the land to the west which had been ceded to Poland after World War II. A peculiar kind of archeologist, Berndt saw a border running through the middle of a foreign country like the shadow of an ancient settlement revealed from the air. One half he put in Western Europe; the other half he left out. It struck me as so exceptional and high-handed that for a moment I considered asking Andrjez about it.

Andrjez had a wife and two children in Cracow. He hadn't met his younger child. For two years he'd been working in London as a decorator, saving up to move his family out of his parents' flat and into a house he would build himself. He'd have stayed closer to home if he'd worked in Germany, and he would have earned more, too, but distaste had held him back. He knew that Poland belonged to Europe – Poland was an old catholic kingdom, whose soldiers once saved Christendom from the Turks at the gates of Vienna. And he felt that Germany somehow pushed it to the margin, creating a gulf or a wall between Western Europe and Poland. By working in London Andrjez had leaped it, successfully pretending it didn't exist.

I decided not to mention Berndt's map, after all. The more we talked, the more Germany figured in the conversation, until I started to wonder whether an obsession with that country was perhaps in itself the hallmark of Polishness, and that being Polish had to do with not being German.

As for the genuine Nazi map, we knew better than to even consider mentioning it. Dredged from the cellar of a shop in King's Cross it showed the whole of northern Poland, from Gdansk down to the old city of Torun, exactly as it was in 1942, under Nazi occupation. Parts of the map showed East Prussia, which had been German for centuries; the rest, though, covered occupied Polish territory, including the Corridor, and there wasn't the least indication of where the borders lay, nor a whisper of Polish – not a city, village, river or forest that didn't have a German name. It was the best map we had, but it was a creepy object; and the creepiest thing of all was that it wasn't old. It had been recently printed, mint off the press; its folds were clean, the paper crisp and white.

We were due to make landfall close to the sinister, invisible frontier of *Ost Europa*; we were preparing to chart our first steps by a relic of the *Wehrmacht*. I was glad to be travelling on a Polish ship, with a skipper who looked as if he'd walked right off the Asiatic steppe. With our boots, our rolled socks, our rucksacks, and our faces turned to the open air, we only needed lederhosen to make a picture fit to hang in Himmler's sitting room.

We sailed on a Sunday. On Wednesday morning we were told to be on deck to watch Copenhagen slipping by, and Elsinore like a stone box. A rash of tiny islands broke out around us. It was a cloudless, windless day, and as we approached a fog bank the sea was like oil. A few scribbles of mist slid across our bows, the signature of a new sea: we stared blankly into a cloud while the horn bleated and the engines, curiously muffled, ran on tiptoe. In an hour or so the mist broke up, leaving us on the oily sea, under the same high skies. We were in the Baltic.

The weather was good: the captain shut one engine down, as if determined not to arrive too quickly, not to miss the meals that still came round relentlessly at eight, and twelve, four and six and ten o'clock, always announced by the steward wearing his thin bow tie and a faint smile that suggested a private joke. We were given nothing to drink but sweet black tea from the samovar until we shyly asked for, and were sold, a bottle of red wine – it tasted like syrup, and derived from more than one socialist country of origin. The mess began to resemble a field hospital, spattered with tea and gravy. Kate found a cockroach baked into a slice of bread and a matchstick in her fruit compote. The compote came out of a jar and suspicion fell upon the fierce cook, who sometimes emerged to have a smoke with us after the captain had retired to the bridge.

One afternoon, five days out of Purfleet, the captain had the remainder of his plate of buns sent over to our table instead of being put away, and we guessed that this brought us very near the end.

Silence filled the cabin, like water; without the frisky accompaniment of the engines every action seemed as slow and idle as the motion of sea plants. At the window a grey derrick stood in stiff disapproval of layabeds in daylight. Shivering in the early dawn we went out on deck to look about at the port of Gdynia.

The sea had gone. In its place lay green water and the tidy edges of the quay, rows of brown containers, a few grey hangars and a perimeter fence of galvanised steel rods. A huge ship called *Feederteam* nosed to mooring without tugs: Mark said he hoped it had brought his breakfast. In the distance rose the Kashubian hills, where people spoke a murky dialect that ordinary Poles found hard to understand (otherwise there were, Andrjez had already told us, no dialects in Poland): but the hills lay west and our attention was focused on the eastern road, towards Gdansk.

Over the ten miles which separate the two ports, Gdynia and Gdansk, we'd hoped to make a leisurely stroll, playing ducks and drakes along the beach, paddling even. But we were well inland

and couldn't see a beach. I stared at a road instead that curved away behind railway sheds and considered the advice my father had given me. He hadn't been very impressed by the hi-tech insoles fitted to my boots, which were supposed to prevent blisters.

'I shouldn't worry too much about them,' he said mildly. 'Foot-rot's the miserable thing. Keep your feet clean. Wash between your toes, and always dry them properly. And in the morning you must piss in your boots.'

'Eh?' I had made him repeat it, to see if I could detect a joke.

The steward announced breakfast.

Andrjez tested us on the Polish they had all been teaching us, words for food and shelter – 'May we sleep in your barn?' 'Where is the *soltys*?' The *soltys* was the village mayor.

'Church?'

'*Koscio.*'

'Priest?'

'*Ksiądz.*'

'Farm?'

'*Dom wiejski.*'

'Amber!'

'Amber?'

'Yes, you find amber today – on the beach!' A jolly couple grinned and nodded. 'Very famous!' We added the word for amber to our vocabulary – *bursztyn* – written out on paper napkins. The cook suddenly burst from her galley and plonked a packet of sandwiches and an enormous pot of strawberry jam on the table; we were touched and tried to protest – the jam weighed two pounds – but there were tears in her eyes as she shared a farewell cigarette. We all shook hands as one by one the other passengers were called away to pass customs and immigration and go ashore.

We were the last called. While we signed documents promising not to import drugs and firearms, and documents that bound us to export nothing included in a list that mentioned sewing machines and underwear, I was summoned into the corridor where a stranger handed me a letter.

We had abandoned any hope of hearing from Professor Ziemnacki, the merest acquaintance of an acquaintance who had suggested he might be able to put us up at certain museums where he was curator. The professor now promised, by letter, to do so and, regretting that a visit to Germany prevented him from meeting us personally, he invited us to go with the bearer to the Gdansk Ship Museum, where we would be given somewhere to stay – vague thoughts of mummies creaking into life and sailors descending from their portraits.

The immediate problem was that the professor expected us to drive with his emissary into Gdansk. Kate and Mark were furious, but there was no way we could really refuse. All hopes of amber vanished with a pop as we followed our new friend to a Polski Fiat parked at the port gates. At first glance it looked as if we'd have to walk there, after all, but years of practice had taught our new friend how to squeeze people in. We were wedged into seats, with packs forced onto our knees; the doors were squeezed shut, and unable to see, barely able to breathe, we drove to Gdansk. I was ashamed to have started like this. I was engulfed in waves of claustrophobic nausea. Yet it could have been worse. I could have peed in my boots, too.

Our host at the Ship Museum watched the canal outside his office window, and gazed at its reflection on the ceiling, a gliding pool of light that swam like carp. Soon he would pile his Fiat with rods and lines and head east, to a small cabin he owned where the sea met a string of reedy lakes, part salt, part fresh.

'Actually this is a difficult coast,' he said, rubbing his nose with his thumb. The Baltic was a young sea, as seas go; shallow, the bed still covered by remnants of the forest that had covered it between the two last Ice Ages. 'So, amber. So, much sand.' The sand was always piling up in bars: the bay of Gdansk was formed by a long arm of solid ground that waved above it on the maps like the arm of a drowning man. The coastline bristled with these spits, or *haffs*, and they wouldn't lie still.

'You like much to fish?' The director asked. I had caught mackerel on a line, and, one evening, standing on a loch's edge, I caught treetops one after another with my flailing cast, and eventually a tiny fish I ate for breakfast. We'd drunk whisky, because it was cold, and smoked furiously against midges. I'd enjoyed it very much.

His eyes lit up. He had been considering the possibility of rigging up a line into the canal but he'd grounded on the difficulty of landing a live fish on the middle of his desk. I looked at the water and thought he didn't need to worry: it was oily green. On the opposite bank lay the first ship built by the Lenin Shipyards after the war, and behind her a row of modern buildings designed to recall medieval wharves, thin and gable ended, with styrofoam walls.

'This fish I catch,' he added, indicating a glum mullet head on a board, showing two rows of tiny grey teeth. There were fish everywhere, in glass cases on the walls and across his desk: I'd imagined they were his.

'No, no, for the museum,' he said, and coughed, because we both knew they were here for him.

He asked about our plans, and I told him we were walking to Istanbul. He nodded. It had nothing to do with fish.

'A long way,' he added, as if he'd just remembered the last time he walked there himself.

At last I asked him how much he wanted for the rooms he had given us – we had a small flat at the back of the museum, behind an exquisite model of Nelson's *Victory*: two bedrooms, a shower, a kitchen and a dining room. He waved his hand and said it would be nothing.

On the *Inowrocław* we had been travellers in the making, scanning the horizon, rubbing wax into the welts of our boots, and scribbling professionally in our journals. Overnight we were transformed into self-catering holidaymakers. Gdansk felt like a place we'd been coming to for years. In a touchingly domestic scene we made a shopping list and went out to change money at a bank – finding that all the shops had banking counters in a corner, as though the people of Gdansk, while standing in line for a loaf of bread, might take it into their heads to change fifty dollars into mixed denominations, and would appreciate being able to do so without losing their place in the queue. This was perfectly true. After forty-five years of non-convertible currency the Poles were playing the markets like Pierpoint Morgans, shifting from zloty into Deutschmarks, catching a drift towards the peseta and dumping dollars heavily on the international market.

They dumped dollars, in fact, with a persistence we found rather depressing. One of the last things I'd done in London was to change all our money into dollars. I had brushed aside Kate's query with an air of weary experience. Everyone, I said, liked dollars.

But the Poles didn't. Nor did the Czechs. The Hungarians and the Romanians, who would have said the earth was flat if it helped make bad blood between them, had cobbled together a common position on the dollar. Later the Bulgars sneered and the Turks wouldn't even accept them. For months the pound rode high. We changed fifty dollars each – we still got a ludicrous sum of money in return, thousands and thousands of zlotys, in notes that had started to mulch down.

Shopping is perhaps the quickest and most painless way to explore a city. The streets looked cobbled and old, enclosed by high brick gables and mullions, tall and thin and faintly Dutch: these looked like the counting houses, stores and dwellings of medieval merchants, squeezing up to the canal. But little in Gdansk was quite what it seemed. Nobody looked like Pierpoint Morgan, after all: they looked as if they ate too much and got too little sun, like the poor in all northern cities; they had curious muscles in their faces, and because cloth was scarce they wore clothes that looked like hand-me-downs: coats that barely reached the knee, suits that gave out at wrist and ankle, short skirts and tight thin jackets. Most of the men wore moustaches; Kate noticed several men pushing prams without babies: like smugglers, or people who expected inflation suddenly to soar.

Mark persuaded me to join him in eating a slab of heavy-looking chocolate cake which proved to be light and crumbly and tasted of nothing at all. In the market a man was selling chickens as fast as he could fling them out from the back of a truck: there was a momentary hiccup when Kate reached the head of the queue but the rhythm rapidly restored itself. Old women stood on the pavement with tiny bundles of vegetables at their feet: a carrot, a parsnip, a swede, skewered together on a length of cotton thread, or a single onion, or bulb of tiny garlic. Packets of Big Ben tea were displayed on car bonnets, and I bought a pair of socks, wondering if they were covered by the export prohibition. I wanted an envelope, and in the end I bought brown paper and glue and made one myself.

Dithering outside a shop that might or might not sell milk, we were hailed by an old man in a beret and a raincoat.

'*Guten Tag! Wovon kommen Sie?*'

I was embarrassed to find myself taken for a German and half-ashamed to be embarrassed. A moment before a white Porsche with German plates had screeched from a standstill down a cobbled street.

'*Wir sind Englander.*'

The man lurched towards us, tilting on a short leg.

'No. Kidding.' He said slowly. 'You know what? I speak English, right? You want know why? Okay, I was in the US army! Sure. I worked as a cook.'

He paused, enjoying our surprise.

'Hash browns. Over easy. Sunny side.' He sang them out like a stallholder attracting attention. 'I got friends in Toronto. Oh, yes. Also Polish men. Good life in Canada. Plenty money.' He nodded, struck by a thought. 'Say, you got any English coins? For my collection?'

I was about to say no when I remembered all the change I'd received from buying matches in Purfleet. I fished out a few coins, amazed by their weight. Polish zlotys would float in a glass of water: it took 15,000 of them to buy a pound. A pound was so heavy and hard edged, so crisply milled, I found it hard to believe, right now, that I had ever exchanged one for mere goods. The old man seemed to feel the same, and hefted the coins appreciately in his palm, whistling through his teeth.

'That's great,' he said. 'Great. Well, so long.'

We watched him stump away, and in a cynical moment I wondered if he had a collection, after all.

It wasn't inevitable that we should start out from Gdansk – the port of Szczecin further west would have done as well – but it was appropriate. Gdansk dominated the Baltic as Istanbul did the

Black Sea. Istanbul was very old. Gdansk was almost entirely new. It was of an age with Milton Keynes, and its outskirts looked modern, in the way concrete buildings from the fifties and sixties look modern and decrepit at the same time. In every direction stretched militarily straight roads between rows of flats, with abnormally wide pavements and patches of receding grass. In the middle, in a rough square mile, lay the Old Town, *Stare Miasto*.

The Old Town was new as well. Parts of it were pastiche-medieval, designed as an exercise by students after the war, and the rest was reconstruction. Sometimes I thought it had been cobbled together out of painted flats and canvas. In the evening, when the cast went home, without the usual daytime crowd of men pushing prams, or military drunks, or mothers in tight fat plum-coloured duffel coats – the buildings looked as if they'd tear if we poked them with a stick.

Gdansk was the effigy of a city that was buried on the spot: a German town called Danzig, blasted to pieces by Soviet guns at the end of the Second World War. After a bombardment that lasted three days, with scant military necessity, contemporary photographs show what might be a termite's nest, or a battered honeycomb.

Founded by German colonists in the twelfth century, Danzig became a trading giant, joining a band of ports and merchant cities in northern Europe that called itself the Hansa and enjoyed the power and prestige of an independent state. Danzig soon shrugged off the authority of its founders, the Teutonic Knights, enfeebled by their defeats at Tannenberg and Grunwald, and put itself under the nominal sovereignty of the victor, the King of Poland-Lithuania. The Polish kings were not powerful enough to extract much from the bargain, and Danzig was in practice free to run her own affairs.

The affairs were many and varied, and made the city rich. South of Danzig the river Vistula wound through a broad plain and carried grain barges to the port, where their timbers were recovered and used to build the Danzig merchant fleet that sailed to Russia, the Low Countries, and England. Carpets, spices, gold and precious stones came to Danzig from the east; goods arrived here from Byzantium, then Istanbul, making the journey we proposed to follow in reverse; from Danzig they were distributed through northern Europe. Meanwhile an 'Amber Road' ran south over the plain, crossed the Carpathians, and descended into Hungary, from where it led south to the Italian city states.

At the heart of a web of trading routes, Danzig became a fine medieval city with a tall cathedral and a huge town hall. If part of my dream of Istanbul was of a city where time ran more slowly than elsewhere, Danzig was a place where time ran very fast, where decisions were always to be made, and risks taken, and a weather eye kept on the conditions for trade; and the events that to most people were merely distant shocks, or interesting rumours, were to the Danzigers matters of immediate concern. The burghers cared if battles were lost or won, if marriages made new alliances, how empires rose and kingdoms fell. More than most medieval men, Danzigers kept their eyes clapped firmly to the kaleidoscope that tumbled their fortunes with the fate of others, constantly trying to gauge its effect.

They had an appropriate talent for measurement, calibration, and the use of scales. In England, where they were known as Easterlings, their silver currency was so precise in weight, so strictly honest, that it was adopted – as sterling – in admiration. To the minds of men bowed endlessly over ledgers and accounts, exchanging one article for another of equal worth, everything had to achieve a balance, everything was quantifiable. The Glory of God was measured in the splendour of the cathedral, the dignity of the city in the grandeur of the Town Hall. Through the ledger, and coin, and patient calculation, the value of Russian furs could be adjusted, day by day, against the value of eastern spices, and in 1700 Daniel Fahrenheit, born in the city, hit on a way to measure accurately the balance between heat and cold. They measured time with enthusiasm, too, and when the first sundial was installed on the tower of the Town Hall the Danzigers thought it was so beautiful they had a roof built over it, to keep out the elements.

Time, indeed, became an obsession. Money and time could be balanced by interest, at so many per cent; time itself, however, was beyond the normal process of adjustment. Life for death was one exchange that couldn't be reversed. Out of their ceaseless activity, their familiar acquaintance with ebbs and flows, glut and shortage, good fortune and ill, came a peculiar dream of immutability. They wanted everything they did to endure, while they knew that nothing lasted.

There was no mention of the thermometer now – poor Fahrenheit earned no commemoration or museum for himself, and the Poles, like everybody else, invoked the name of his victorious rival, Celsius, to describe the unusual early April heat. But the cult of Arthur that flourished here was embedded in the fabric of the city, where the *Arturshof*, the Hall of Arthur, was built by the side of the Town Hall. Statues were raised to him, and these early businessmen extolled the chivalry of the Round Table. They claimed that the king was sleeping, ready to wake: rejoicing in a fable that alleged to hold time itself at bay.

From England, Arthur was followed by the plague, thought to have entered the city in rat-ridden bales of English wool. Plague was a recurrent torment after that, and in 1602, during a virulent outbreak, the Danzigers believed that Antichrist had arrived. Beyond the gates, corn bolted and began to rot in the fields; farm beasts strayed; villages died and the roads between them disappeared. Fugitives from the plague began to wander in search of plunder or safety; the city closed its gates, too late, for already there were houses shuttered up, and soon there were none left to close shutters, lock doors, or guard the strongrooms. Some who escaped infection starved; others went mad. Plague was a spectacle so grotesque, such a dizzy overthrower of human effort, it defied rational comprehension. The Arthurian romance of eternal life turned sour. The myth distorted under pressure and the gift of life, a mystical blessing, reappeared as a terrible curse. For while Danzig was in the grip of Messianic fears, people were told of the Wandering Jew, and of his visit to the city.

The story appeared in a pamphlet printed in Danzig in 1602: it was the first mention of the Wandering Jew in northern Europe. The bishop of Schleswig, Paul von Eitzen, found him in Hamburg in 1542, sitting in church, very tall, very still, concentrating fiercely on the sermon, beating his breast and sighing when the name of Christ was mentioned. 'He wore no other clothing, in that very hard winter, than a pair of trousers badly worn at the bottom, a cloak reaching to the knees, and over that a mantle reaching to the feet.' The soles of his feet were two fingers thick, and hard as horn.

He explained that his name was Ahasuerus, and that he had been a shoemaker in Jerusalem at the time of Christ. In his ignorance he held Jesus to be a false prophet, 'a heretic and seducer of the people', so that he joined the crowd that bayed for his crucifixion, and rushed back to his house as soon as sentence was pronounced so that he could watch Christ passing by.

Weighed down by the Cross, Jesus leaned for a moment against the door post of Ahasuerus's house. 'The anger of the Jew rose up more than ever, and with curses he ordered him to pack and be off to where it was fitting for Him to go. Then Christ looked sternly at him, and spoke to him with meaning: "I WILL STAND HERE AND REST, BUT YOU MUST WALK." '

The Jew put down his child and followed Christ. He witnessed the Passion. Then he walked out of Jerusalem, never again to see his home, or wife and child, but wandering in foreign lands 'one after the other, until the present time. When, after many centuries, he came back to his land, he found it all laid waste and Jerusalem destroyed, so that he could no longer recognise it.'

Eitzen asked him for 'a true account of all kinds of things which had occurred in the countries of the East after Christ's birth and times. He gave a satisfactory account of that, so that they could scarcely wonder enough.'

He ate and drank little, seldom spoke unless spoken to, but spoke each language like a native, never laughed; and when he was offered money he took no more than two shillings, which he gave to the poor, saying God would provide for him. He attacked blasphemy. He had to 'endure his portion', he said, 'until it pleased God to call him forth from this vale of sorrow to eternal peace'. Only then would he cease to wander, searching for death.

He was met in Madrid in 1575, by Dutch ambassadors to Spain. He was known in Bohemia; at the beginning of the seventeenth century he entered Hungary. He was seen in short order at different ends of Europe, and he once overlapped himself, being reported simultaneously in Poland and in Russia. But it was the Danzig pamphlet that brought him to the attention of Eastern Europeans in general, and the Germans in particular, and supplied them with a new vision of a man who could not die. He was a far cry from Arthur; he was no hero; he carried the weight of history on his shoulders, and he was horribly dispossessed, friendless, exhausted, a wanderer.

Danzig recovered from the plague; the fear of Antichrist receded. But a new fear struck the merchant princes. Though they remained as busy as ever, their wealth was shrinking. The cause was Dutch competition, made ferocious by the discovery of the Cape route to the Indies. Danzig had distributed Eastern goods that reached it overland; now the Dutch were cutting it out, and the Hansa as a whole was in decline.

The Flying Dutchman was the Wandering Jew afloat. His story was a piece of Danziger spite. 'By God!' cried the Dutchman, 'I shall round this point if it takes me till Doomsday!' as winds thwarted his course around the Cape. His curse rebounded on him in full measure. Not only was he to be seen, under full sail on windless seas, by ships in distress; he was said to hail ships and try to give them letters to carry to Amsterdam. And anyone who touched the letters, or agreed to carry them, was shortly doomed to wreck.

But Danzig itself was doomed. First the mercantile glory withered away, for against the rushing volume of trade in Western Europe and overseas, this part of the world was a backwater, and Danzig a city up the creek. The day of city states was over. Danzig became a city of starchy-collared Prussian bureaucrats now drily engaged in totting up tax returns and local agricultural yields.

And at the end of the Second World War the city vanished. Its people scattered like fugitives from a plague city; the fabric of the city was destroyed, like the Jerusalem of the Wandering Jew. The *Arturshof* crumbled to dust. Even its name became a thing of the past now that Gdansk stands where Danzig stood, and if the modern city has copied some of its buildings, Danzig itself is gone like a Boojum.

On the outskirts of Polish Gdansk they made trouble and ships;

in Stare Miasto they made believe. We spent the evening trying to think up suitable words to a 'popular song' tolled by the bells in the Town Hall, with the unlikely, and emphatically unironic title, 'We shall never abandon the land of our fathers.' Mark fiddled with an enormous radio that drained the lightbulbs in order to warm its valves. Kate set about making a chicken stew in a big saucepan. I polished our boots with the proprietary wax, working it with my fingers until it was warm and sank into the leather, hoping no-one would point out that the boots were hardly worn and didn't need dressing, because I was polishing them for psychological advantage. I'd peeped at the maps and seen a maze of thin blue lines and next to no roads.

On the boat we had drawn up a route through Poland that would take us to Cracow, 300 miles south and not far from the border with Slovakia. On the smaller maps it looked as if we would just drop in a straight line until we reached Częstochowa, more than 200 miles away, and then turn southeast for the last leg into Cracow, skirting the edge of the Beskid Hills; as though no obstacles lay between Gdansk and Częstochowa, only the Vistula curling lazily across the page, drawn here and there by invisible declivities. As soon as we transferred our plan to more local maps, though, problems arose.

'These blue lines...' Mark murmured, peering over my shoulder. 'Can we jump them?'

I frowned. I didn't know. There were an awful lot of them. I had an uncomfortable vision of missing the further bank and being dragged out, sodden and cold, to spend the night in an open field. 'We could take the roads, instead of going across country,' I said. 'But none of them lead directly to Malbork.'

Malbork was to be our first destination. It lay about forty miles southeast of Gdansk, offering us a reasonable trek to establish how far we could travel in a day; and it was the site of Marienburg, Mary's Castle, the medieval headquarters of the Teutonic Knights. The professor had promised us a night there.

'If there are roads there are bound to be ways of crossing the streams,' said Kate. 'I think we should go across country.'

'Better take the main road,' Mark said.

'That'll be twice as far.'

Arrival

It was stalemate when we ate the chicken. Looking back, I think we should have been celebrating instead. It was the best meal we ate for six months.

Northern Poland Tends to be Flat

There was an angry hiss and a pop as the flame went out. Mark dropped a teabag into the kettle and we drank the brew in tin mugs, scorching hot, sweetened with spoonfuls of strawberry jam from the enormous pot. The kettle rolled down the bank and into the water. We fished it out with a stick. Eventually Mark and Kate stood up and hoisted their rucksacks onto their backs; and as soon as I saw the straps biting down on their shoulders I knew I was done.

My back ached. My legs were bruised. I had a crick in my neck and my shoulders rang like beaten anvils. Kate and Mark were prancing impatiently on their feet but mine had received the bastinado. When I stared weakly up into the blue sky I felt scorched hips and torn calves, and I could tell my vertebrae like a rosary.

I'd been mugged by a kilo of socks and a cheddar cheese.

But the others pulled me up, handed me my pack, and set me tottering down the road like an ant with a sugar lump.

Small fires crept along the ditches to devour the grass, although the flames were invisible in the bright sunshine. Everyone called it hot for April. In central Poland, further from the coast, they'd talk of drought, carry barrels on their carts, watch the thin soil bleach as white as sand and drink beer without regret when the samovars ran dry. Further south were the mountains, where snow and mist always lingered into summer.

But here on the polder, where our walk began, cautious farmers still kept their stock indoors, ignoring the sunshine that had followed us from Elsinore, where the captain made us come on deck. This showed the farmers to be shrewd: unbelievably it was about to snow.

When we walked from Gdansk the sun was up and bells rang congregations up the cobbled streets. We impiously breasted the flow, consoling ourselves with the thought that our walk to church had only begun, and would end, miles and months later, at the foot of St Sophia. Gdansk disintegrated into sheds and fields.

Hochzeit, Landau, Sperlingsdorf: tiny birds twittered in an avenue of willow. We threaded lanes between meadows and ditches and small canals. Polish maps showed a blank white space with a village or two and the main roads we wanted to avoid. Only the Nazi had a local's grip on the place, and named this polder country, all grazing land and water meadows, Danziger Werder, giving way to Marienburger Werder later on. The Nazi knew a place to cross each dyke, and would warn where the going was likely to be soft; he showed us short cuts, and pointed to hamlets the Polish mappers didn't know.

For the Nazi, of course, it was 1942. But the roads were the same, and the wooden houses, bright with coloured paint, were old enough to figure on the map. Even the ducks waddling up to the picket fences, and the chickens picking up their skirts and fleeing from us on the road, had ponds and yards that were down on the map, exact. Only the people had changed, and in the days that followed we discovered a land of exiles, a Polish crust that kept breaking over country that was German fifty years ago.

Today I was more concerned with cheese. I carried a one pound ball of cheddar in my pack, obeying the suggestion made to me the previous week by a man who writes professionally about Eastern Europe in general, and Poland in particular. He had been encouraging. 'But you'll miss the taste of cheese,' he'd said.

I was beginning to think I could live without it. In that book, the bearded walker had warned that for every ounce you carry you shift half a ton over an average day. You lift that ounce again and again and over the miles it all adds up. The cheese weighed 16 ounces. It was approaching midday. Stamping along I worked it out.

Four tons.

Four tons of cheese! I broke out in a sweat. The cheese, had I known, was sweating too; at last it burst as I plodded on, and impregnated all my clothes before time with the smell of old socks.

'Shall we stop for a bite quite soon?' I suggested, as soon as I had caught up with Mark and Kate, four tons ahead.

Mark nodded appreciatively.

'I've got that sausage,' he said.

'But don't you miss the taste of cheese?' I asked, my eyes narrowed. It was a good question. It threw him off balance for a moment, and before he could think of some suitable sausage-shedding riposte I'd thrown off my pack and begun scrabbling at the straps that stood between the cheese and the fresh air.

We ate it in a field for lunch, our backs to the breeze, and later, by chance, we found a smart restaurant where they sold us beer at the back door. The menu was made of knobbly leather. The list was written in Polish, very tiny, and ogre-ish German, very large; *Rindfleisch, Schweinfleisch, Sauerknochen.*

After Sperlingsdorf we came to Zugdam. Suchy Dom, argued the sign at the village boundary. It was already dusk, the bogey hour when villagers would be taking a last look around and locking up. It was a terrible time for three strangers to loom up, asking for shelter.

Two farmers turned us away, politely, anxious looks upon their faces. The *soltys*, the village mayor, came to the door in a vest and scratched his armpit; he didn't have a barn. Did we have a tent? Camp where you like, he said.

We didn't have a tent, but it seemed easier to nod and walk away. We camped on a haystack in the end, some way outside the village. Mark was pleased, feeling like a guerrilla chief, or a wounded airman behind enemy lines. We made tea, ate a handful of biscuits, and crept into our sleeping bags gingerly, trying not to drop anything.

'What a superb haystack,' Mark crooned. Somehow Kate had become knotted into her bag and couldn't make it reach above her waist. It was too dark to do anything about it, so she put on all ten jumpers. As I slipped deeper and deeper into the crack between two prickly rolls of straw I heard Mark mumble a toast to the haystack, 'the first of many'. The sky was clear and the stars looked frozen. In a voice fat with contentment Mark reminded us that sleeping bags worked more efficiently if the warmth of the whole body was allowed to circulate freely inside them. 'You must take off everything, all your clothes,' he said. But nobody moved. Kate pointed out that she wasn't actually much in her bag. I pointed out that Mark himself was wearing everything but his boots.

'But I don't really need efficiency,' he replied. 'My sleeping bag is very warm.'

There was nothing to be said. I folded my arms over my chest, and dreamed of cheese and a huge black dog that had reared at a gate, like a mutant bear.

A string of cackling ducks flew overhead, all but invisible as a crescent moon sank orange in the east. I dozed off. Hard puffs of wind brought the light.

Our bags were wet with dew. Kate had dreamed of pulling things out of her pack, including high-heeled shoes and a leg-shaving machine. We packed up speedily and set off back to the road. Pollarded trees made blobs above the low mist. Kate spotted a wallet on the road, containing cash, a driving licence and the ID of a young man with a moustache, and every twenty yards or so we picked up small tins of Heinz chicken and sweetcorn.

Farm dogs barked as we entered the next village. In front of the half-timbered village hall we sat on the green under a big tree and pumped the Primus. Storks had nested on the hall chimney. People were wheeling milk churns along the road on trolleys and bicycle racks; as the mist cleared we laid out our bags to dry off. Children carrying satchels on their backs crossed themselves in front of the church on their way to school. At eight o'clock we deposited our finds at the Posta. The post mistress, rather surprised to have her grille choked with money and sweetcorn so early in the morning, began asking questions we couldn't understand until, forgoing either a reward or an investigation, we fled.

That first day, and the next, we stumbled across a landscape that was as flat as the map itself until Malbork – Marienburg – reared up on a bluff, glaring across the river as we approached.

Marienburg was the cornerstone of the Drang Nach Osten, eight centuries ago, built when Prussia was a forest. In the forest lived a race of peaceful Slavs, the Prus, who spent their time fishing, hunting and martyring the occasional German prelate who crossed the Elbe for their enlightenment. For they were pagans, more blind than the Saracens in Palestine. The Order of Teutonic Knights, which was formed in Jerusalem and who found themselves unemployed after the fall of Acre, petitioned the Pope and the Emperor and were granted crusading rights over the pagan lands east of Germany. They fell upon the Prussians, taking control of their coasts, their fields and forests. They built castles and churches, and filled the empty land with German colonists.

Marienburg, the Knights' headquarters, was the largest, best-fortified castle in Europe, and it was never taken in battle until 1945, when it fell to the Soviet army after a siege of seven months.

Castles that reached the end of their useful lives used to grow old and ruinous and picturesque. Nowadays they are given over to restorers, working like undertakers primping with wax and cotton wool and rouge, preserving and improving a body once the blood is drained. There's a powerful temptation for the heirs to put the body on display. Lenin had wanted a simple burial; but the Bolsheviks needed him around, looking fresh, bestowing legitimacy on whoever possessed him. Perhaps Malbork fell into that category. Turrets stood proud against the evening sky as we approached, and the setting sun slipped along smooth walls.

The professor had promised we should stay in the castle that night.

At the top of an outer bastion we were given a room fitted up with grey carpet tiles and pine beds. The loos were on the ground floor, down fifteen flights of ill-lit winding stairs, and once or twice I rushed up the steps with the devil at my heels.

Der Teufel! We were tired, but we were very hungry, and went into the town for something to eat.

The town fell away from the castle mound like rubbish; at the bottom the road dwindled to a heap of garbage against the piers of a deserted flyover. There were three bars. The first had beer, but sold no food and banned smoking. The second bar allowed smoking, but had neither beer nor food. The third bar sold food and drink and let you smoke but everyone was fighting drunk. They kicked chairs and dabbed fists at their enemies, while we slunk to a corner table and pointed nervously at a dish of beans displayed behind a sheet of glass.

The food was so bad it suggested the canteens of an army on the move, probably in rout; we gobbled it miserably as heavy bodies hurtled past or crashed into our legs. The men of Malbork drank as if they wanted to be anywhere else but here; and if not out of Malbork, then out of their heads at least. When we crept back up the hill men in blue overalls slid around the pavement clutching bottles, and punching each other outside the liquor shop. We made a foray, took a bottle of wine, and drank it in our room; it was thick and sweet and gave us fur teeth and hangovers while we were still drinking it. When we went to brush our teeth the toothpaste had disappeared.

The sheets were cool and clean but I was afraid now that every Polish town would be like this and every village like Suchy Dom, coughing us up like bad germs to spend the night on chilly haystacks.

Behind the studs and iron that bound his turret door, Marek inhabited a snazzy world of stripped pine, poufs and fitted carpet. 'We will explore points of contact,' he'd announced, when we met him at the castle gates.

In his kitchen we were greeted by cheerful German voices, and the sight of a young man in a silver metallic jump suit. We all said 'Hi.'

I recognised a point of contact right away. We were hungry. They had food. They had German cheese and German butter; honey and jam and boiled eggs; they had plates of wurst and salami, and hot white rolls with golden crusts. They had pots of freshly ground German coffee. Since Gdansk we had eaten a pound of cheese, something like dog food (lungs, I think) in a gruel, and a plate of beans that tasted like soap.

Marek offered us some coffee. That was all. A point of contact shrivelled up and died.

Marek was the educationalist at Malbork. The Germans, four young teachers from Hamburg, had brought the food with them, and were over to arrange the details of The Game, to be played during the Summer holidays.

'This is a learning game, of course. For our young to understand medieval life.'

'To live in a medieval way.'

'We live here. We work together: baking, singing, everything medieval.'

'You eat medieval food?' I asked, squashing crumbs from the tabletop with my finger. The group leader hunkered down over his boiled egg, and I watched a smooth ball of white come away with a trickle of yolk from the middle. He held it in mid air.

'Sure. On our last evening we cook a pig on the fire.' He swallowed the egg.

'Two pigs,' added his colleague. 'And sheeps.'

There was a rumbling noise from under the table.

I wanted a cigarette but there was something about the flat that said no smoking.

The leader took a clean bite of pumpernickel, smeared with butter.

'And we have walkings,' he said. 'In the forest. Like – *wie sagt man?* – singers.'

'Minstrels,' I suggested.

'Exact. All the young sing, and walk in the forest. Marek must make surprise.'

'Surprise?' we echoed.

'For example. Polish young will make like robbers, to attack the group.'

'Or lepers, also. To beg for food.'

I glanced at Marek. He seemed unperturbed.

'Do the two groups, I mean the Poles and your children, get on well?'

'You see, the year is fourteen eighty. It's OK.'

We must have looked blank. One of the teachers said:

'This year, Poles and Germans are not fighting.' She giggled.

Marek had a map of the area showing all the local paths, which helped the teachers pipe their gartered and besnooded children through the forest to their next encounter with a leprous Pole. We pored over it covetously.

'Is there any way of buying such a map?' I asked excitedly. There had to be maps like this to the whole of Poland.

But Marek was unhelpful, pointing out that this scale of map was prepared for government departments only. 'Not what you can buy in a shop,' he added sniffily. Relenting slightly, he said: 'All through Poland we have many long walks, on paths. They are marked with colours. You can follow one to Kwydzin, perhaps.'

'And is there a map which shows where they run?'

'No,' he said.

On our way out, crossing the courtyard, we sadly assembled around a pink stain on the ground. Someone had sprinkled a little sand about. Kate tentatively identified it as the remains of the Euthymol toothpaste, which must have fallen out of her pack the night before. Someone had trodden it flat. The toothpaste belonged to a fragile battery of potions to alleviate the barbarity of life on the road. Mark scuffed the remains with his boot. He liked to brush his teeth by rubbing them on a corner of his shirt.

On the day we left Malbork we spent the morning doubling paths through a wood, and in the afternoon we blundered through a hamlet away from any road, where dirty children stared open-mouthed and curtains twitched at the windows of a concrete block embedded in the sand. We crossed a ragged heath and entered a forest as dusk was falling. Pine needles slurred underfoot and the sand track churned like a ship's wake. We followed red marks on stones and trees until it was too dark to see them and we stood irresolutely at a fork in the track.

Through the trees a house light burned.

We crept closer. A dog plunged against its chain, scenting our approach. Somebody moved at the fence, a silhouette against the dim light cast from the farmhouse porch. Our footsteps were muffled in sand, but I could hear my own breath, the dog's growl, and the creak of the wicket where the farmer leaned.

Out in the shadows I felt like a watching ghost.

'*Dobry wiec*,' the farmer said suddenly: good evening There was a question in his voice. We broke out into the light. Mark took off his hat.

We explained we were lost. The farmer offered directions, adding that we had ten kilometres to go. He saw the look that

41

must have crossed our faces because he took a step back and opened the gate.

'Please come in,' he said. 'You can sleep here. My name is Leon,' he added, shaking hands, while the dog's tail thumped in the dust.

Leon did more than let us in – he pulled us from one kind of journey into another, where there would be no more haystacks. We'd been ghosting through the landscape, eating and sleeping and moving on down a kind of tunnel that might open on Istanbul – moving like a band of peculiar earthworms, all alimentary tract, but blind: so that Suchy Dom might have been Zugdam, and every step was fraught with disbelief. But from here, right the way across Eastern Europe, someone was ready to shelter us at night, in a barn, or in beds, in straw or feathers. Often we'd be fed as well and talk, in broken languages, until our heads began to nod. In the morning we'd try to pay, but as a rule our offer was rejected with dismay, and we were given something – bread or sausage – to keep us going through the day. In the hours of light we plodded south, making encounters close to dusk, founding friendships, learning a language; we took soundings from the country, and anchored ourselves at night. Our walk became more of a daily exploration than one long haul to Istanbul.

Leon's impulsive gesture stirred the first ripple of trouble: because while one of us, at least, felt that walking was warranted by hospitality like this, another had an eye on Istanbul, and didn't want to be drawn in, over the threshold, from the quiet shadows into the light.

After the gloomy arcades of frigid pines the kitchen was yellow and hot. We were seated at the kitchen table. Leon fetched a jug of milk while his sister fed us liver sausage and carved great wedges of bread, holding the loaf against her chest. Mark was taller than Leon by a head, and scarcely less broad, so old Mrs Lis, Leon's mother, clapped her hands and made no secret of her admiration, winking at Kate and giving me a commiserating chuckle. I tried to look bright but I felt pale and earnest and ridiculous.

Kate was too tired to eat much, but Mark and I had to struggle to rein back. Mrs Lis told her son to make us tea and he swung the kettle to the stove, riddling the grate. I was mesmerised by the stove. It was built of bricks and clay. It heaved up through the wooden floor like a stifling mushroom, brilliantly white-washed, past the riddling pan and the oven doors, mounting higher and higher by shelves and rings until it flattened out, six feet tall, broad and long to take a mattress in the winter. A thick black pipe festooned with drying socks and vests shot through the ceiling overhead. It was the kind of stove that was built in the north before the house itself. When the ground was cleared the *zdun*, or stovemaker, would be called in to set the hearth and raise the stove, a job too skilled and important to be undertaken by anyone else. The house, of wood and wattle, was wrapped around it.

This one was wrapped round Mrs Lis, as well. She was round and fat, rammed into a high-backed chair like a dropped weight, generously shelved at bust and lap, planting two stout mottled legs on the floor and radiating a stovish warmth.

'Istanbul! Oy oy oy!' she cried, raising her hands and then miming her legs worn away to the knee. 'On foot! No hitching! Oy oy oy!'

Leon had raced us round his farm – the barn, three cows, a suckling sow and a pallet of piping chicks under a low-watt bulb: I saw generations of Lis giants, sweeping back the trees, planting a stockade, raising a farm in the forest where the track forked.

I was wrong. Mrs Lis began to speak about somewhere so flat and treeless you could see the curve of the horizon. She smoothed the air with an outstretched hand, palm upwards, swaying from side to side. It was really beautiful, she said, and she pronounced it with long vowels: Ukraine, where she'd lived as a girl, 500 miles east. She shook her head. She'd left like all the other refugees, by cart and on foot, taking lifts, using the train, carrying next to nothing: fleeing her homeland as it was sequestered by the advancing Soviet army, pushing their borders closer to the west. (Leon seized a broom and swept the invaders across the floor – '*So – wi – etski!*' The Russians were pulling out of Poland. His mother smiled.) She had never really liked it here; it wasn't Lis country at all. She sketched waves in the air. It was too hilly.

We'd walked for days without a rise or a prospect. When I

looked at Mrs Lis in sleepy astonishment she yawned, and smiled. 'This was a German farm,' she said.

We'd pestered Mark to make a drawing: now it was growing late. Leon laughed and joked and struck poses at the table while Mark measured him with a pencil; but soon he yawned, and smiled sleepily, and his eyelids began to sink, while Mark stayed half an expression behind, rubbing out, redrawing, racing to catch up.

'There,' he said at last. Leon jerked upright.

'Waa – uh?'

It was a portrait of Leon fast asleep.

They put us into beds, a double for Mark and I, a single for Kate, in a sitting room at the back of the house where all the sofas folded out. We lay in our sleeping bags and talked about Mrs Lis' journey, and the fresh warm milk; and remembered the chill of the forest, until our responses came more slowly, and finally stopped altogether, and the only sound in the house was breathing.

It snowed the next day, rather feebly, like dandruff; in half an hour it was over. In the small town of Rijewo I plucked up my courage to ask a chemist for a laxative: to my relief she spoke good German and sold us a chocolate button. Outside we found Mark being thanked by a drunk for entering the war on the Polish side. Mark was looking gracious.

Kwydzin – another old German town, Marienwerder – had a hotel close to the railway station. It was the first we'd seen, and I wished the Germans back immediately. The walls were nicotine, the sheets too small for the beds; the carpet was a grey rag and nylon curtains choked with dust hung limply across the windows. From the state of the loos it was obvious that every guest had stopped off in Rijewo to pick up the chocolate button.

The functions and foibles of the body were becoming obsessively interesting. We filled our days with innumerable minute experiments: wearing our socks outside our trousers, perhaps, or no coat. In Gdansk we made a pact never to wash our hair again, thanks to a woman someone had seen on TV who claimed this was the secret of her glossy locks. Anyone could follow her, she said; it took three months to achieve results. We decided to try it out and ditched a heavy bottle of shampoo.

For a week our hair had been getting heavier. In Kwydzin I started to scratch.

Mark woke up to an enormous blister spread between his toes, having dreamed of amputation in the night. He peered crossly at his foot. He had always scorned our boots; I was secretly ashamed of them as well. They were Italian. They came from a long line of crocodile loafers and thin-soled brothel-creepers, with an indelible whiff of Gucci handbags and tight-bottomed trousers. They pampered our feet, like a pair of suave waiters. Mark's boots were made in Lancashire, cousins to tacketty boots and hobnails. They were manly and bluff. Now Mark had to lance his blister using a hot needle, not daring to meet our eyes.

Father Topowski turned on his heel.

'In Poland speak Polish!' His cassock billowed angrily as he stalked from the church.

'Priests,' snorted Mark. Mark's anti-clericalism seemed uncharacteristically continental. It stemmed from an afternoon he'd spent tramping around Yorkshire looking for a willow he could make into a walking stick. He had stopped to rest in the cool of a church, where the vicar found him, dishevelled, fast asleep, slumped in a pew with a billhook in his hand. Mark woke up to find two detectives preparing to question him about a recent murder. The vicar had flitted around at a safe distance, and put his sacristy at the policemen's disposal.

The passengers on the *Inowrocław* had told us to go to the church if ever we were stuck for shelter, and I had thought we looked rather quaint, leaning on our sticks at the church door, bowed by our packs, waiting patiently for the priest to emerge after Mass. But he had been a long time changing his robes, snuffing the candles, drinking the communion wine; when he saw us he seemed annoyed.

We introduced ourselves in Polish. He kept interrupting to say that he didn't understand, tapping his foot impatiently. It was odd, when less well-educated farmers got our meaning easily enough.

At last I said: '*Sprechen Sie Deutsch?*'

And he shrieked: 'In Poland speak Polish!'

We took a few helpless steps after him, and he wheeled on us impatiently. *'Milicja!'* He waved his hand as though he were shaking his fist. We weren't sure if he was advising or threatening us, and we had to dawdle at the roadside to let him scooter out of sight, before we turned up the unmetalled fork on the forest side of the tracks.

Hamlets roosted in the gap between the forest road and the railway line. We approached a woman with a clutch of small children, to ask for water. She darted quick looks up the way we had come and put her hand to her hair; Mark and I waited by the gate while Kate drew water, the children crowding round inquisitively. A rickety wooden barn leaked comfortable straw but she was alone and we thought it better not to ask for shelter.

We were resigned to sleeping in the wood. We made one last sally down a track into one of the little villages, with a brick schoolhouse, farms presenting yards and a wicket fence to the track, and, miraculously, a shop which was still open. We entered for supplies.

Like most Polish shops the shelves behind the counter were almost bare, except for a few loaves of bread which might have been there for days. Polish bread was always rather tough. I asked for bread. A tipsy farmer followed in, kissed the ladies' hands and shook the men's, asking what we were doing.

'Istanbul? On foot?' The shopkeeper was amazed. 'Where do you sleep?'

It was the practical question most settled people asked, and it couldn't have come at a better time.

'In barns. Is there anyone in the village who might let us sleep here?'

Mark and Kate, having reconciled themselves to sleeping out, were eager to get settled before darkness fell; a conversation now risked us blundering through forest at night. The people put their heads together.

'Perhaps you should see the German woman.'

They directed me to a farm across the way; Mark and Kate remained to finish shopping.

I found two men in the cow-shed, one plump and dull-eyed with a page-boy haircut, the other dark and saturnine. He looked me up and down and asked for my passport, which he read studiously aloud, turning the pages with dung-smeared hands and struggling slowly through every word from Afford the Bearer until he arrived at the Polish visa and started trying to decipher the consul's signature. The light was failing; I suspected that he would turn me down after enjoying himself with the passport. Both men offered cigarettes. I took the passport reader's Mosne 'Strong', which gave me hiccups. Kate and Mark came up and together we had to explain where we'd slept the night before. He walked backwards and stopped, making a sleeping posture with his hands on his cheek: when we understood we said a barn. A reassuring fib.

The dark man's wife came out to join us, her round and smiling face done up in a kerchief.

'May we sleep in your barn?' We asked, pointing to a big building of wood and plaster which enclosed the farmyard.

They shook their heads. No. It was too cold. The woman smiled and said we should have some tea.

We left our packs and boots on the doorstep. At the end of the room stood a tropical fishtank – this in a country where it was hard to buy an envelope. In the kitchen a shrunken, beady-eyed old woman with a pinched face and slightly protuberant teeth was peeling potatoes; she wiped her hands on her apron and shook hands.

We were invited to sit on a sofa in a long thin room like a railway carriage, facing a wall of shelves, recesses and small glass-fronted cabinets with a display of children's toys – dolls, trains, spaceships and cars moulded from gorgeous plastic. Meanwhile the room was cunningly transformed: parts were folded out, unclipped, swung round, tucked in: by a sort of wooden origami a table and bench were conjured up.

It wasn't poverty, especially, or lack of space, but an economy of cold, fitting three rooms into one wrapped around a source of heat. The table was laid with a small feast – *crostini* of mushrooms and tomatoes, slices of bread and sumptuous battered flounders. The two men passed out bottles of beer and insisted we eat; Theresa joined us only when nearly everything had gone and when we apologised for eating so much her husband mimed secret stove-side snacking in the kitchen, and squeezed her affectionately.

When the table was cleared the grandmother lowered herself onto a chair with her knuckles pressed against the table top.

She smacked her lips.

'*Das Bier ist gut?*' The villagers called her the German woman: her voice was reedy. We said the beer was good. She watched us steadily. 'Ach, was, not so good as city beer. Gdansk, Cracow, Warsaw – they know about beer there. This country stuff has no strength.'

She pursed her lips, unsmiling, watching us. The fat friend shifted slightly on his chair and put his hand to his glass as if he meant to drink; instead he slowly rocked it back and forth. I didn't think she was German – it wasn't her first language. I wanted to ask, but her peppercorn stare made me uncomfortable.

The TV hollered at my back. Nobody watched it, but they wouldn't switch it off until they went to bed. It ran old films, serials, quiz shows and the occasional documentary – there had been one about the Katyn massacre the night we stayed with Leon Lis. The presenters from Warsaw were dressed in suits; the women had aggressive shoulder pads and tidy coiffures; in farmers' kitchens they managed to look weird. Country conversations, however, were always conducted at a shout, a habit among people who spent most of their time out of doors; the TV was turned up in competition. Since nobody ever paid it any attention it jabbered and blinked all evening like a demented relative nobody even noticed any more.

Over a frantic whirl of violins, I raised my voice.

'You speak good German.' Behind me came the sound of a coughing engine and the cluck of chickens scattering in a yard. The old lady pursed her lips again and blinked warily.

'Miz Abby come! Miz Abby come!' A smooth narrator began translating into Polish.

'*Ich bin ursprunglich Russisch*,' said the old lady: Russian by origin.

Mark's eye flickered towards the TV set. 'Why, hullo Charles. Yes, I'm home.'

'From the Ukraine?'

'And a mighty fine thing, too, Miz Abby. Welcome home.'

'*Nicht, nicht.*' She frowned. 'I was born in Donetsk. Factory city.'

I've checked on Donetsk. It's a city north of the Sea of Asov; it was never Polish. She was Russian for real, then: why here? Why speaking German? And why did the villagers call her the German woman?

Kwydzin, she told us, was a German town, and this had been a German farm; but Grejewo was Polish.

Their first offer was to let us sleep on the floor of the empty schoolhouse. Later they suggested we stay in the house, where there was a sofa and carpet and it was warm; but it was impossible to guess where the family themselves might sleep, and we didn't want to crowd them out. Theresa walked us over after we'd said good night. Grandma sat at the table, thoughtfully picking her teeth.

The schoolroom had benches around the walls and a broken sink. We had our sleeping bags out on the floorboards when the farmer arrived with his quiet friend and a bottle of *schnapps*. Glasses were found in a cupboard: we chinked them together and said *Prosit! Nasdrovie!* Cheers! He explained how to knock the liquor back and stop it with a glass of water before you breathed, to prevent the afterburn from roaring out of your nose and making you sneeze. Theresa returned, and we talked about her uncle; the farmer drew a diagram and dates on the first piece of paper that came to hand, showing how her uncle had spent the war in London, and returned to Poland. When he saw that he'd written across the back of my visa form he made a good play of the Malbork dungeon. We examined his stock of German: *schnapps, prosit* and *Hande Hoch*. We all knew that. Eventually he turned the bottle wistfully upside down over Kate's glass, and they left cheerfully.

On the floor of the old schoolroom I lay awake, thinking it over. Through the skinny quilting of my sleeping bag the floor was knuckle hard. Once it rained, and the cracks and plops that followed the downpour kept me alert. 'In Poland speak Polish!' the priest had screamed. But the German woman – who was she? How had she wound up here, reefed on an obscure little village on the northern plain, jetsam churned up in the wake of war?

In the morning, the schoolroom windows were cracked with frost; outside it was warmer. A breakfast of smoked pork, blood sausage studded with little cubes of fat, a glazed loaf of hard unsalted bread and a chicory drink was waiting for us when we went over to the farm to say goodbye. We asked if there was anything to see in Grundiaz, which we planned to reach before evening. Alexei laid his hands on the table and said: 'Grundiaz is very beautiful.' His wife gave him an enquiring look and shrugged her shoulders. The old lady sucked her teeth and her mouth puckered with a smack.

'*Das ist ein kleines Stadt*,' she said.

Kate gave the daughter a cashmere jumper before they walked us two miles down the forest road. I took a photo, and we waved goodbye.

On the print they look weaker than I remembered, almost sickly. The pretty granddaughter has a thin, peaky face; her grandmother's eyes are sunken in their sockets, her mouth seems awry. By contrast the three of us look startlingly healthy, weatherbeaten, cheerful.

My feet felt less like roasting puffballs since they'd cooled and shrunk. Although my legs still had to be helped into bed at night they didn't get drawn on the rack while I was asleep. We had slipped at last into a rhythm, which made everything easier and less exhausting, like a big whisky, or television. My boots swung up and down like dumbells. I stopped wondering why we were here, gaining so slowly on the road that an observer in a balloon would probably assume we weren't moving at all. After the first chilly mile in the morning our feet and hands warmed up. It was true that my pack annoyed me. Whenever I took it off I felt that I was about 70 feet tall, with long spindly legs, and that I could walk ten leagues in as many minutes. As soon as I hoisted it up again it gripped me like the Old Man of the Sea, a fat, unwelcome passenger; and for all my attempts at cinching the waistband and adjusting the shoulder straps I still sensed it enjoying the scenery over my bowed head, teetering up there like the headress of a character from Peking Opera, only heavier.

After the pain, your body grows entertaining. Frankly it is all you've got. To your left the ground is ploughed and flat. To your right, flat and ploughed. The road ahead dwindles into the trees that line it; behind, the trees eat up the road. You could grow a beard. Tonight you may get a chance to cut your toenails, to stop them growing through your boots; you have not yet found the right combination of light and privacy to perform the operation. Being hot you could stop, take off your coat, roll it up, strap it to your pack; and perhaps you will be too cold instead. You think of your unwashed hair, rising and falling like a cake, though it looks alright, if dusty, perhaps; and soon, when you stop, you will swap your socks around, left sock to right foot and vice versa, which may resemble wearing a new pair. And perhaps, swinging your stick, you'll start to sing.

We sang a lot. We chose songs by theme – sleep songs, roaming songs, food songs, drink songs – mostly food songs. We were always hungry. Shy animals in the forest fled the approach of a trio of Fats Wallers shouting 'Fish! Fish! Fish!' Farmers treading behind the plough found themselves asked to do the mashed potato.

When the rhythm of walking was smooth I had the sense of turning a drum with my feet, watching the scenery scroll slowly by. Turning the drum made my feet ache, but there were very few cars, no white lines or traffic signals, only ploughmen taking their horses to the fields, tractors towing trailers with pigs; and the occasional bus. The roads of Poland are beautifully planted. From a little rise, or an upper window, you can see where roads run across the plain by following the line of trees, slanting between the furrowed open fields. The soil was pale, like sand; and the trees were just coming into leaf, as fresh to the landscape as we were.

Poland was a country with a top and a bottom but no sides, only this plain rolling west and east to Germany and Russia. The land was destitute of natural barriers, with nothing to stop a people on the move, the spread of language, or a marching army.

Medieval Poland was a sprawling empire, its gigantic borders touching the Black Sea in the south, the Carpathians, the Urals, and the Baltic: an empire that spread outwards like a pool from the Vistula until it reached some distinctive, defensible line on raised ground. Poles met face to face with Ottoman Turks pushing north from Istanbul, and the two camps were interlocked, almost like friends, dependent at least on each other's enmity. Neither empire was prepared for the new powers rising against them. In the seventeenth and eighteenth centuries the Tsarist empire in the east, resurgent Prussia, and the Habsburg empire all broke through Poland's extended lines of defence: then central Poland was doomed, as well. The Poles had nothing to fall back upon, only this vast, near-featureless plain where armies could easily march and wheel. In 1795, claiming that the Poles were incapable of governing themselves, the three powers blithely carved Poland up between themselves, leaving a little principality to rule itself in Cracow. From then until 1918 there was no Poland at all.

From time to time we passed relics of one occupation or another. The Germans, for instance, had laid branch lines to carry troops, or POWs, or Jews destined for the extermination camps that they built in occupied Poland. In town squares stood the liberators' tanks, graffitied now; wagons on the railways stencilled with cyrillic letters. Even little things could remind one of occupation, like the endless ticketing and receipting in triplicate that bedevilled every transaction from extending a visa to buying a bowl of soup – the kind of bureaucratic frenzy that overtakes empires everywhere, from the British Raj to the mandarin court, as if the rulers would stop the people's mouths with paper, and buy their loyalty with a wild proliferation of pointless jobs in the service of the state.

And Poland sometimes felt like a bureaucratic device. Without protection from the landscape, it seemed to exist by fiat only, for as long as Germany or Russia were prepared to allow. No wonder Andrjez on the boat had been so anxious to define Polishness: Poland was something that had to be continually asserted, or it might vanish. Outside Grundiaz we had lunch with a teacher at the local school. We talked of one thing and another, and finally he announced to us that three Polish diplomats had been killed in Beirut, in retaliation against Poland's decision to fly Soviet Jews to Israel. It was a shocking outrage, he said, but we could tell he was pleased. It was recognition of a kind.

Grundiaz was a Prussian factory town, in workaday red brick: brick school, brick barracks, brick tenements and brick government buildings; from a bluff above the river we looked back on a roofscape feathered with smoking chimneys: from soft coal that burned in flats and offices and factories, sank in the streets, singed the brickwork and the pointing and the people's lungs, and lent the whole view the atmosphere of a Doré engraving of the London slums. It had the look of a city that would have turned people to communism once.

It was full of promises. It promised work in its steaming factories, producing things nobody wanted. It promised the buzz of commerce, throwing open its shops on the Sunday – only there was nothing in them to buy. But the most outrageous promise of all was made by an old man who had overheard us asking for insoles in an empty shoe shop. In German he advised us to visit the market. '*Dort konnen Sie alles kaufen – Schuhe, Autos, Mädchen.*' (You can buy everything there: shoes, cars, girls.)

In an open field behind the main square they sold the junk of junk. People were crouched over piles of black plastic fittings tossed in a vermicelli of electrical wiring, looking for a Fiat part or a bit off an old radio. They bargained for a rain-sodden cluster of components that had once belonged to an elderly vacuum cleaner. They made offers on a castor wheel, a turned chair leg, a jamjar. *Autos*, *schuhe* and *mädchen* were in desperately short supply. There were Russians who had crossed the border with a ragbag of tea, toy cars, bottles of Stolichnaya vodka and TV sets that they displayed on the bonnets of their Ladas. Men in brown sheepskin coats held out their hands, rings winking from every finger, while loudspeakers crashed out angry, discordant rock music at a deafening pitch.

Nobody had much to dispose of; no-one could afford to buy. Grundiaz's poverty, like the plain, went level and unrelieved.

'Likaspeekadinglish?'

He wore a suit, a watch chain and a furry wig. The *soltys* wore blue cottons and a shirt unbuttoned down his chest. The dog barked and the wind slammed the door behind them.

'We are English,' I said finally.

'Like, ah, wayafrum? Like, ah, Youessay or what?'

'We're from England,' I said.

'OK, OK.'

'We're walking across Poland, er, walking on foot. Sometimes we sleep in barns, *stodoła*. We wanted to ask the *sołtys* for somewhere to sleep the night.'

'Walking? Like, ah—' he made a small bustling motion, jabbing back his elbows.

'Yes.'

'Wayasleep? You want like a room? How much you pay?'

Before now, everyone adamantly refused to be paid. We had no idea.

'You pay American dollars? Waddya got, English money? You got dollars in England, right? Polish zloty, OK?'

We settled on 20,000 zlotys, about £1.50, and shook hands.

'My name is Stan, right?' He sounded anxious. We laid our rucksacks down in the porch and removed our boots and followed them in.

From the eighteenth century Poland's chief exports have been tole, fruit, timber, fur and people. A constant drift away to America, Canada, Brazil, Israel and Western Europe became an avalanche after Partition, after the failure of the 1830 uprising against the Russians; in 1864, and in 1905; in the 1930s and 1940s and in 1968. Like the Irish, who also farm and drink, the Poles have had alien rulers, and emigrate with a noisy patriotism inspired, perhaps, by the fear of being gobbled up by more powerful neighbours.

Stan had come back. When we saw the sausage, the boiled eggs touched with mayonnaise and the thin slices of pâté, it was obvious we'd interrupted some kind of party. Beyond the table stood a wooden bed and the inevitable wall unit full of things produced to fill wall units: china figurines, dimpled copper things, souvenirs from around Poland. The walls of the room were stencilled in vertical patterned strips.

Stan introduced us. The *sołtys'* wife was a heavy woman, wearing braids pinned up just as she had worn them years ago for a wedding photo, tinted up in rouge and flesh. Supper was over and a small boy stood near the table in his best trousers, braces and a clean white shirt. A slightly older girl sat on the edge of an armchair, wearing a flowery frock.

Stan smoothed his trousers, took the head of the table, poured himself a small vodka, tossed it off and asked to see our passports. Out of the wind, I had to fight to keep my eyes from closing. He selected a silver-topped biro from a small rack of pens in his inside pocket and began jotting down our details in a notebook.

Occasionally we'd shown our passports to farmers who had held them in their big hands, slowly turning the pages until they reached the Polish visa which they read silently, mouthing the words. But Stan knew passports well. He wrote down passport numbers, visa numbers, and our names, ages and places of birth. It was, I thought, like US Immigration.

'This is OK, right? This we all gotta do? You good guys, we good guys, but . . .' He pulled a troubled face. 'Normal, right?'

We agreed it was normal.

He gestured to the remains of the feast.

'Eat.'

Stan lived now in Chicago. His wife came from somewhere close to the Russian border. Her clothes were those of an oriental potentate, a nomad princess with the Sears catalogue and a charge card: a loose knitted black jersey dusted with gold thread, her shoulders inflated by giant pads supporting a mayorial collection of glitter. She wore lots of make-up, and her blonde hair was elaborately set; rings sparkled from her fingers. She had lived in Chicago almost as long as Stan, but spoke no English.

Stan had left this house when his parents were still alive (the farm had since passed to the *soltys*, his maternal uncle), and he now worked as a nightwatchman in a garage. He made a fist and inhaled through his nose.

'Youessay. Great business,' he declared.

It was a gripping performance. Stan, after all, had been born right here, on a windswept farm by a clinker road – there were proto-Stans in half the farms in Poland, in jerseys and blue cottons and thick-soled shoes. We could tell that after fifteen years as a nightwatchman in Chicago he barely spoke English, yet to look at – and his relatives watched him carefully enough, listened to his broken English with amazement – he was the very image of prosperity, shiny and foreign like a real Yankee. His wig was glaring, but perhaps it was meant to be – why splash out on a wig if people will only think it's your own hair? The Melting Pot was more like a stir-fry: the flavours intact, but all the ingredients tossed together to give them a coating of American sauce.

'My son speaka English good, right?'

His son had, in fact, lapsed into silence after a moment of volubility. 'Hi,' he had said with a squirm. It was hard to judge.

'Very good English,' we said.

'Like, her name is Ron. Ronnie.' Ronnie: the ultimate. Ron should turn out to be a railroad king or an electrical magnate. He'd drop the complicated consonants that finished his surname; do morning paper round and night school; and burst from the ranks with hard work and a Great Idea. A Pork Baron. The Silicon Mogul. I felt quite excited for Ron.

I produced my last Camels and offered them round. The *soltys* fetched three thimble glasses and poured us vodkas. We toasted America. With rather more enthusiasm from the locals, I thought, we toasted Poland.

And then to our surprise the visitors stood up to leave. Stan had driven across from his in-laws on the Soviet border and now they had an appointment further west.

'Say, ah, like you gotta packacamel? I pay you.'

But it had really been my last.

'Too bad.' He smoothed his wig carefully with both hands while everyone made their farewells.

The *soltys* came back into the house and sat with us at the table. As a boy he'd learned German at the local school. Later all the teaching itself was carried out in German, and he had needed a pass to travel in his own country. '*Vergessen, vergessen,*' he mumbled – forgetting deliberately the German language, and the Occupation.

We were travelling south? He was silent for a while. Then he began to talk in a rush. He started miming, brushing the back of his head and patting his cheeks. Something about the south.

He brushed his head again and his hair stood on end. He pointed to our feet and began counting imaginary objects on the floor, raising his hands higher and higher as if sculpting a mountain in the air.

'Piles of shoes – he's speaking about Auschwitz,' Kate realised. 'That's what he saw in the south.'

The *soltys* nodded wearily.

'Poland,' he said. 'Very beautiful.'

The following night we reached Torun.

The Podolia had been purpose built at the turn of the century as the Berliner, standing on Wilhelmstrasse opposite the neo-baroque theatre. Now the street commemorated a Polish revolutionary and the hotel, renamed after a lost province of southeast Poland, was suffering from hypothermia. There was, at a glance, too little money circulating. Its once scarlet trappings had grown pale; its extremities were shut down; it no longer communicated with the outside world. It had just enough energy to croak a demand for money and to supply a thick fug of central heating to the surviving rooms. In the downstairs restaurant an attempt to revive it with alcohol was proceeding in the normal Polish way.

It was fantastic, the way people drank. They found a bar and knocked back shots, chasers, whole bottles. Later, we'd meet them on the road, staggering home: and because there were so few bars we would try to guess the distance to the next from their gait or their breath. Of course when we found someone actually lying in the road, or holding onto a tree, we looked about, because bars were easily mistaken for agricultural depots or concrete cow-pens. Drunks became part of the landscape and we expected to see them every day, although they never quite lost their capacity to astonish us, any more than the landscape ever lost its astonishing flatness.

As the sun set the country could look suddenly sad and blank. The wind whipped across the sandy fields, ruffling the thin spring shoots, blowing in our ears. It wasn't hard to imagine winter up here in the north – the sheet of snow, the tideless Baltic, never deep, immobilised under a thin sun and all the rivers jammed with cold. Only the avenues of trees would feature on the plain, since the border between fields was nothing but a strip of grass, a temporary mark as low and flat as ploughed earth; but even those avenues would be ruled by the wind, corridors it could race along like an avenging legion, through villages that never had any depth, but grew like streamers on the roadside, blown into line.

There were forests – acres of woodland through which we'd walk for hours, even days, away from the wind, out of the sun; where we spoke quietly, as though we were in a church, and where we experienced the illusion of following the song of a particular bird, or the *tocatoc* of a woodpecker, retreating before us. We always had the forests to ourselves, and never met the woodman who marked the trees to be felled with a painted cross, or who had made a clearing where the bare trunks were stacked; only in the bright forests of silver birch did we sometimes glimpse a shadow that might have been a deer, or a pair of storks beating their wings slowly upriver. None of the forests seemed old (like an English wood with oak and moss). Most were plantations, ranked gloomy and angular against the fields' borders, where birch and pine could be planted and felled within a generation – as if the forests could move, and alter their boundaries, and belonged to the same windy landscape as the open fields, the avenues, the villages blown into line, and all the rivers that in recorded time had shifted their course like whips in the air.

Drink was the bunker on this landscape, and the men nestled into it, turning their backs on the draught that blew through sober life, with its work in the open, raising of families, and church. They hunkered down in the attitude of freezing men to drink, curling their hands around the bottle, and when the fire burned inside they vomited like Roman senators and staggered away with swollen roasted faces. They drank vodka and lager by preference, cold, thin drinks, which weren't what we wanted when we were dog tired and needed courage and sugar. But the Poles, who always seemed so gentle, drank what they were given, like children; and overdid it like children not knowing when to stop; and toddled out; and if they came to blows it was always silly and predictable, like Tears Before Bedtime.

Hungarian goulash, rice from the south, and even the beer, though Polish, intended for export: supper at the Podolia was surprisingly good. Halfway through I dashed away with an overpowering feeling that I was about to be sick. Perhaps it was exhaustion; perhaps the hotel was too hot; probably I'd overdone it on the goulash. I lay on my bed for half an hour, feeling unwell, with a pain in my leg that felt like a grinding bone. I blamed my insoles: they were supposed to prevent jarring, not crack my femurs. Mark's blisters, at least, seemed to be getting worse. I pondered the fact that only Kate was still perfectly sound, and I wondered if the same thought had struck Mark, and if it were true; and when I felt better I hobbled down to the restaurant to investigate. Mark was onto the icecream and they were both trying to discourage an actress from repeating the same phrase in English, over and over again, as she wobbled round their table; and somehow the thought slipped my mind and instead we went to bed, snoring in the incredible heat.

Anyway, I knew what Mark would think. Yesterday, when we'd stopped in a clearing to make tea, Kate had unslung her pack, stretched stiffly, and made the ritual remark, that the rucksack seemed to weigh a ton.

'You should try carrying the primus as well,' Mark said.

'As well as what?' Kate asked. Mark fiddled with the pump and didn't reply. I changed the subject, although I could have pointed out that Kate's pack, weighed down by maps and the parcel of cashmere jumpers that we used now as presents, was only slightly lighter than Mark's. We had weighed them all before we left London. Mine was heaviest, but I'd junked the radio since then and I was literally tearing through my *History of the Jews*, ripping out each page as I read it, and throwing it away.

Mark allowed himself to believe that Kate was carrying very little; and Mark's beliefs, I was starting to see, had a way of rooting themselves firmly like bindweed.

He kept his head down, his shoulders slightly stooped, hands in his pockets as he scuffed along the verge. Later, when we struck the first hills, Kate skirled past us on a wave of exhilaration, striding so fast that neither of us could possibly keep up. I found that towards midday or dusk my legs grew square and fell like hammers, whereas they flowed, like perfect numeracy, on a burst of sunshine or a frosty morning. But Mark's pace never changed. When he lifted his eyes from the road he never remarked on a change in the light, or a curious view; he just bumbled along as if someone had wound him up and set him down pointing south.

He was impatient of maps. Kate and I knew that the Nazi map

stopped at Torun, which lay on a curve in the Vistula marking the southern border of old East Prussia. Like Danzig, Thorn was founded in the thirteenth century by the Teutonic Knights, who erected the towers and bastions that even now bristled above the river. At first, the protection afforded by the Knights attracted merchants and settlers to the town, but as the Order's power began to wane, and its demands grew, the burghers of Thorn transferred their allegiance to the Polish crown, extracting privileges in return that made them all but independent, and Thorn a virtual city state. In the centre of the square that forms the centre of the city, they have left a great Town Hall, foursquare and turreted, built with the skill and expense reserved elsewhere for palaces and cathedrals.

Outside the Town Hall, in 1769, a fight broke out between Catholics making a procession to the church and a group of Protestant students, who jeered the papists – mainly Poles, as the students were mainly German – as they passed by. The fight became a riot, dubbed The Tumult of Thorn in English history books, but known to the Germans as *Der Thorner Blutbad*, or bloodbath – the ideal pretext for Frederick the Great's part in the Partition of Poland seven years later. The Prussians had countered the independence of the Town Hall with a gigantic Post Office on the square, satrap of Berlin.

Although Torun is now a solidly catholic, Polish city, jeering is not a forgotten art. As we walked through the square one morning a group of boys fell into step behind us. '*Deutsch Schwein! Deutschland Schwein!*' they began to call – though not very loudly – and when Kate, hotheaded, swung round on them and shouted, they simply melted away into the crowd.

We searched Torun for new maps, although Mark dragged his feet. Maps made him nervous. They had to be read and discussed. Points of view might differ; an argument might spring up; someone would eventually have to yield to logic. There was no knowing what sort of entanglement a map might lead you into. Better to keep your head down and follow the signposts; better not to chance shortcuts and argy-bargy, Mark reckoned. Left to himself, he would have sprung to the main roads like a bullet to the breach;

and he brightened up when the last possible shop assistant had shook her head.

The search for maps took us past a prosthetics workshop down a narrow alley off the square. A jointed human leg hung in the window. Into the room behind it, scarcely more than a cupboard, were squeezed a workbench, two chairs, two prosthetic workers, one fat and small and the other tall and thin, in leather aprons, and a hanging jumble of plastic hands, surgical boots, padded bras and articulated elbows and knees: all so tightly squeezed together that it looked like a struggle for light and air from which only the two men in aprons had emerged alive.

Both men were well into their seventies and spoke good German, although none of us could think of the word for insole. The fat man spread his fingers.

'Unfortunately, we do not have these, ah, in-the-shoe-comforters ready made.' He bent down and peered at Mark's boots. 'And if we did, I doubt it would help. You have very big feet.'

'He would need his in-the-shoe-comforters specially made,' I said.

'For these feet, certainly.' He lifted his pince-nez for another look. 'We can make them,' he added.

'I have a terrible pain in my leg, here,' I said jealously. These men were allegorical. Everything about them and their tiny shop was faintly implausible, as though their presence was a celestial error; tomorrow they might be found and gathered up, and the wall would seal up and the alley be as blank and empty as before.

They measured our feet in socks, gravely sketching round them on sheets of brown paper. the tall man put his hand through a necklace of false teeth and fished out a book whose yellowing diagrams showed the internal configuration of feet. The two of them put their heads together, pointing and discussing and nodding.

'Come back the day after tomorrow,' they said.

Two mornings later we shouldered our packs and trudged down early to the workshop. Each insole was made of two pieces of hide glued back to back around a series of rubber lumps that would support the instep and encourage our toes to form an arch, as prescribed by the aged foot book. In my boots they felt as if thumbs were gently rubbing the soles of my feet as I walked.

Over the river the main road thundered away towards Łodz, the Polish Manchester, which lay smack on our route to the south. We meant to avoid it, for no-one had a good word for a place whose grey and angry suburbs sprawled for miles, and whose centre was only a concentration of its suburbs. We took a track off the road and plunged into a pine forest.

'SMIERC!' said a red sign at the forest's edge, which we ignored. 'SMIERC!' said a sign 100 yards further on.

'It reminds me of something in Russian,' Mark said.

We trudged on. A heavy tractor had crossed the track and lumbered into the forest, leaving an imprint on the mud.

'Must be logging,' I remarked.

Before long we were brought up short by a high barbed wire fence in the trees. From the other side we heard the hoot of a locomotive and a train clattered by invisibly. When it had gone silence fell. We stood baffled by the fence, wondering why the forest was so still.

For another hour we blundered about, hoping to strike a firm track that would lead us out of the forest, and eventually we found a metalled road. The asphalt was marked with a white stripe at five hundred metre intervals. After a while we wondered why there were no cars.

'Why are all these trees dead?' Asked Kate.

Mark scratched his chin.

'That's right, I remember. In Russian *smierc* means death.'

We slowed down, digesting this. An open field lay ahead.

'I can see tanks,' Kate said.

Mark and I groaned in disbelief. 'They're stooks,' I said, and trudged on.

'No, I promise they're tanks.'

One of the stooks began to move.

We had been walking into the forest for hours, and now we couldn't get out. We fled. The forest was immense. We couldn't be sure how *smierc* would find us: coming from a soldier's rifle, perhaps, or just lurking insidiously among the dead trees. There were no birds. Perhaps our hair would start falling out. Once we cowered in the undergrowth, hearing a patrol pass by. At best we'd be arrested and thrown out of Poland; at worst they'd find the US Air Force maps and shoot us.

My feet were aching and bruised. The rubber lumps had changed from gentle thumbs to fiendish fingers, grubbing and poking at the soles of my feet. Afraid or not, we had to stop to remove our boots. Mark prised the rubber free; I threw the whole lot into the trees, cursing the scoundrels of Torun.

When we made our way down a dingy high street it was already dark, and a neon sign over a doorway was gathering dust. We pushed the door onto a hangar full of drunks. The barman said there was nowhere to stay. We looked between the grinning bucolic faces and the puddles of slopped beer, and asked our way to the railway station where we caught the last train back to Torun.

We did escape Torun, breaking from Prussia into country that had been Polish forever, and in the first village we entered all the men looked alike, with pale blue eyes and long chins.

Bread grew scarce, and we couldn't think why, until we saw the countrywomen baking cakes, hogging all the flour they could lay hands on in the run-up to Easter. We stopped in dried-up ponds to munch yellow sponge with poppy seeds, dry as drought. For water the farmers loaded barrels on their wagons, and travelled a mile or so to the deep well; we allowed ourselves a few short lifts with them on the grounds that the horse, at least, was walking. We'd sit up at the back, lurching from side to side as the wagon creaked.

After the fiasco of the orthopaedic insoles Mark and I were shy of experimentation. Kate, on the other hand, pared down. She began by picking the German logo off her pack and finished by discarding her knickers. Her stock of cashmere jumpers dwindled as she gave them away. Eventually red blotches appeared on her legs. They weren't painful or itchy, but coming so soon after our detour through the forbidden zone they caused consternation. It was only later, in Cracow, that someone mentioned asphalt rash, apparently harmless, which afflicts pilgrims walking to Często-chowa.

Since we were heading for Częstochowa too, people often assumed we were making a pilgrimage. We didn't struggle to put them right. We were curious to see the city that everyone called the spiritual capital of Poland.

Shrines stood by the road like holy milestones. At first I thought they marked some grisly event like a car crash or a murder; but they existed on paths as well, half-hidden in the tall grass. The humblest, nailed to trees, were nesting boxes for a tiny roosting virgin. Sometimes from little chapels built of stone Christ on the Cross watched passers-by through an iron gate.

The shrines were often old. From their position on paths that hadn't been made into roads we could tell they'd been erected when people still went on foot, travelling in groups, like caravans, for protection. As life was guided by church service and confession, so the physical way was marked with reminders of the faith, leading the traveller through to journey's end.

The shrines were comforting. It was always uncertain where we would sleep, or eat – whether we would eat – or who we'd meet; we couldn't control the weather or the terrain. We were helpless as the believer is helpless before the inscrutable will of God.

Mark didn't scare easily: you could tell that from the way he walked. Kate, looking from side to side, remained nervous and alert and her mind would boggle in an instant. She could put the wind up me. We felt the road wasn't always safe; that in some intangible way it was rife with menace and malignity. Our voices rang with foolish temerity in forests that seemed dark to us. Once or twice we hid to avoid approaching footsteps. We took care not to wander after twilight, and we were alert to every abnormality – an abandoned car, for instance, or a derelict cottage, rare sights in a country where plastic bags were hung out to dry.

This anxiety was unspecific, not absurd. We read fairy tales obliquely, so it is easy to forget how they document travellers' unease – how far they actually presuppose a widespread understanding of that unease.

All manner of trickery and deceit is practised on the simple young man out to seek his fortune or the dutiful daughter carrying food in her basket. The path follows the trajectory of life: and along it lies both dangers and rewards, the harsh lessons of experience. Duller, perhaps, to remain at home: but how much safer! All tension and anxiety begin with a shove from behind – a journey, an expulsion, a migration.

Plainly the shrines were to protect the traveller from dark forces haunting the road. Djinn, ghouls and dybbuks prey on wanderers, encouraging people to keep their bounds and not to move abroad at night. Movement makes for fear, and the road is the focus of uncertainty to villagers born and dying in a single parish. Villagers have all they need lying to hand: they don't look for links and ways. On the contrary, roads that spring up from God knows where bring an unwholesome rabble of intruders – traders, peddlers, tax collectors, soldiers and vagabonds. Things disappear; diseases spread. In Polish Prussia, people themselves had wandered from the east. But here, in central Poland, we noticed an initial hesitancy that greeted our appearance at a gate, and we were asked more often for credentials.

We stopped mentioning Istanbul – it worried people, so foreign and faraway that even to us it had begun to sound sinister. We said we were going to Częstochowa.

A pilgrimage! Pilgrimage brought us within the ambit of the Church, the great opponent of idle movement, which had ordered restlessness by appointing holy walks, and countered the essentially unsettling, semi-pagan character of roads by planting shrines and blessings on them. It was true that we were out of season, since the great Częstochowa pilgrimage wouldn't take place until June; but we were foreigners who might be expected to be ignorant, and at least our motive was clear.

Georgy bore us home as trophies from the *gospodar*. His father returned from the fields and greeted us with huge shouts, pumping our hands, until his bellows were drowned out by his daughter's pop cassette. She switched it on in the kitchen, and nobody seemed to mind.

All evening the machine spat tapes and demanded to be reloaded. Hour after hour its speakers woofed happily like an indulged family pet. Supper was prepared to the Beatles: slices of wide home-made loaf, sausage and boiled eggs washed down with tea, during which we were only able to conduct a little high-decibel small talk and bellow our protests when they put us to bed under enormous white eiderdowns.

Into farmhouse bathrooms, like a thief, came stealing a new influence. An unframed print of the Madonna that had hung alone above the bath for years was suddenly cohabiting with a steamier namesake. The boys from Wham! were making a comeback from the cistern and a German band, all leather and long moustaches, were rocketing to fame with a sticker on the towel rail. Sylvester Stallone, two inches high, laminate, glinting with effort, took out the toothpaste jar and everything it stood for.

Yet conversation struck up on the strength of a sticker in the loo had a tendency to go adrift. No, he had not actually heard Michael Jackson. She was not absolutely sure which one we meant by Madonna. The band she liked came from Warsaw, and they didn't have a sticker. But they were quite good. To prove it she switched on the tape recorder and blasted the farm with bass rolls and riffs and angry singing.

Later in Cracow they explained that peasants supposed anything from the West was good, giving a deprecating shake of the head to express sorrow at such an avalanche of tat. But it seemed to us not that the farmers revered all things Western but rather that they were accustomed to sharing everything with their children as people in the city were not, where everyone worried about housing and fumed about the shortage that obliged married couples to share a tiny run of rooms with parents and siblings. In the country children were expected to stay at home, certainly until they married and ideally after that as well. More room could always be found: and more hands would be welcome on the farm. Everyone knew the same people, went to the same festivities and worked together during the day. So when the children introduced pop the adults didn't see they were supposed to mind.

Easter

Maciej was a photographer – weddings, births and reunions. Creeping through forests and fields in his spare time, hoping to get his lens up close to a vole or a bee, he liked to catch the dying sun through the grains on a stalk of wheat. It was the plain that drove him to miniaturise his world, fixing his position among a myriad of tiny things. Isa pointed out a canvas of swirling greens and browns and said 'Dark period,' smiling. She spoke a little English.

Maciej had called us off the street, where we were trying to slip from the embrace of a gang of drunken boys, to offer us tea. When we took off our boots at his front door we noticed others wedged into a rack beneath the coats, and a stick lounging against the jamb. Then for the first time in a private house, we went up stairs.

'To Istanbul? Wonderful!' Maciej seized an atlas and began to plot our route. The first man with a staircase: the first to think that our journey sounded fun. Most people commiserated. Isa wondered what we ate.

We wondered too. In the evenings we were often given something by the people who put us up – bread and butter, cheese and cold meat. During the day we sustained ourselves on an erratic supply of bread and sausage, hoping to strike a country restaurant. These *gospodar* were primarily drinking-holes; if they were honest they displayed their shrivelled food behind a glass counter, but otherwise they handed you a long typewritten menu with entrées, starters, meat dishes, vegetables, puddings. Holding the menu, you asked what she had. She had *schabowy*. You all decided to have *schabowy* and she wrote a big figure three on the pad, cleared the menus and went to the kitchen. There was something atavistic and surreal about the process, the way the menu had the day's date written at the top.

Schabowy was Wiener schnitzel's poor relation – Mark had promised to slip a couple into his boots if we didn't find him better insoles. It was seldom cooked all the way through. We imagined that any rustle in the undergrowth might be the shy creature itself, bunching its filaments and tendons to flit through the forests like an earth-bound flatfish.

Isa wrinkled her nose when we told her about the *gospodars*, and gave us golden schnitzels, soft as bread, under a mound of crisp green salad. We meant to have tea; we wound up staying for Easter.

Maciej was also a scout master. Scouting in Poland was more than bare knees and dibdibdib. It was a dissident act. For years the authorities had been pronouncing the scouts disbanded, but powwows went on in forest glades, and old ladies were helped across Poland's trafficless streets while the Young Pioneers went begging for recruits. Maciej was as proud of the scouts as he was of the Catholic Church, and relished the Western leanings of both. The scouts served us as well, for Maciej had a range of excellent maps, and canvas camp beds larded with pine resin from the forests.

That Easter night, after sunset, he led us around the cemetery. Each grave was lit by a candle in a jar. Families wandered between the stones of parents or perhaps grandparents, though none of the inscriptions were very old, except that on the tomb of a Pole who had fought with Napoleon in Russia: there was a tilted stone shako on the lid, and the Nazis had spared this when they destroyed the cemetery and its record of Polish dead. They had razed the Jewish cemetery, too, near a synagogue that had since become a shop. The Jews had mostly lived around there; in little houses with wooden shutters and thresholds on the street.

At 5 am the fireman's band played a grisly dirge on tubas and trumpets, to the crash of a bass drum, and we followed the entire town widdershins around the church and the host was dipped to the rising sun. The church was the gift of the fruit-bottling millionaire who established the town's only industry between the wars; inside the walls were pendant with apricots and grapes and pears, spilling from cornucopia generously tilted by rosy cherubs; it was a lot of fruit to bear at 5.30 in the morning, along with the crush of the congregation standing in the aisles, and the sleepy faces of the firemen who had maintained the traditional vigil in front of the lady chapel, axes over their shoulders. I stifled a yawn. Mark was engulfed in a drift of white lace, surrounded on all sides by tiny ladies perky in mob caps, red ribbons and starchy pinafores. I saw him close his eyes and wondered if he could sleep like a horse, standing up.

Two hours later we stumbled out again into the sunshine. At home, Isa's mother had laid the Easter feast in a sombre downstairs dining room. Silver candlesticks gleamed heavily in light strained white through muslin curtains; the cloth was spread with cake, fried fish, tea and painted eggs. Painting eggs was a Byzantine tradition that had worked its way north in a thousand years: I took their appearance at the table as a cheerful omen, a promise that we'd reach Istanbul in the end. We were halfway through Poland now, and the intention that had seemed almost fanciful at the outset seemed far more plausible now.

Maciej poured us tots of bison-grass vodka and emptied the bottle over the Easter cake. He talked of going north to find work on a Scandinavian building site. He and a few friends would take a car up through Lithuania, to Estonia and Finland. Like Andrjez, he needed the money to build himself a house. And just like Andrjez, he wouldn't work in Germany.

Later that day, back on the road despite Maciej's and Isa's protests, fears tumbled in my mind, confused and uneasy. In some versions of the tale, the Wandering Jew cannot stay anywhere longer than three days; in others he must be off by morning, or within the hour, or in the time it takes to eat a morsel of white bread. In Brittany he remembered fields where an ancient forest stood; at Matterhorn he walked through a city, but a thousand years later found only the mountain. On the Baltic it is said that he must sleep on a ploughshare on Christmas night, and wander until he finds a harrow standing upright with its two points touching. In Polish and Lithuanian renditions most of all, he longs ceaselessly for rest. Those who relayed the story instinctively recognised the exhausting insecurity of incessant novelty: it is harrowing to be a stranger, never settling, forever casting ahead to the next turn in the road.

The Poles cast nervously ahead; long memories reached back to the glories of Poland-Lithuania, to the invasions of Russians, Turks, Prussians, Austrians. They remembered, like witnesses, when Poland was extinguished. Now the Russians were going: but the Germans were growing strong again.

This Polish fear was one I'd shared since that moment on the boat when I saw the peculiar border on Berndt's map. It was a scarcely palpable anxiety, like the quality of light before a storm. From the West, the light appeared to fall brightly on Germany, revealing a sober, cautious people who wished to be responsible Europeans and whose vague air of humility contrasted wonderfully with their industrial success. But that light slanting over Germany from the west slid shadows across this side of Europe: unsettled memories, dark suspicions, a host of guilts and resentments. An atmosphere of unspoken tragedy hung over towns and villages: in the symbols of communist victory, obelisks and plaques; in the shade of an empty synagogue; in the half-ruined avenues of trees that led nowhere at all, and seemed like a relic of something we'd all forgotten, like standing stones: these things could be laid at Germany's door.

We steered for Częstochowa like sailors taking a sight on the coast. Away from the Vistula the soil began to thicken up. On rainy days it clung to our boots, so that skirting the edge of a field a sticky clay stacked up under our heels and put us tottering onto the road like Chinese courtesans. But this was the only impediment we faced, and we rode it out like a shallow swell at sea, keeping our bearings to the south. It was all easy, a little dull; the landscape was unassertive; roads could run here or there, and when villages fell into line along the road the very positions people adopted on the landscape seemed arbitrary.

The Poles so wanted to settle, and live securely, but they had settled like water birds on the surface of a lake, folding their wings as they landed – and it sometimes seemed that a single report, a clap or a gunshot, would beat them lightly back into the air, and leave the lake as glassy as before.

I tried hard to shake this odd impression off: it belonged to the shadows. It was by building, after all, on thoughts like these, that the Germans once imagined they could winnow the Poles and the Jews like chaff from a Reich stretching east to the Urals.

We were almost over the imperceptible watershed that divides the Vistula from the Warta. The Warta, too, flows north, but joins the Oder on Poland's western border. The shape of the wells had changed with the water: from buckets on a rope they had become nodding donkeys, and the long spar that hung suspended in every farmyard would crack our heads in bad light. And now there were gentle hills at last, though obscured by forest, as though hills were an embarrassing frolic of the landscape best hushed up.

Easter Sunday was jaunty with weddings. From one village to the next we glimpsed white lace, combed heads and unfamiliar suits; we waved to cortèges of tooting cars. In a torrent of sudden rain we stood in the shelter of a kiosk and watched a party gather in the village hall. A bandsman sprinted through the rain with an accordion on his back. That night the farmer we hailed across his gate supposed we were Polish crooks on the run pretending to be English wayfarers; fortunately his daughters found the notion of the three of us sleeping in their barn hilarious, and persuaded their father to see the joke. Huffing with suppressed amusement the whole family watched us spread our sleeping bags. They really wanted to see us tucked up like chrysalises in the straw, but at the last moment the farmer roused himself and shooed them all out, leaving a light on so that he could come back later. The cattle through the wall snuffled and knocked their wooden stalls. Cat's paws crackled over the straw around us, trailing smaller noises. Kate woke around four o'clock and saw our host standing by the bailer. Then she fell asleep again.

Morning broke; all the cracks in the barn turned bright. From somewhere outside came a muffled shout of laughter. Someone flung back the door, leaped into the straw, and poured a bottle of cold water down Kate's sleeping bag.

Mark made a rapid rustling noise and a lot of him vanished under the straw. A hearty young man with a splendid black moustache stood grinning and panting like a happy dog, but his bottle was empty and I began warily to dress. The farmer's wife, an eager witness to the outrage, explained through her laughter that only unmarried girls were wetted today: wet Monday. Mark emerged from the straw. Kate, modestly enfolded in an icy sleeping bag, whimpered.

In the farmhouse kitchen the farmer's daughters were in a fever of excitement, entertaining the moustachioed young man and his friend, the policeman. The two boys had been playing accordion at somebody's all-night wedding party; the farmer's wife scuttled about with cake and tea while the moustachioed young man made jokes at the policeman's expense, laughing very hard in anticipation of his own next joke, and setting the kitchen in an uproar. Under a hail of jests, clutching a creamy cake, we stamped away.

The pigskin water bottle made an excellent water pistol. I had squirted the farmer's daughters to effect and later, carried away by the spirit of the thing, I squirted an absolute stranger who passed us on the road, expecting her to squeak with surprise. Instead she walked on without turning her head.

In the next village the wetting was in full swing, but it didn't look much fun. Mark and I took up flanking positions beside Kate and tried to look tough as little boys caught little girls and doused them again and again. Grown men with buckets loitered at the roadside. At the edge of the village six big men were trying to squeeze themselves into a baby Fiat, from which we concluded that somewhere ahead there was a bar.

For a nation of drink-lovers, the lack of bars in the countryside was baffling. All they needed was a parlour laced with alcohol, like the small cafés you find across the continent. We'd trudge thirsty and hungry for hours, through village after barless village, wondering how the Poles had earned a reputation for black marketeering all through Eastern Europe when they were too unenterprising to open bars at home. A bar – any bar – was a sure-fire thing, I imagined.

In olden days the country inns were run by Jews, numerate and sober; for which reason absentee landlords employed Jewish bailiffs on their estates. Almost anywhere in the countryside, Jews were better educated than their neighbours. So Jews ran bars and Poles did not. The sort of Pole who would open a bar had probably been led away to the city already, perhaps even to America.

Some days we tramped along Indian file, thinking our own thoughts. I used to think walking cleared the mind. But instead with so much time for pondering, walking seemed to induce obsessions, revolve them and wind them tight. These were not elevated thoughts. Phrases from songs I'd never even liked lodged in my head and played in a loop for hours on end. We argued over characters in *The Archers*. And I had never read a book as slowly as I was reading the *History of the Jews*.

The German *Drang Nach Osten* may have whirled the Jews along in its wake: or – as Koestler argues – found them already in possession. The shift to the east was not all push on the German side, nor was it always led by cold steel and fanatical Christianity. Almost every ruler in Central Europe had invited German settlers in at one time or another – Conrad, who allowed them access to East Prussia, or Stephen of Hungary, or Catherine the Great, when she placed the Volga Germans. All across Eastern Europe German merchants and craftsmen dominated towns and town life to the point where they became, to all intents and purposes, cities of German culture, obedient to German law and confessed before German prelates. For centuries the language of the streets in Gdansk or Torun, in Cracow or Levoca, Buda, Kalingrad or Sibiu, was German.

Unless it was Yiddish. For each was a great Jewish city, too, with synagogues and schools and Jewish doctors, lawyers, tailors, merchants and innkeepers. Two relatively sophisticated, urban, mercantile communities had expanded through Eastern and Central Europe almost in tandem, presumably in competition with one another, but each also drawing from the other. Their languages entwined, since Yiddish, the lingua franca of European Jewry, owes a lot to German (though less than was once supposed, when philologists dismissed Yiddish as a German cant, much as they treated Romany as a mere argot of thieves.) Now both Jews and Germans had vanished from the place.

Until the days of Napoleon, at least, almost every town in the region was powered by Germans and Jews; outside towns there lived nobles and peasants who spoke – insofar as anyone noticed or cared – the language they were born with. These were the great divisions of Eastern Europe; for until the First World War, at least, there were no states of the sort that were emerging in Western Europe by the time of Henry VIII or Henri IV or Philip of Spain, with a population speaking one language, abiding within recognised frontiers. In the East there were only empires and their cities, bound to a particular ruler by tradition, by force, by interest, or by all three, in a state of continual flux. It was this world that Danzig watched, as a fisherman watches a sheet of water; the world of shifts and reversals and passing glories out of which stepped the Wandering Jew.

At one time the King of Poland ruled Poles, Germans, Jews, Ruthenians, Ukrainians, Tartars, Cossacks, Russians, Lithuanians, Hungarians, Romanians, Armenians, Greeks, Slovaks and Szecklers. Stefan or Istvan Bathory, King of Poland, Hungary and Transylvania, was the first European ruler to preach religious toleration – and no wonder. He governed Catholics, Lutherans, Calvinists, Muslims, Moravian Brethren, Orthodox Christians, Orthodox Jews, Orthodox Christians who recognised the Pope, Unitarians and Uniates and Nestorians.

Religious affiliations counted for more than language, social standing for more than religion. For languages and faiths were irretrievably jumbled up, between one village and the next, between one house and its neighbour. But peasants were peasants, mountaineers were shepherds, anyone might be a townsman, and the nobility was noble, and spoke French if it liked. Long afterwards, Patrick Leigh Fermor stayed, in the 1930s, with a stream of aristocrats from Germany to Moldavia who could all, it seems, recite Homer and speak perfect English, and who felt that their position was declining. And Arthur Rackham, in 1915, asked a Galician peasant, near Cracow, what nationality he belonged to, and was sent away with a flea in his ear.

'Belong to? What are you talking about? I belong to this place. I belong to here!'

At Gorki Grabienski an old woman leaned across her fence. She spoke rusty German. At fourteen she had been taken to Germany to work in a gang sifting rubble after air raids. Later she worked in potato fields, digging from dawn till dusk. The rubble damaged her hands; the icy mud ruined her feet; she came home at nineteen, already an old woman. From the way she spoke of her son indoors we guessed he might be an idiot. She'd always worked hard, but it was difficult selling produce now, and all their savings were lost in the inflation. If only they had a cow!

'If I had my time over,' she said, fierce suddenly, 'I'd have stayed in Germany.'

Then she made a hopeless gesture with her hands. 'You need the sound of your own people around you, in the end,' she said.

Lech lived by the railway line to Silesia, hoping to catch a wife. He had silver teeth and sat in the kitchen of his parent's farm combing his hair neat. From the farm you could hear the hoot of engines and the soft knuckling of wagons rocking over points, *tocatoc tocatoc*, for much longer than you thought possible. Coal passed up the line, grain, oil, tractors, steel rods, engine parts, refrigerators, but no girls alighted on the station at Grabie.

Lech's father had a soft face and high, pink cheekbones. He believed English was a German dialect.

'*Haus*,' he said.

'House,' we replied. He beamed.

'*Mann*,' he said. '*Bett. Tafel, Ja.*'

'Man. Bed. Table. Yes.'

He chuckled excitedly and pointed to his wife. 'Frau.'

'Wife,' we said. He pretended not to hear.

But she was astonished that the English believed in God. 'In Christ?' She moved her teeth about in disbelief.

On another farm, Aileena had caught a sailor for a husband. They were to marry in a week. Aileena's mother showed us a photograph of the boy and said he was short, but when Kate pointed out that he looked strong she agreed, pleased.

When we left in the morning, Aileena gave us a coloured picture of a priest. Kate gave her a cashmere jumper.

On both nights Mark and I shared a bed.

Kate was the navigator, filleting the map so deftly for paths and byways that for days we dropped south without touching the main roads. When she was happy with a shortcut, Mark shrugged to show he didn't believe in it. This irritated Kate and seemed deliberately hurtful. Mark then went quiet, refusing to be drawn into the argument that would begin when I took up Mark's unspoken position, to rescue Kate from the suspicion that Mark had shrugged his shoulders principally to hurt her. On the contrary, I'd be saying, Mark has a fair point.

The trouble was that Mark had shrugged his shoulders to hurt Kate, and his point wasn't fair. Very soon I'd tie myself in knots trying to defend the indefensible. Kate would be baffled and enraged. Mark, the unwitting perpetrator of the whole thing, would trudge on ahead, firmly pretending not to hear.

In Mark's mind this walk was an Edwardian event. It was *Boy's Own Paper* stuff, and in the *BOP* there were things a chap did that he did without girls. He was abroad at last in an age before plastic; an age when peasants dwelt in humble cots and the only travellers on the road, bar pedlars and rogues, were amateur sportsmen and gentlemen-painters, his very own prototype. Everyone could be allotted a role: his, to be striding out with a box of paints and a hearty laugh; peasants', to live in their cottages and treat him as an eccentric. He disliked complexity as he disliked the fiery tangle of roads and paths on our maps; and he shied instinctively from questions, enthusiasms or arguments. I came to see it in the very way he walked when he stepped ahead, a black hat on a pack swaying over a pair of moleskin trousers, not looking round, steady-paced.

He had a stubborn determination to move on, not to linger or loiter on the road to Istanbul; so at Warta we never cleared up the mystery of a bright yellow Stuka dive bomber that sat in somebody's garden, but pressed on until we reached Sieradz.

For two weeks, since we'd left Torun, the countryside dealt us farms, fields, forests and flooded rivers; Sieradz, which we reached after dark, brought smoking factory chimneys, crowds battling for buses, faces preoccupied in yellow streetlight. Smoke and shadow lay across the city, with the tubercular hack of old buses, and the silence of factory gates, where dark oil stained the road, and the tenements exhaled damp like tombs, and cabbage water.

The hotel stood on the outskirts next to the prison and combined staff in an effort to save money, making it almost as hard to book into the hotel as it was to escape prison. An axe-faced old woman made us dig through our packs for documents that had lost their significance months before: currency exchange certificates, for a start, which weren't issued any more, and the forms we'd used to apply for visas and which we were carrying for no particular reason except that we tended not to throw anything away. She stood with her arms folded and a look of passive triumph as we upset all our careful packing, and took the slips without a word and summoned a Mongol woman to show us to our room.

In the hotel restaurant we were met by a stiff maître d'. A greying cloth hung over his arm and his maroon bumfreezer was stained with gravy. He showed us formally to a table, using the cloth to wipe his nose and three glasses. We ordered beers and had our *schabowy* imaginatively clothed in a slice of cheese. Men in suits with puffed white office faces ordered food and pushed it away untouched, very wisely, leaning their elbows on the table and pulling heavily at their beers.

Below our bedroom windows a young couple hooted with laughter, and slowly he began to sing, rather sweetly, in a voice clogged with drink. They made love on the stairs but exhaustion got the better of prurience and we fell asleep, faintly disturbed by cries and happy shrieks that echoed through the party wall.

Sieradz seemed less apocalyptic by daylight: the factories and tenements were peripheral, and the cobbled square in the old town was surrounded by two-storey houses with enormous sloping roofs: medieval buildings re-ordered by eighteenth-century fenestration and faced in stucco the colour of pipe smoke. Sieradz had been founded by the king under German law, but it was a humbler, dozier city than Torun and lacked its industrious brick, its perpendicular buildings soaring with wealth and civic pride. Sieradz looked like a county town, more Polish than any other city we'd seen, more provincial.

In treacherous felt galoshes we skated across the polished floors of the local museum. With delight we discovered a Turkish scimitar and the helmet of a janissary, steel bound in brass, with Koranic inscriptions etched around the brim. What child of Christian parents, snatched from a Balkan village, had been raised to wear it, in bitter hatred of all Christians, in fervent devotion to Islam, and fanatical loyalty to the Sultan? Where had he fallen – on the

Pripet marshes close to Kiev, or at the gates of Vienna in the west? And which Polish lord had won it, bringing it back in triumph to Sieradz?

Whoever had won it, we could see at a glance who claimed it: behind the scimitar a collection of portraits – crude, ill-proportioned canvases – gave us a glimpse of Sieradz high society around the middle of the eighteenth century.

They were all wearing fancy dress. There, for instance, was the captain of the *Inowrocław*, a vast Mongolian, drowning under a scarlet cloak of silk and a fur-edged jacket. A bristling wheel of astrakhan crowned his head, and thirty golden eagle buttons marched two by two down his belly. A young gallant – his face to one side, but his mustachios painted flat – held a languid scimitar across the shoulder of a jacket of pale blue silk, worked with gold thread from throat to cuff, and stuck with what looked like rubies.

The women were peahens in their provincial echoes of fashion, compared with this battery of male vanity, these swathed, extreme-cold-weather fops. I peered at their faces coldly: little faces buried in finery. Like buttons in fat upholstery.

These men had a passion for Polish history, for trumpeting the glory days – aping the dress and manners of their forebears who a century earlier harried the Turk when he brought his armies to Ukraine, and rode down the janissaries when they loitered, insolent, before Vienna. The nobility claimed a link with the fierce Sarmatians, a Scythian tribe who roamed the borderlands north of the Black Sea in Roman times. Sarmatism at its best was a grand fib, a gorgeous pose. At its worst, adopted with enthusiasm by Poland's squirearchy, the *schlachta*, it endorsed conservatism so bull-headed it was almost mad. By the beginning of the eighteenth century, the days of Polish empire were done. The crown itself was bought and sold. In parliament the *schlachta* chose their kings by election: they took bribes from every possible source – French interests, German interests, the Vatican candidate. Every noble had the right of *Liberum Veto*, by which he could bring a debate to an end simply by rising to his feet and saying so. The result was chaos – or rather what the *schlachta* proudly called anarchy. The smaller gentry (all the sons of counts were counts, and their sons counts as well – countless counts) had the same official rights as the great magnates, which allowed the squire to huff and puff and extol the virtues of what he was pleased to call Democracy, in a state of Anarchy, while creeping fulsomely to the great magnates; who disposed of the only power left in the moribund realm, the power to make appointments and distribute sinecures.

Sarmatism was arrogant, snobbish, xenophobic, posturing and provincial. It offered sloth and negligence for policy. France, Prussia, Austria, Russia and Turkey circled Poland's borders watching each other jealously to see who would make the first move against the Commonwealth – which had no army, no public services, no diplomacy, no leadership, no direction at all. Peace reigned, by a hair's breadth, and the landowning classes did well; while peasants remained at subsistence level, their surpluses leeched off by the squire, through rents and dues and a manorial monopoly on liquor sales. Jogging along in a mood of comfortable ease, vetoing any attempt to make them pay tax, the gentry were stolidly Roman Catholic, treating the village priest as a family chaplain, at the same time credible and superstitious, keen on gewgaws and jawjaw, a collection of powder puffs, fogeys, bletherers and parochial tyrants. They had half-shaved heads, half-Turkish dress, and wore the *kontusz*, or greatcoat, slung off at one shoulder; considered themselves to be the Polish nation (serfs not included) and grumbled about everything that went on beyond the farm gate. The result was that in 1793, when Russia, Prussia and Austria at last hit on a way of partitioning Poland between themselves, the *schlachta* had nothing to fall back on.

There was resistance, the Confederacy; its leaders claimed to value scratch armies and fought *la petite guerre*, before they were crushed by Russian regulars in 1794. There would be risings, too, brave words for Poland, and barricades: yet the rising of 1846 in the south was never suppressed by Austrian troops – it was nipped in the bud by peasants who didn't belong to the Polish club. The Austrians gave them freedom, and they turned ferociously on the squires and the lords, who hadn't so much as considered them before.

But there was endearing swagger in the way the Captain wore

his bear-skin mantle, and dash in the cavalryman's epaulettes, big as broomheads.

Out of Sieradz, green shoots met the frost crunching underfoot, Winter merged with the coming Spring. Mornings like these meant rain in the afternoon: floppy hats, cold trickles down our necks, and trousers drenched at the knee where water cascaded off our plastic coats.

The road lifted its head, sniffing the air. Treading along its back we felt it rise, slowly, like a dog that has heard its owner's footsteps in the street. It shook itself in a great loop and broke suddenly with exhilarating violence into a succession of tight swoops up the flank of a hill. From here we could see the chimneys of Sieradz, clusters of trees, and an enormous forest that stretched ahead into a smoky blue horizon. At the summit stood a wooden church with an onion dome, and a village green between tall trees, and a pond, wooden farmhouses, railed paddocks, and other houses half-lost between shrubbery and the steep escarpment where we stopped for tea.

I took off my boots and wiggled my toes in the sun. They looked like something lost down the back of the sink. I had a corn on my little toe as well, a half-ounce stowaway that bit like a loose pebble. Mark kept offering me a razor blade to cut it out, and I was always putting him off. We made tea and ate jam doughnuts. Way beneath us a carter charioteered along a track, standing up to encourage his horse, followed by the speck of his dog.

The *soltys'* wife leaned against the cupboard, watching him eat his supper: a big grey-haired old man sitting ramrod stiff in front of a plate containing a piece of buttered toast.

When he had finished she boiled a kettle and reached onto the top shelf of the dresser for a screw of paper, from which she put a pinch of tea into each glass. From another bag she filled a glass bowl with sugar, and brought out the end of a loaf and a bit of butter from a tin, apologising that the bread was stale. Tomorrow, she added, they would have had fresh.

Kate forbore; Mark and I took a slice each and buttered it very finely, chewing as slowly as we could under the anxious gaze of the *soltys'* wife. The *soltys* got up and stood by the dresser, magnificently tall; he requested one of my cigarettes and smoked it carefully. He'd forgotten his German, or so he said. He had worked there for five years and in 1946 he came back. She was a square-jawed woman with sharp eyes who had left her home near Lvov in 1943, retreating before the Russian advance.

They had recently sold their farmyard to a private company that had bought up the local collective farm. They had no running water and the earth closet stood on the wrong side of the barbed wire fence. It belonged to an Arab, said the *soltys* gravely. We thought we'd misheard.

In the morning, beyond the village, we stared at a sign which read ABDULLAH NEMEH AND SONS LTD. There arose a wavering vision of minarets, white villas, a snatch of cobalt sea and a string of camels ridden by men in flowing headgear. Abdullah rode at the head; sons ltd lurching along on slightly smaller camels. I saw him say, this land is good; he paid cash. His sons stayed. They would slaughter a sheep for travellers, prepare shashlik and pilau on an open fire. I closed my eyes. Mark had often described Nemeh family cooking. Aubergines stewed in the cauldron; pitta, with cold cucumbers. I opened my eyes. In the concrete yard a Pole in blue overalls and a cap leaned over the railings, smoking a cigarette.

Two days later we arrived in Częstochowa.

Heart of Poland

In June the village banner is unfurled, knapsacks are stuffed with bread and sausage, the priest bestows his blessing, and bands set out from the boundary shrine to follow the Częstochowa road. Old women in cloth boots make the journey on foot; young men, and parents with children on their backs; farmers and activists, workers and seminarists; a swelling pilgrim flood that surges a million strong towards the tower of Jasna Gora, and the chapel of the Black Madonna, a holy, patriotic, collective pilgrimage, to the shrine they call Poland's heart, or soul.

Częstochowa was also a textile city, pop. 570,000; we should have entered with gritted teeth, but page by page our guidebook had sunk scrumpled and illegible and soft at the bottom of someone's pack. Flying by wire, with everyone congratulating us when they heard where we were going, we imagined Częstochowa to be somewhere between Canterbury and Melk.

It was, in fact, the kind of city we'd been aiming to avoid. It possessed Malbork's air of desperation, Gdansk's ugliness on the outskirts, the sottishness of any Polish town, and a leery misery all its own. On sooted tenements algae dried like bruises. Factories, curiously wired-up and puffing, ringed the city and stained the ditches orange and green. It was the seedy anonymity of the area around the railway station that proved Częstochowa was a big city, where we found a flophouse, and where a gang of skinheads strutted in short jeans and army boots by the traffic lights – and where that night, in the ill-lit street, a man grabbed Kate.

Under our window, trains clattered to and fro; trams whined on their tracks. Two women in the corridor were locked in combat, tearing tufts of hair from each other's heads, screeching and clawing, both trying simultaneously to kick their way into the lavatory where a spidery little man with bad teeth and thin hair stranded by a comb had locked himself in. In our room we crunched bedbugs with our nails – real live bedbugs that sprang from gloomy novels by Zola into our pyjamas. Out of the window, over the roofs, we could make out the bright white neon star that shone from the tower of Jasna Gora.

The light was a lure to the innocent and unwary. The pilgrims came in droves, year after year, and they had given Częstochowa the atmosphere of a frontier city, overly mobile, a place in which strangers tended to collide, where factories were built in the hope that the prevailing wind would export the smoke and dust; and where the locals preyed on the people passing through. The man who grabbed Kate ran away when she screamed, as if all along he'd been trying it on; and everything was expensive for Poland – the food, the hotel – everything was worse and shabbier than it would have been elsewhere, while the bedbugs themselves seemed to suggest that too many people had slept in the room.

The avenue to the monastery was old, dull, yellow-sided, smelling like all the city of soft coal. At the top stood the pasty concrete tower of the Polorbis Tourist Hotel which was made for Party junketing – conference chambers, monopod ashtrays and antimacassars on all the chairs. We ate boiled eggs in mayonnaise, thin gruel and a tough *schabowy*. In Reception a German tourist was interrupting her telephone conversation to find out the name of the city she was in.

'*Częstochowa*,' said the receptionist.

'*Was? Tsches –* '

'*Częstochowa.*'

'*Tschen, tschesch – wie ist das?*'

The receptionist repeated it slowly. '*Częs – to – chowa.*'

'*Ach, mein Gott*,' snapped the woman, and had the receptionist write it down. '*Aber das*,' she said, unsmiling, '*ist keine Name.*'

The heart of Poland was a fort. It stood on an artificial hill, shaped like a star after Vauban's principles of defence. Much of the building was seventeenth century, but parts had been added and subtracted: the last extension had been made by the French on their way to Moscow. They intended the fort to protect the so-called Duchy of Warsaw that Napoleon had carved out of the partitioned state, but the Duchy was a puny monster, dependent on Napoleon, and it died within three years, in 1813; Jasna Gora surrendered to the Russians without a shot being fired.

It hadn't always given up so easily. Jasna Gora became legendary for its stubborn resistance to the Swedes in 1654, when almost the whole of Poland had acquiesced in the invasion of Charles Gustavus, the Protestant King of Sweden, who held out the prospect of a Baltic empire under the Swedish Crown. The Polish King, Jan Casimir, fled over the border to Silesia – Częstochowa truly stood on a frontier then, which ran through the hills at Częstochowa's back, where the city guards a passage over the Warta river. Hills! Silesia is Polish now – the centre of Poland's industry, inherited from its erstwhile Prussian rulers, the largest source of coal in continental Europe after the Ruhr – but in Jan Casimir's time, and for centuries before that, it belonged to the King of Bohemia. With Charles Gustavus in command of the country, only the abbot of Jasna Gora stood firm for the Catholic king. The Swedes settled down to starve the garrison into surrender, but when the Virgin Mary herself took a hand, catching enemy shells and lobbing them back into the enemy camp, the seige had to be raised. News of the monastery's stubborn resistance spread through a kingdom already shocked by Swedish profanity and desecration; to general surprise a rebellion, led by the southern mountaineers, drove the Swedes from their conquests within the year.

The fort had another moment of glory, in 1764, when the Confederates occupied it and held out against the Austrians marching in to partition Poland. The Confederacy, established in the eastern town of Bar, was a belated effort on the part of Poland's landowners to resist Russian interference in Poland's internal affairs. Carried away, perhaps, by their own martial rhetoric and fine Sarmatian garb, the gentry raised a scratch army against the Russians, a task for which they were signally unprepared, having spent the better part of a century eating and reading the Tarot. The armies of Austria, Prussia and Russia squashed them flat, and proceeded to the First Partition, which took large bites out of Poland and rendered further partitions almost inevitable (one of the Confederate leaders fled to America, where he was to fall fighting the British at Saratoga, and so become one of the first Polish emigrants to the United States). The fort once again held out against the invaders, and only gave in when the Partition was an accomplished fact.

We stopped at the foot of the mound. For a fort claiming to guard strategic alleys into Poland, Jasna Gora's walls looked too low; its moat – filled in now – far too shallow; its central tower so high it seemed possible to reach out and snap it off. And anyway it was a monastery, full of monks – extra mouths to feed in time of war.

Perhaps I was approaching Jasna Gora from the wrong end.

The origins of the icon of the Black Madonna are mysterious and obscure. According to legend, St Luke himself painted the likeness of Mary and the Holy Child on a board of cypress wood taken from a table in Nazareth. St Helena took the icon from Jerusalem to Constantinople to be one of the other-worldly treasures with which Constantine hallowed his new city on the Bosporus. Later, by the same account, the Emperor Nicephorus gave it to Charlemagne: perhaps in token of the Eastern emperor's recognition of his Western partner. For hundreds of years it lay in the castle of a Ruthenian prince, before a descendant, Leo, attempted to have it moved to Opole. But the horses stuck fast, and in a dream Leo learned that the icon was to be placed in the new monastery of Jasna Gora, where it has since remained, refusing to budge, growing wondrously heavy when assailants have tried to drag it from the spot.

The experts agree that the icon is Byzantine – it came from the unreal city. It has been in Poland since the thirteenth century. I wanted to see it very much.

The congregation squashed in around us. The chapel was small, considering the number of pilgrims who could be expected to turn up after walking, perhaps, for miles, and for whom this moment had to be an ecstasy. We stood, for there was no room to sit: no room for pews or chairs amongst the giddy press of muffled farming people; barely air to breathe, between their warm breath and the sweet pricking scent of frankincense, twisting gravely from the silver ball. A bell tolled; cymbals crashed; our neighbours crossed themselves and muttered prayers as all eyes turned on the silver iconostasis. Slowly, at last, the doors swung wide, and over the thick air cut the sorrowful gaze of the beautiful virgin.

She is, indeed, black – coppery soot. Her face is long, her mouth small, her eyes slanting and wide set, her nose straight. Her child sits very upright, hand upraised, head inclined. Three scars on the Virgin's cheek are left from a Hussite raid on the monastery in 1430.

Prayers escape from moving lips like tobacco smoke: prayers for wealth, no doubt, and health, a mother, a brother, child, crops, lumbago, eyesight, lameness. Not only is there a young man on crutches with his head bowed, but in the weird battery of votive offerings that adorn the walls hang tin legs, tin hands, hundreds of spectacles without glass, aluminium crutches, tiny photographs, school badges, crystal and coral rosaries, silver hearts, cameos, pearls, lockets, rings, medallions, scraps of writing, and names.

The bell tolls; the congregation kneels to take the host; finally, chalice is wiped and napkin folded, jug and platter tucked away in a cupboard under the iconostasis. Many eyes are closed as the silver doors swing shut.

And then – out! The priests glide away like Chinese dolls. Out! Stewards are scooping the people through the doors, into the light and away from their prayers. The boy on crutches has his eyes shut tight, and isn't moving with the rest.

Out! The schedule's too tight for miracles. Nuns in grey habits are sweeping us out with their brooms, scattering sawdust across the floor, and even the young man must swing away, just catching my eye as he lumbers past. And I look away, embarrassed.

Jasna Gora embarrassed me. English, Protestant, passing through: a peeping Tom on every count, it seemed to me here as if we were spying on someone's private rituals, or reading their diary. It was obvious now why the pilgrimage to Jasna Gora was barely known of in the West, compared with the holy walk to Santiago de Compostela, for example. We weren't particularly wanted here. The Church didn't want us bursting in as it preened in the mantle of Polishness – in garb as Polish as the *kontusz*.

The museum, like the votive walls, proposed candidates for remembrance, each exhibit recalling a moment in Poland's history. There was a rosary of dried bread from Ravensbrück concentration camp. There were some of the spoils of Sobieski's rout of the Turks outside Vienna in 1683 – a glorious, thankless escapade that had brought Poland little more than ostrich feathers and wonderful turtle-shell shields. Lech Walesa was on display – as an icon, haloed. Above all, there were medals, row upon row, most of them won by Poles in foreign armies, fighting without a country for any side that might grant them one: Napoleonic medals, crosses and sashes from both sides in the First World War; bronze medals struck for Free Poles after Monte Cassino – a desperate battle into which Polish troops were thrown in force, as desperate men without a country: that made them fierce; dispensable, too, perhaps.

The atmosphere of a beleaguered fort went well beyond the rows of medals, the Turkish spoils, and the muskets racked in the armoury. Despairing of temporal power and elected kings, the Poles had racked their country onto a higher plane on which it was inviolable. Swallow the idea expressed at Jasna Gora and Poland was a religious entity, the Poles themselves a chosen race. Their queen was Mary, Mother of God – they gave the Black Madonna a coronation in 1714 – and she stuck by her people, unlike so many kings of flesh and blood, unlike Henry of Valois, who chucked over the Crown as soon as he heard that the throne of France was free, galloping away from his subjects one night after ruling just three months; or Jan Casimir, who scampered over the border when the Swedes broke in, and raised his head again only when his throne was saved at Częstochowa (where he came to give thanks, as well he might); or Władisław, who spent more time in Hungary than Poland, and died at Varna on crusade; or all the nobles to whom the Crown was ever offered, and who tried wriggling away from it: unlike them, the Queen of Poland stayed put, and suffered with her people. Her scars have always been preserved in restoration. Political exiles chose her as their patroness – Polish Siberian Woman – and she was the best, most faithful queen Poland ever had.

And all through the nineteenth century, when you couldn't find

Poland on the maps, or Polish diplomats at any court (except the Sublime Porte, which always refused to admit to the disappearance of its ancient foe), this spiritual Poland, ruled by Mary, survived in the meeting of patriotism and faith: *Polonia Semper Fidelis*.

I could grasp this much, but I wasn't a Pole, and I didn't feel comfortable to find the Church hijacked by national feeling. The Church was peddling a line, working God and the Poles and the past as a decorous version of the three-card trick, until you couldn't be sure any more which was which. Pilgrims were hustled in the city; and in the monastery fort, too, they were supposed to fall for the patter.

Just outside the monastery, across a gravelled slope beyond the scimitar shaped bridge, a row of shops was selling trumpery mementoes – papal nightlights, plastic virgins, holy water, John Paul T-Shirts, rosaries and key-rings. The shop assistants lumbered wearily along their counters and they were also selling playing cards and pop cassettes and fluffy, irreligious toys and there, by the door as we went out, not *Polonia Semper Fidelis* but a poster with a Union Jack and the unmistakable whoopee-cushion lines of Samantha Fox.

And a step beyond we were rushed by gypsies. They wrapped their hair in printed scarves, piratically; they had bad teeth and gold rings, shabby cardigans, patterned blouses and skirts falling below the knee, with heeled sandals. Their skin was scaly with dirt. They were the first gypsies we had seen, and they came at us like pigeons flapping up from the pavement, jabbing lapel pins into our clothes, screeching for Deutschmarks. Kate and I were thrown off guard and flustered by their close-range yammering into producing money – but the pin buckled against Mark's thorn-proof waistcoat, and left his assailant speechless with surprise.

From here there were hills. Frown lines appeared on the maps from the effort of reading contours; crow's feet, wrinkles; squiggly roads, zigzagging rivers. Geography squashed up close.

We broke from the city over a fractured waste of leaking drums, rotting refuse and dried bones, watched by a group of tired men in overalls waiting for the bus. We struck a marked trail, leading from one bluff of karst to the next: the Trail of Eagle's Nests to

Cracow, popular with Polish hikers in the summer. It was still empty, and the hostels and hotels that catered for walkers along the way were closed.

Towards evening we passed between two craggy rocks in a field. Behind us lay the broad plain, the view of Poland we were accustomed to, flat and fielded, broken here and there by forest and indistinct low villages. But ahead stretched a new and rumpled landscape of hills. Something had changed: the Baltic sandlands were at an end, and we were heading into the hills and the mountains of Central Europe.

The marked route took us out onto the road at a particularly dramatic moment. The road swept around the flank of a hill and suddenly Olsztyn Castle stood across the valley, a giant broken ruin. I felt at last like a traveller: given my staff and a wild and romantic scene to gaze on, I lacked only a cloak and a feathered hat, for the evening was growing chilly and even as we watched the castle mass grew darker and less distinct, furring its edges with the outline of the hills beyond. With new vigour we set off to reach it, and in a few moments it dropped from sight.

We scouted for beds in the *restauracja* and drew a blank. The waitress was scolding a table of drunken farmers who sprawled in overalls and gumboots making ruminative noises, and she could only suggest we took the last bus back to Częstochowa. The *soltys'* yard was dogless and silent; but the view from the next ridge was unbroken forest, as far as the eye could see, and we turned back.

We appealed to an old lady with a teasing daughter.

'You've got a barn for these people, mother.'

'Ah, very small.'

'Big enough for three.'

'It's cold, very cold.'

'Plenty of straw.'

'No, not very much.' Everyone was grinning.

Marek stepped in.

'I have a barn. Come.'

He ducked his head and set off at a half-run to his house.

'Come.' He giggled bashfully.

Inside he rushed about to switch on the TV and the radio. He began to stuff the stove with twigs to make tea.

While we waited for the kettle to boil he snatched up a book and pored through it feverishly. He stopped at a photograph of a Spitfire. 'English. Polish.' Between the pages were coloured pictures of weapons, carefully cut out of a magazine. He scrunched them into a little ball and tucked them under the kettle.

He ricocheted around the house to fetch us things to look at. A portrait photo of him in national service, the boots we admired in the photo. He stood just out of the light in the next room and played a quick burst on his bugle. He pressed us to watch some TV: a woman with enormous pink shoulder pads interviewed peasant farmers. Standing in dung with her crew and her suit and her modulated TV tones she was a visitor from outer space, not Warsaw. He fetched a photograph. It was a standard colour print, very neat about the edges, showing a big woman sitting in this kitchen.

'My wife,' Marek said: and his tone was a mixture of pride and sorrow. She had run off with their little boy a year ago and he still hadn't seen either of them. He clocked in at work, clocked out, and returned to an empty house where he batted about like an abstracted moth.

'Come,' said Marek again.

Kate stayed behind with the TV and her plastic bottle of liquor, toping merrily while she watched a mini-series starring Sophia Loren as a first-generation immigrant in New York.

Marek led straight up the hill at a breakneck speed, with a torch; I carried mine and made some feeble jokes about too many cigarettes. In the dark, in his castle, he lost all his diffidence and shyness. He didn't slow down on the rock-strewn summit but flung himself about from tower to dungeon. Two towers stood on the top, and a keep built out of a huge cave, from which secret passages ran out to the cave-kitchen and the deep cistern. I stood a moment in the cave alone: thousands of ghosts whirled towards me and I scampered out with my hair on end. It was a good castle. All about was inky black, a starless night, and only the odd glimmer of a cottage light in the distance way below.

Hills and valleys now hemmed our path, and villages, no longer strung out along the road, began to huddle for protection. Other castles stood where the passage of armies might have been expected.

Our muscles began to ache: stamping, climbing, braking muscles; going downhill we stubbed our toes on our boot-ends. At night we asked as usual for barns, although the hay was now so thin we might have slept badly had Kate not discovered Five Crowns Polish brandy.

The brandy was a phenomenon. Except for the language, we'd arrived in a new country, where bars were more frequent and more salubrious, where the houses had eaves and the shrines grew tall and thin like sentry boxes. From hilltop villages, where the water was pumped to the level of the street by turning a wheel, we had views of swooping valleys, flocks of sheep, and woods. The crops themselves were more advanced, and by filling the fields with tall green shoots they suggested prosperity, a long way from the impoverished sands of the north.

We reached Cracow in three days.

Cracow

Trams make me think of Emil and the Detectives, the man in the chocolate hat. The clang of the bell, the electric hum, conjured up black and white photographs from the 1930s, of men in Homburgs and wing collars, shops with striped awnings and German-Jewish names. 'Central Europe', like 'Successor States', belonged to the two decades between the wars: before, people would speak of the Austro-Hungarian empire, which included Cracow; afterwards, the Eastern bloc.

Everywhere there were flowers: sold by the tramstops, sold in armfuls on the square, proffered singly by gypsy women in the restaurants at night. They were new to us: no-one grew flowers in the countryside; nobody sold them in other towns. Certainly Cracow could thank Austria for this: the flowers belonged to Habsburg etiquette, *Küss-die-Hand*, and I noticed, when I presented a bouquet to a woman at the hiking club who'd found us a map, that she was as ready with a vase as a hospital nurse.

Cracow's formality was metropolitan. In Rynek Główny it is said to possess the largest medieval market place in Europe – although the currents of trade that pooled in the square slowly dwindled to the mere provision of vegetables and meat (that large and homely market, too, declined in favour of the vendors of costumed dolls, basketware and folksy weaves). Now the square is mainly for pigeons and passers-by, but the currents for a time were very strong indeed. Cracow could claim to be the first civilised city a merchant would reach if he came off the steppe with furs, wax and honey; a city which sent grain to the north, and amber south, took carpets and spices from Anatolia and the Levant, and German clocks and cloth, clipping much of the exchange between east and west, north and south. Cracow's burghers – mostly German then – could ally their city with the Hansa, and attempt, at least, to defy the King in his own capital. They built a city to which Polish noblemen later brought Italian architects, and Turkish spoils, and plenty of money and society.

From a table outside our favourite café, identical in every way to the café on the other side of the Cloth Hall, except that its staff were friendly, we'd sit and watch the world go by – and there was no question but that it was the world, or one world, anyway, a particular self-composed society: of Jesuits in cassocks, striding confidently to confession; of elderly *flâneuses*, coiffed and made up, still interesting, quite imperious with their small coffees, a trifle knowing, wearing suits very carefully patched and darned that were content to whisper the 1940s, when things were still properly made; of kids in jeans and T-shirts; a young woman walking a Great Dane; a covey of nuns; an academic in bicycle clips; and once – eerie, bewildering sight – a black-curled Hassidic boy who crossed the square in a crisp black frock coat, and disappeared in the direction of Kazimierz, the old Jewish quarter. And as we watched, we felt ourselves watched, too: which is the sensation peculiar to great European cities.

The gypsies were watching. There was a fat gypsy woman who lounged, chewing gum, against the pillars of the Cloth Hall, playing Fagin to a ragged group of big-eyed children (though not so many children as at first appeared, since the little girl in a tattered skirt who stopped by our table in the afternoon, and dabbed her hand to her mouth in a peculiarly Indian fashion, was also the little boy who had begged our change there in the morning: we caught him out and he laughed and settled down nearby to play). The gypsies, like mudlarks here on the endless flow and ebb of a metropolis, worked the stranger's carelessness with small money: they wouldn't have lasted two days in Sieradz or Torun. The gypsies also sounded the 1930s note again, like trams: as Ruritanian as the marching band and proclamation we heard read aloud to an empty square one Sunday morning. At the top of the tower that stands alone in the square we saw a photograph of a military parade that had drawn up down below on the eve of World War II: bunting out, bandsmen in caps, politicos in cockaded hats, and

– pathetic and incredible – a corps of cavalry, in shakos, whose lances glittered in the sun.

After a night in a hotel we moved to a room in Wawel Castle, provided by the invisible and munificent Professor Ziemnacki. Wawel Hill was Cracow's answer to Windsor, Westminster Abbey and the Tower of London rolled into one: the royal palace was there, and the cathedral in which Poland's kings were crowned and buried up until the seventeenth century; the whole hill was walled and turreted. Our room was in a utilitarian garrison block built in the last century by the Austrians; we travelled through the courtyards of the royal palace, and pulled a cord at the guard house to be let in; from Wawel, our eyrie, we swooped down on Cracow like hunting monarchs. At night, when the tourists had gone, and the offices were closed, the central court was dim and silent, but for the distant tramp of the honour guard on patrol, and the periodic tolling of cathedral bells.

We browsed through the bookshops off the square, full of lavish Russian art books, relevant Polish novels and secondhand books in German and even English, too, rescued from who knows what attic in the city: the *Empire Book For Boys*, Southey's *Life of Nelson*, a Tauchnitz edition of *Moby Dick*. On Florianska we found a bar tricked out in a glorious style of baronial Art Nouveau and attached to a cabaret, dark and dimly lit, where intellectuals by the fistful sat and smoked, and where a cloakroom attendant would take our coats, sell us matches and cigarettes, and exact a tiny sum for use of the facilities.

Outside the very grand hotels these people haven't existed in the West since the First World War; no doubt, they are doomed to extinction here, but for now they are numerous: members of a sub-official class who first achieve some minuscule sinecure and then cling on grimly, performing their near-valueless tasks to the bitter end. Offices employ them neither quite as doormen, nor yet as receptionists, but merely to sit and watch you come and go. Below the cafés on Rynek Głowny they supplied lavatory paper at a price, sheet by sheet. They inhabited all the public places of the city and their doyenne, without doubt, was the woman with orange hair who sat in a booth at the entrance to Wawel Castle. We approached her to buy a ticket: large queues formed behind us. We opened negotiations through a slab of glass. Her voice, authoritative and negative, issued from a crackling loudspeaker. She refused to sell us a ticket. She quickly lost patience with pantomime, with the tapping of watches and the flourishing of cash but she spoke no foreign language, and folded her arms. The Japanese stood bewildered, Frenchmen wrung their hands and Germans turned sadly away. I saw people who had travelled hundreds of miles to get here burst into tears of frustration and disappointment. And the extraordinary thing was: it wasn't her job to sell us a ticket. We didn't need her at all. We could just walk past.

And in a way these half-invisible door-people confirmed that the city was alive. They formed the smallest capillaries of an organism that was there to leech you. The countryside and market town will exist very well without you, while you are exactly what the city needs. Cracow, very grand yet slyly attentive, rifled our wallets, issued us tickets, directed us here, displayed itself there, and prestidigitated with ceaseless patter. The country towns, by comparison, had stage fright; they were awkward with visitors, with a slightly repellent shyness. Cracow's efforts to retain your eye and interest were a form of practised flattery.

We rattled out one evening in a tram through the grimy nineteenth-century suburbs and the filthy post-war overspill of concrete blocks. Cracow had deceived us slightly: it was closed to cars, and largely walled, and it was almost possible, from where we were living in Wawel Castle, to suppose that the Renaissance centre was Cracow cap-a-pie. Almost, but not entirely possible: for when the wind set in the wrong quarter people wore surgical masks in the street, and wept; statues turned up sinisterly blank faces, and elaborate stone corbels had been wiped quite smooth. The architect who had invited us to visit had told us to watch for a basalt monument to a Soviet admiral and we got off the tram when we caught sight of him, scowling at a small park as though he looked forward to joining the Soviet withdrawal.

We had trouble finding the house, matching coordinates on a grid-iron pattern of streets that reminded me strangely of a smart Delhi suburb, but we found it eventually and rang the bell.

Stanislaw didn't suggest we look over his house, as I

half-expected he would. It had become a comfortable ritual for the night, like cocoa or the bedtime story. We'd stand in a mix of dung and straw to admire the weaning sow. We'd lean across stable doors, slap cows, murmur to chicks, and befriend – with just a grain of self-interest – farm dogs chained to their kennels. The inventory was always short: four cows and half-a-dozen pigs made a farm seem prosperous; but half as much would bring out the same smiles of pride, the same comfortable nod at the way things were getting along. Every farmer liked to make his rounds, and seemed to like sharing the walk.

Stanislaw sat us on a sofa – a real, unconvertible sofa. A picture window with sliding doors gave onto a small courtyard; the ground floor was open-plan.

'It's a design for hot-weather countries,' Stanislaw explained. 'The deal fell through, so it got built here instead.'

I was right about the Delhi suburbs. Stanislaw's wife had prepared plates of elaborate canapés. They must have taken hours, snipping the herring, chopping the eggs, slicing up the sausage, arranging it all on squares of hard dark bread, like edible brooches. She sat at an angle on her armchair, sipping mineral water. She was rather beautiful, tall and blonde like a Scandinavian, but expressionless; she asked polite canapé questions, from an invisible hostess's checklist.

Stanislaw's career to date was a perfect echo of Poland's post-war history. It had opened in 1946, when he landed his first big job. He graduated at the end of the war, having studied at the underground university. He was a qualified architect, eager to practise; a new man, unattached to the past.

'I was sent to Gdansk,' he said. 'The city was in ruins. Really. They said the Germans destroyed it, like Warsaw, but, you know, I had my own theories about this.' He smiled knowingly.

'My first task was not architecture, no. In the rubble many things. So every night the city was disappearing. It was a black market for beautiful stones, carvings, all these things – were taken out by Swedish ships at night. So we made a curfew. An ar-chi-tec-tural curfew.'

The goverment wanted the new Polish Gdansk up and running

as fast as possible, as a counter against possible German irriden-
tism.

'We had to build workers' housing, very quickly. In the centre
I can only make the façades again. Behind the houses there used
to be alleys, courts, many little places. But it was impossible.
Many records were destroyed – and we didn't have enough money.
So behind we just build flats.' He shrugged.

'Today I am not so pleased with their condition. Workers
cannot look after such properties very well.'

After his success at Gdansk, Stanislaw went south to design
Nova Huta. It was hard to imagine what he would say about it.
Everyone hated Nova Huta. They hated the factories, ten miles
out of Cracow, that poisoned their children. They hated the grim
Stalag housing, the parade grounds, the crumbling concrete, the
heavy monotony. They hated Nova Huta because it represented
the submission of their country to Stalin and Russia.

Unlike Warsaw or Gdansk, Cracow had emerged from the war
relatively unscathed. It had been mined by the Germans but the
mines had failed to go off. But it was crammed with refugees from
the east, inevitably opposed to the border changes that would
deliver their homes to Russia. The authorities saw Cracow as a
kernel of opposition, where aristocratic influence (aristocrats stood
to lose their great eastern estates) might establish resistance to the
regime. Privately they decided to bring the city to heel by swamp-
ing it with workers.

Nova Huta was a Soviet-style monster of heavy industry, a
booming prestige project that would conjure up a proletariat to
carry socialism another step forward.

'You visit this man?' Andrjez had asked. 'In Cracow, we call
him The Mad Confectioner!'

Stanislaw was not worried about his role at Nova Huta. He
described, in neutral terms, the immense brief he'd been given:
thousands of flats, integrated services, shops, laundromats, roads,
hospitals, police stations. A whole satellite city was to be built
from scratch.

The place had shortcomings, he said. His instructions involving
new methods of construction and unfamiliar materials had often
been misunderstood. And the whole project was pinched on costs,

so that poor materials were substituted for those he'd specified. 'It was much too fast, much too cheap,' he explained.

Then he played his trump card. 'This was an exciting time in the world, you know. For architects the fifties and sixties were a time of experimentation. Festival Hall, South Bank, Coventry Cathedral, in your country: amazing buildings also. Have you see the Byker Wall?'

And slowly he began to nudge Nova Huta away from Stalinism, away from the suspicion of punishment, until he had lined it up with a broad movement in architecture across the world.

'I think we may all have gone too far,' he said with a rueful smile.

He had just returned from a symposium in London. 'I make one little joke. I include one or two slides of Nova Huta. Nobody noticed when I discussed it as a post-modern work. Then I told them it was built in the 1950s. It was very funny, they were so astonished. Of course, we had to call it socialist realism at that time.'

He had lunched with the Prince of Wales. 'He is truly concerned about the environment.' I could almost hear the bandwagon creak as Stanislaw leaped aboard. The Prince and several other eminent Europeans had agreed to establish a new conservation group. It would concern itself with pollution in Europe, ancient buildings, and historic sites. It would lobby governments at the highest level – something Stanislaw, always in favour, would doubtless enjoy immensely. At a stroke he had furnished himself with credentials that were apolitical, pan-European and concerned.

Stanislaw's reasons for becoming an architect rang true. Desolation frightened him. Towards the end of the war he had walked the eastern reaches of Galicia – a part of Poland lost to the Russians, then to the Nazis, and at last to the Russians again for good. Instead of flourishing villages inhabited by Poles, Jews and Ukrainians, good harvests and stout houses, he walked for several days through an utterly empty landscape, among ruins and burnt fields.

He was proud of Gdansk. Rebuilding cost four times as much as building new. 'We have a passion for our culture,' Stanislaw said. The communists had even been prepared to pay for rebuilding churches.

Money was spent in towns, at least. Cities had been knocked flat during the war, and the communists had to replace them. *Sehenswurdigkeiten* too, like Malbork, were restored. But of 10,000 great country houses, which had come through the war damaged but not lost, just 800 had survived land reform and clearances.

They left holes in the landscape. Sometimes we passed the mouth of an avenue and followed the sweep of the trees towards a clump of brushwood or a lowly depot full of steel drums.

But Poland has been contracting for centuries. The Swedes destroyed her castles in the eighteenth century; in the nineteenth, how many of the bright and ambitious slipped off with the hopeless and despairing to the New World?

Stanislaw claimed to have seen a document circulated Top Secret to all the Soviet embassies and high officers in the satellite states, outlining a plan for the subordination of those countries to the Soviet Union. Polluting industry was to be built in the satellite states, as close to urban cultural centres as possible. The planners had chosen to settle steelworks upon one of Poland's most fertile farmlands, at Nova Huta next to Cracow. There low-grade steel was produced using ore imported from the Soviet Union and brown coal brought from other parts of the country; the profits never matched the capacity of the farmland.

I tried to find out how he had come across the document. It sounded like a green version of the Protocol of the Elders of Zion, with the Russians in the Jewish role.

Slovakia

Mountains are baffling. The landscape is folded and concealed. A distant peak steps out in a shaft of sun, while nearby hills are lost in haze. Low, hanging cloud creates a false horizon; snow-capped peaks make a phony sky; shade cuts the valley deeper than it really is. A village appears at a blink and vanishes again as the road turns.

Your sense of scale starts to oscillate wildly. The going is hard and the climate lurches between extremes. It is futile to talk in miles, or try to gauge distances on the map, when half the distance is uphill, or over broken ground.

Words and customs stumble on the passes. Mountaineers, living aloof and undisturbed, seldom meet strangers. The terrain gives them little scope, but having learned to read the mountains, and survive in them, they are reluctant to give up what was so hard won. They tend to be harder, and wary. Highlanders build wooden houses with wide and sloping roofs; they gather by clan and are potentially inbred; they enjoy music, and carving in wood, and a reputation for meanness. People accuse them of having minds as narrow as their valleys.

For centuries the Slovaks tilled and pastured, unremarked. Slovakia, the northwest tip of the Carpathian mountains, belonged to Hungary. From here the Carpathian chain bows out eastwards across Central Europe like a buttress, or a question mark. Formerly, Hungary lay within this loop, securing the mountains in its own defence when it was strong, and expanding towards Trieste and the Adriatic to the southwest. When it was weak – when the Turks broke in from the south in the sixteenth century – Hungary took to the hills, sustaining itself in Slovakia, and Transylvania to the east, while the Hungarian crown passed westwards to the Habsburgs in Vienna. Slovakia came under Austrian jurisdiction. Transylvania, the walled-in plateau, remained aloof, paying dues to the Turks, managing its own affairs, until the Turks were pushed down the Danube, and the reconquered kingdom came into the hands of the Austrian dynasty in 1699, and Transylvania submitted to their rule.

Long after the Turks were put to rout, Slovakia was a land of castles, Hungarian nobles, serfs and small German towns that lived off the passing trade. Some of the serfs spoke Hungarian, many spoke a language akin to Polish and Czech; but the languages they spoke were of no significance. The Slovaks were serfs, and had no voice; they never had a voice. Philologists compiled the first Slovak grammars and dictionaries in the mid-nineteenth century, for purely academic purposes. By the end of the nineteenth century a bare handful of Slovaks could boast a university education – a Hungarian university education. Yet within twenty years they were counted as a nation. The Austro-Hungarian empire collapsed at the end of World War I, and the Czechs, lobbying the Allies, insisted on the creation of a Slovak state.

Czechs were the teachers, the architects of the new state, and they, with exceptions, taught the voiceless Slovaks to speak. When Nazi Germany annexed the Czech lands in 1938, Slovakia was set up as a puppet state, ruled by a fascist Catholic priest. After the war, the country was reunited as before.

Czechoslovakia looked far too thin. Viewed on the map, from west to east, it had the dimensions of a country. From north to south, from top to bottom, it looked like the tail of Prague's comet; a no-man's land, mountains in borders, a barrier we'd vault in a moment. The maps linked it to the Hungarian plain below like a lid to a saucepan.

The border post lay across a stream in a gully between the pines. Nobody else was crossing here – the guards seemed to be waiting just for us. My Polish visa was out of date. From the Czechs we needed to get an internal passport to present on our way out, showing that we had slept in registered lodgings and changed an obligatory $15 a day. We also needed money.

I was so jumpy that I left my stick on the Polish side and had to creep back for it later, worrying at every step that the Poles would decide to examine my passport closely, after all. We were so keen to get away that we asked no practical questions, and scouted no good routes. The post was too small to have a bureau de change. We didn't even have a proper map.

The road from the border spiralled up between pines and a wall of granite, and curved in a bald valley by a wooden chalet with green shutters and a wall stacked with logs. A hiking trail sign-posted in blue took off into the Tatra mountains. The treeline was very low. Above it, snow was skulking under rocks like white mascara. The mountain tops were black. The trail led over the mountains to Novy Targ; the road fetched up there, too, skirting their base. We stuck to the road, and far too long after dark, when the forests around us had blackened into night. Kate was frightened and all of us were tired; we clumped into town. We'd been fooled by the map; we were grindingly tired, and penniless, a thread away from arguments and tears. On the empty road we'd passed nothing in 20 miles but spa hamlets awaiting the summer season, deserted even by dogs, cold and unfriendly behind their screen of pines.

The hotelier denied she had a room, before peering upwards through the window, into the dark, watching. Then she led us through trees to a chalet full of sleeping scouts and gave us three clean beds.

The whole of Slovakia leaves a roaring void in my diary, with one exception, written in a field of flowers above the walled town of Levoca. In the hot sunshine we'd watched a thunderstorm swirl through the next valley: an odd feat, like Victorian picnickers spreading their cloth to watch a battle; but the mountains forever trembled on the brink of storms which flared out of a blue sky like tribal warfare on an edgy border.

'Someone's coming,' said Kate suddenly. I saw nothing but flowers, meadowgrass and the steep avenue of stunted chestnuts which led to a church on the summit of the hill. Every year good Slovaks gathered here in procession and toiled up for a Mass; we'd missed them by an hour, and when we arrived they were coming down again, an avalanche of Slovakian *babushki* in dirndl skirts and pleated jackets.

'It's men.' She meant men with a missing prefix, as in 'plane or 'phone.

'Axemen?'

'Come on.' She was on her feet. I could hear the drone of male voices, dropping from above. Why should I be alarmed? I snapped the diary shut and together we fled downhill.

Levoca was founded by German merchant colonists in the middle ages: Leutschau. It was a small town with a defensive wall and a square surrounded by low buildings with high tiled roofs. In the middle of the square stood a Gothic town hall and a huge Lutheran church; the buildings were a colourful medley, because frescoes decorated the plaster between the beams.

To the Slovak eye it had a fault: it really looked its age. If tourists were ever going to be enticed to stay it was essential the town should look less cruddy and ill-kempt. A visitor might go back to his friends and say: Slovakia's a mess. It's backward. The people live in sagging houses. They haven't replaced their windows in centuries. They take over a country and then they let things slide.

And the world would tap its collective copy of *The Good Soldier Svejk*, and roar with laughter. The Slovaks could see the sly old Czechs in Prague – smiling, and making apologies for their country cousins.

They reacted in frenzy to this thought. Forget health care, barefoot children, rickety old women. A strenuous effort had to be made to improve the appearance of the town. The fading frescoes were repainted in snappy acrylics that would last. Houses that bulged and buckled could be improved by knocking them down and building back up with breeze blocks and mould-resistant render. Still the town walls were mottled and pockmarked, and the gateway onto the market place, rudely bruised and battered by the passage of countless carts, was as yet untouched. There was a lot to be done, to jolly up those terrible poky shop-fronts that might leave visitors with the impression that Slovakian trade was still in the eighteenth century. Meanwhile someone – anyone – had to deal with the crackly old paintings in the local museum.

The picture restorer had attempted faithfully to bring the past alive, using whatever force seemed necessary. Banished were gloomy aristocrats and stiff-necked counts; banished, the sneer of cold command, the reasoning eye. Eyes should be nice and round, with decent pupils; frown lines and smile lines required shadow, preferably with a half-inch bristle. The sitters beamed with complacent satisfaction, every one, their great wide mouths ready to break into sloppy grins. They'd had, no doubt, their passions, jealousies and feuds; now they were all one big happy family, with a single, ruddy outlook, back to life like vampires after blood.

Probably we were not expected to visit Spissky Hrad before the tourist board had got to work. It was barely ten steep miles from Levoca, where two valleys converged on a small plain, from which rose a hill with gently sloping sides and an outcrop of rock on the top. We saw the great wall from a long way off: the wall, and ruined turrets, and the keep. We climbed the hill. From Spissky Hrad the view was broad; from here, soldiers had controlled one of the easiest passages from Poland into Hungary.

After the military regularity of the castle, after the prissy fakery of Levoca, the lower town of Spissky Hrad seemed unkempt and a bit wild. The centre of the town, where three roads joined – one to the castle which lounged majestically on its hilltop in the background – was a triangle. The buildings around it were shabby and worn; the render patched with earth and bleeding the old lime greens and russets of distemper. Almost vanished Gothic lettering suggested shops and trade. Where the town straggled towards the castle the buildings lowered and seemed poor. Kate recognised a synagogue from its empty pediment. The old Jewish quarter was now the home of gypsies: small and dark, their children with tufty unwashed hair laughing at us and begging crowns.

It rained and we all ran. The gypsy children ran with one hand held above their head, a gesture that reminded me of Indians in the monsoon. The storm burst, as well, with the force of monsoon rain. In seconds the triangle was flooded, and people crammed the carriage gates and doorways. Before long we couldn't see across the street. Lightning flashed greeny-yellow on the rain, and the water swirling around our feet was flattened, foaming at the edges. All of a sudden the rain stopped. In the silence the water gurgled along the gutters. We took it for a lull and raced to the hotel.

The hotel café was dark and steaming. We ordered tea and glasses of beer, and shared the last table with a gigantic old lady who was working her noisy way down a bottle of vodka. My eyes were stinging and my nose felt cold.

We slid our packs to the floor and sipped our beers.

'Aaaaaaaaa,' said the old lady.

'No,' she said, jerking her head. She paused.

'Aaaaaaaa,' she said. Her eyes closed. 'No.'

We understood about one word in ten. She had five children. There was one – Prague – foreign – mother! Good boy. Good boy! My son. Gone!

She reached out to take Mark's arm in a massive hand. She yanked Mark's arm from the roots and tightened her grip.

Mark could not move his arm. Two tears rolled down the old woman's cheeks and she dragged Mark's arm towards her and planted his hand on her bosom.

'Aaaaaaa – no,' she said. She rocked back and forth. Mark lunged to and fro. The glasses on the table tinkled and jumped. Kate and I sat mesmerised, watching Mark and the old lady rocking together. Mark's expression, as he lurched over the table for the tenth time, was desperate.

'Aaaaaaa – no. Aaaaaaa – no.'

'I'm stuck,' Mark said.

'Aaaaaaa – no.'

'Let's go, Mark.' I said. The old woman leaned back. 'Aaaaaaa – '

As Mark swung past he gritted his teeth and said: 'I can't get away.'

'No. Aaaaaaa – no,' keened the old woman. The tears coursed down her cheeks. Outside it began to rain again.

South down the valley, at the end of a winding avenue of poplars between low hills, stood a fair-sized town with industry and railway lines, Nova Vies. The museum displayed old plush, brocade and clocks. An old photograph of the outside of the museum showed horses and carts, a gig, and an inscription on the pediment in a language we couldn't figure out. Outside we looked up, but that inscription had disappeared.

On our way out of Nova Vies, to avoid being caught for our missing stamps, we went furtively by the police station where a gypsy in a pink tracksuit and handcuffs went up the steps between two uniformed policemen, and grinned.

For an hour or so we dared a storm which sent the buttercups ducking in the windy grass. We sat out the downpour in a bus shelter, munching chocolate, and made for the gorge when the rain had swept by. The road was narrow and we had to hang our packs out over the metal crash barrier whenever two trucks passed. Mark took the opposite verge and was nearly squashed between the rock and an overtaking lorry, but eventually the walls opened out and a village sprouting from a bed of lumber provided a place to eat, festooned with antlers and boar tusks.

We ate voraciously, as usual, before heading up a lane towards the summit. Meadow stretched to the firs, and a series of elegant clapboard villas climbed the road, each with a verandah and a screen of perforated wood which reminded Mark of houses in Anatolia.

We stopped and stared at an abandoned villa, carved and shuttered like its neighbours. Now it was greyish-black with sun and stabbed with slimy blades of damp. Clapboard started from the frame, the empty windowframes reproached the brambles in the garden. The roof had shed its shingles, and tufts of grass had sprouted in the rafters. Like a rotting hulk the house sank quietly at its mooring.

Rain and snow-melts had washed our track, revealing slabs of granite shot with brilliant ores and veins of quartz that twinkled, incandescent, underfoot, polished by water and picked out by the sunlight falling through the leaves. Near the top we gingerly rested on a rickety chaise longue, leaking springs and damp. There was no room for speculation: however it had arrived, it belonged to the grotto, to the green leaves overhead, the jewelled floor, and the mulch of leaves it sat upon, making a salon in the open air. We spread our maps.

Rivers sprouted here like wires, away from a twisted empty line that resembled a river of white on a printed page. The summit was just above us. It struck me suddenly that all the rivers on the map – the Warta, the Vistula, and the Lis, running north, and the Tisza curling south onto the Hungarian plain, originated from this line. From Gdansk we'd been moving uphill, wading into the meandering current of the Vistula, the Warta and the Lis. But on from here rivers had a purposeful, direct look to them: we'd be tumbling with the stream, with thousands of streams joining and swelling to reach the Tisza, which dropped like a plumb line to the Danube, flowing east to the Black Sea. It was an exhilarating moment, as if the countryside were about to change direction, and swell at our back to carry us on.

'We are sitting,' I pronounced, 'on the exact watershed of Eastern Europe.'

Kate smiled. The sunlight had fused the wisps of her hair, and her bare arm across the back of the chaise longue appeared to fit a slot of sunshine between the shadows.

Mark shifted uncomfortably.

'My bottom is soaking wet,' he said.

'For this moment half the rivers of Eastern Europe have their source in our trousers.'

Mark stood up.

'Not at the top yet,' he said.

The summit was eerie, fog-shrouded, slightly burnt. Birches stood singly, bare-limbed, black, oddly bent as though they were being pricked and hobbled by the gorse bushes around them: as though they had been advancing, but found the rocks and thorns too difficult, and had stopped to listen to us pass by. The bracken was green. Only the fog moved: it snagged and grew ragged on the branches, gliding very silently and slowly over the ground, searching for something. There was no sign of the sun, just the grey light; and our breath made great clouds of vapour which drifted off with the searching fog, creeping over the rocks, hesitant and intent.

We were glad to emerge onto the empty road close to a hostel marked on the map. It had steep gables and dark windows, and an entrance at the back, and inside two men sat at a table; they looked up and one of the men took himself off without a word while the other served us tea and chocolate bars from a little kiosk in the corner. It was a relief to hear our own voices. A thin heat radiated from a stove and an impenetrable home-made map was spread across one wall.

We sat rather proudly in the silence, storing the secret of our walk from the man in the kiosk who would think we were holiday walkers, out for a day's hike in the mountains.

He asked at last if we wished to stay the night. In the fog it seemed later than it really was, four o'clock – three more hours for walking; four hours, perhaps, till dusk. We hesitated. Was there a village on the other side of the hill?

Some consequence of the silence that greeted our arrival, the way the other man left silently, the fact that we hadn't explained ourselves, or been asked for any explanation, engendered a kind of small pride. We were greedy to press on at that moment towards Hungary, downhill and with the stream: he shrugged and nodded, jerking his thumb over his shoulder. We had a brandy and left.

The descent was more precipitous than the rise. The path looped like dress braid stitched over the belly of the hill and we plodded round and round on a mulch of moss, leaves and trickling water. The air was damp, but clear again. Once we came out onto a view over the valley below, and caught a glimpse of whitewashed farms and a blue steeple, before the path sank into a glade of beeches banked in moss where we sheltered from a squall. We left the forest by a small farm, and greeted the young farmer hewing wood outside his barn.

A pity the farm was so little – it made us shy of presuming on the cheeriness of our encounter. He said there was a bar down the road, maybe it was a hotel, he wasn't sure – but they had excellent beer. We pushed on through the village and crossed a railway line where, just above the station, we found the bar in a row of cottages, approached by a few stone steps without a handrail.

In retrospect I see only a series of small mishaps which we could have interrupted at any point before it was too late and every opportunity had vanished. The upshot was far from disastrous: we only walked late, and slept in the open. It was only one lost night. Proportionate to all the other nights spent in homes and barns and hotel rooms, it was nothing; but we didn't have such a sure sense of proportion any more. It seemed, weirdly, like a watershed of our own from which we tumbled with growing abandon and velocity, smashing our rhythms, colliding, rebounding, breaking from something fragile that lay between the three of us like the slow fog.

The landlady was not warm and the local men over their mugs and cards seemed tired and incurious. They spoke quietly, and breathed loudly. There was, when we asked, no accommodation in the village. The woman shrugged behind the bar, and served a customer with beer. She might have thrown the question to the room: something – a barn, perhaps – could have turned up then. A hint of her hostility prevented us from asking around ourselves; even the way she poured our beers expressed the feeling that this place was hers and theirs.

The hostel was too far back and up. There was, though, a hotel a few stops back up the line. With the beer Mark and I realised that we were very hungry. Here there wasn't even the prospect of food.

We might have asked the railwaymen for shelter in the snuggery where they sat with flasks of coffee and a hot meal sent over from the village. They were friendly and helpful, inclined to be optimistic about the hotel, and advising us to go back and wait in the bar until the train was due. There we should have used Miss Marples to affect an introduction, for the bar was now transfixed by the TV set. Cars with belted bonnets flashed up lanes, people poured whisky from decanters, spinsters pruned their summer roses. We waited meekly for the train instead and blew our last chance drinking *palinka* with the driver and guard in their cab up front, watching our headlamp devour this narrow gauge spaghetti in the dark.

At Vlech we got out. The wind was cold. With a toot the train burred away into the night, trailing a small red lamp which hovered eerily across the darkness and was suddenly pinched out. We groped through the empty station and by the feel of tarmac underfoot made our way towards a red neon sign, beneath which a pair of glass doors led into a bright lobby.

There was nobody around. Emboldened by the silence we left our packs behind the counter and trailed noisily through lemony corridors and up narrow flights of stairs, calling and knocking until we got a fright when a door slammed in the distance.

The janitor appeared at length in his vest and a pair of trousers, scowling as he scratched his armpit. The hotel was closed. At first we didn't quite believe him. We thought we had heard wrongly, or that he was muddled; we argued, hoping that someone with more authority would appear. After a while we grew desperate. We made propositions. But he wouldn't let us stay in the hall. Kate, on the verge of tears, pleaded with him to let us simply crouch on the inside of his glass doors, rather than wander, freezing, through the mountains all night. We stood astounded under the neon sign as he bolted the doors in our faces.

Mark had been the first to admit defeat and clump out of the hotel – a tactical error, as I pointed out. We were now very hungry, very sleepy, and cold. We were also lost. The hotel wasn't in a village.

'There's plenty of moonlight, and we'll keep warm by moving,' Mark said. 'We don't have to worry about lorries and we can watch the dawn.'

In the less-than-perfect moonlight I couldn't see his face, but I knew the Jack Hawkins look that matched the voice. It would be set in an expression of eerie resolution, carefully pieced together from crucial volumes of *War Picture Library*.

'Against which,' I replied, 'we can set the fact that we've walked one mountain range today already. We haven't eaten since breakfast. And thanks to the train ride we don't have the faintest idea where we are, or where to go next.'

At that moment an enormous white shape flew out of the bushes at the side of the road and lunged at Kate's head. I heard her draw breath.

It was an owl, I think. Villagers who had heard the scream were nervous of opening their doors to our knock; they put their heads out of upper windows and urged us on with eager promises of hotels. After a while they stopped even looking out: the windows were shuttered and drawn, the inhabitants fast asleep, or faking it. At the edge of a smoking reservoir another hotel did actually appear, just more dark and secured against us than the last. Eventually a woman emerged in her nightie onto an upper balcony. We explained that we were English. Could we sleep here?

'No, no.'

'This is a hotel?'

'Yes, yes, hotel.'

'Can we have a room?'

'No, no, no room.'

'Thank you so much.'

Astoundingly a bus stopped just up the road. We panted on board. 'Hotel?' The driver rubbed his chin, and grinned. 'Da, da, dobre.'

We dozed as the last passengers were dropped off, and on his homeward run he woke us up, pointing through the black windows of the bus.

'Hotel?' we asked incredulously.

He made a gesture. We climbed out.

There was no hotel. He meant a private house, perhaps, where rooms were rented out; but the owners had evidently gone away. There were only a few people in a small village for us to frighten, before we crouched down against a hooded fence that passed for a bus shelter.

Kate and I shared a bedroll and gave one to Mark. I imagine I slept. Kate dozed, keeping an eye out for the glint of steel in the bushes. Mark folded his arms and drew his hat over his face and began to snore. One o'clock came coldly. At three it rained and we pulled ourselves in as tightly as we could, draping anoraks over our legs, rummaging for every scrap of clothing in our packs. At four a dog began to bark, but we were too tired and frozen to move. Half an hour later a bus may have gone by without stopping. The stars were fading into grey. We got to our feet.

We rubbed our kidneys, cracked joints which had gummed up in awkward positions, tried to blow life into our cheeks and clapped our hands. By half past ten we were back outside the bar at Blech, turning our steps towards the sun.

We started with all the brightness of exhaustion, brittle and alive; and the day brought a transformation, another break with the easy rhythms of the past months, another prop kicked aside in the gathering rush to the south.

I felt as though I'd lost a layer of my skin, like the bruising of impending flu, as we started up the hill out of the village. A cheery farmer and his wife pulled us off the road to drink lemonade in the cool of their half-underground kitchen: outside it was already blazing and windless. We filled our bottles with water, and they gave up trying to give us a short cut, good-humouredly, knowing as we did how strangers make long work of them.

It was gone noon when we stood puffing at the top with a clear view straight out ahead and south, to Hungary and the plains. We took off our packs and sat on a log to stretch our legs. I smoked a BT, the classy Bulgarian cigarette. Then we started down.

Geography seeps in through the soles of tired feet. In Poland, for the first few weeks, our aches and pains, our unwashed hair, my corn, Mark's wretched insoles were subjects of minute interest and keen discussion. The landscape could be held at bay while it remained flat and predictable – its notes had been monotonous and undemanding. In Slovakia the landscape showed its teeth.

We got smacked by the turnabouts and hills. For ages I'd planned to grow a beard but now, despite the sprouting bristles, the entertainment value seemed low. Even Kate's rash, a perpetual source of interest, had evaporated on the mountain tracks. Before long we were punch drunk, dropping the songs and talk of packs and feet for the knowledge that we were utterly lost to the road and its whims, and the uncertainty of a landscape that could suddenly buckle or drop away, or deal us pasture or woodland at a stroke.

The more lost I felt, the harder I clung to the idea of the road behind us. Up ahead everything was confused and exhausting and unknown and nothing made sense – but in retrospect it could be linked up and laid out like a chain. Walking made a pattern, a route-memory which could be followed step by step, like the return of a migrating bird.

Never steep, never narrow, the long gentle inclines led us in loops around the spur, travelling now east, now west, a bit down and a few yards south. Sometimes we would short circuit the loop and crash through precipitous bracken and a hatch of fallen branches to reach the lower straight, building up a dangerous momentum, trying not to pitch headlong; more than once I almost spitted myself on my own stick. Feather-headed with lack of sleep, bruised by lack of rest, we wound ourselves into agonies of boredom. The tall beech forest was full of changing light and filtered sunshine, birdsong. At the same time it was screechingly dull.

Around four o'clock I started heavy breathing. I had fallen into an abysmal panic with the puny efforts we were making to dent either our altitude or a sense of forest infinite. As gorgeous loop succeeded loop, and we faced about and about again, and nothing changed, I had one of those visions of hell where the sinner must empty the Atlantic with a slotted spoon or roll a boulder up a mountain. My entrails actually hurt with exquisite boredom, as though vultures pecked them. A car rolled past us and vanished in the distance of the road ahead. For full five minutes we plodded after it, until its roof reflected a ray of sunshine through the trees, about a hundred yards below us and a few yards south, going back in the opposite direction.

The day passed. At the bottom of the mountain Summer came. The sun pulled long shadows across the road. Crickets whirred lazily in the seeding grass. The hills were thickly wooded, forests of beech for which the Carpathians are famous (there is a region further east called Bukovina, land of beech, which was once the furthest province of the Austro-Hungarian empire, and now lies on the Romanian border with the Ukraine). We turned around to see where we'd been, and found, to our astonishment, that the mountain had disappeared. In its place stood a fat bellied hill. For a moment it seemed almost supernatural, as if we'd been pushed through a hole in space, and stepped out somewhere hundreds of miles away. Only that morning we'd been shivering in mist, up to our bootstraps in mud and edelweiss.

We slurred our words like drunks and teetered from verge to verge. A peculiar sound met us up the valley, a sequence of weird cries. As we approached the cries began to connect, though they remained unintelligible. It sounded like a railway announcement but by the time we reached the village we recognised it as a Madonna song, blasted at coruscating pitch from loudspeakers hung along the road. An old lady clipping a hedge in her garden waved as though she might be stone deaf.

We stumbled into a bar and shut the door. It made little difference.

We ordered a couple of *palinkas*. Mark had tea.

We reached Roznava just before dark. The border lay less than a day's march away. But not, it appeared, the crossing. The receptionist double checked while we had our breakfast and confirmed that a crossing existed for locals – for locals and Italians and Austrians and Hungarians, the old inhabitants of the Habsburg empire – but we would have to go 30 miles further south to the nearest international border point. This meant two more days in Czechoslovakia, unless we wanted to cross at night.

Mark had made up his mind. Every day we spent in the country cost us $15, by law. If we couldn't show that we'd spent it, they'd be entitled to make us pay up at the border.

'I think we'll get away with it,' argued Kate. 'It's an old rule. We'll tell them it's been abolished.'

'But what if we don't get away with it?'

'At the worst we'll just have to deposit the money at the border and use it to come back again one day.'

Mark stuck out his lower lip.

'I am never coming back again,' he pronounced, shutting off one of life's possibilities with depressing certainty.

'You might come back from Istanbul on the train,' I said.

'I'm going to fly,' he retorted impatiently.

'But Mark, one day – '

'No. Never. And I won't risk it.'

And that was that. Kate and I decided to try our luck and Mark changed his precious valuta at the bank, took the receipt, and went shopping. I was quite jealous when he and Kate returned with boxes of pastels and the Czech version of a Rotring pen, made up in neat parcels.

Neither of them quite met my eye when they joined me at the

pavement café on the main square, where I was reading a scrap of guidebook to Hungary and drinking wine. The place was full of men with black moustaches and sallow skins, very talkative and lively. Gypsies, I supposed.

'What else?' I said.

'There's a bus to the international border point in an hour.'

Hungary, said the guidebook, was the land of milk and honey. I didn't hesitate.

Into Hungary

The bus was registered in Budapest. It was a glossy high-flanked beast which snorted impatiently as fifty old ladies tried stuffing it with foam rubber. Mattresses were cheap that season in Slovakia.

The old ladies prattled in a sing-song of long and short syllables, divided into clicks and rattles and strange rubbery vowels, as weird as the writing on the sides of the bus, or over the shop-fronts in the town where we had stopped. There were many Hungarians in Slovakia still; near the border they were closely concentrated, with bilingual roadsigns, shop-fronts and town names. Slovak always took precedence, of course; only the improvised placards of road-side flower sellers or ice-cream vendors gave pride of place to the strange language: *Viragbolt*, *Fagylalt*.

It was five miles to the border and five miles beyond it to the first Hungarian town. The old ladies told us to get on the bus; the driver said we weren't allowed to cross this border, confirming what we heard the night before. We weighed our chances. If we arrived on foot the border guards would have time to check the regulations governing our visas and stamps. If we accepted the old ladies' advice we might slip through with the crowd. The driver shrugged, and gestured to his empty seats.

At the border they made us stand apart while the old ladies had their passports cursorily checked. The border post was flat-roofed like a petrol station, and the sun slanting underneath was dry and hot. A Slovak customs officer in a costume reminiscent of the Afrika Korps removed our passports; Mark began pacing up and down.

'Keep still,' I said. 'You're making us look nervous.'

'I'm not nervous,' he said.

'You're attracting everyone's attention.'

'Nobody can stop me doing what I want,' he said.

There was a venomous little silence.

'Come on, Mark. I don't want them starting to wonder about our exchange receipts.' Mark had his, of course; Kate and I were hoping to bluff.

In reply he gave a little shrug. He moved in dwindling circles, and finally stood still. The other passengers began to scramble back onto the bus, and not until everyone was aboard with the engine running did a Hungarian official dash across from his office with our passports. We were through.

The guidebook dismissed Ózd in half a line. It lacked museums, old houses, dignified public buildings; there were no statues or theatres or great restaurants or zoos. Ózd had a seven-stacked steel works, a second-class hotel, and a bookshop; it had red wine, white rice and spicy meat. Ózd was in Hungary, and it felt like a holiday.

Leaving the next day we were addressed in German by a man who had recently walked to Eger with his son. 'And long before that, too, when I was a Boy Scout myself. Before the communists got rid of them. So you must walk now to Eger, too. It's the most important place in Hungary. It is where we Hungarians defeated the Turks, who ruled our country for one hundred and fifty years!

'Baden-Powell!' he cried, saluting with three fingers.

Kate went into the bar first. She wore her skirt, a thin silk T-shirt and her hair in a tail, because it was so hot. Inside, the same faces I'd sat among across the border, wrongly assuming that they were gypsies: men with dark eyes, and down-turned thin moustaches, and their cheekbones burnt raw. Some of them glanced across, then looked away. The barmaid's face was pinched and rough. She didn't understand us at first; she grinned, and showed grey teeth.

Tacked to the wall behind her was a curious magazine photograph of two spinnaker-rigged yachts. Their sails had billowed out in a following wind. I thought idly that it was an odd choice for a landlocked people. The sails looked, really, like enormous breasts.

There were photographs tacked to the walls all round. I looked at them for a moment, then back at the photograph behind the counter. They were, in fact, enormous breasts. The walls from the ice-cream machine by the door to the liquor rack were festooned with pouting, pirouetting nudes. It was like standing in a soldier's locker.

The barmaid helped me sort my change. Mark swallowed his coffee at a gulp and sat staring into his empty cup. Kate drank wine.

They were all dressed in blue cottons like the Poles, white vests, gumboots or fat-soled shoes, but the blues were fading into mauve with the sun, and the way they talked together over wine was miles from a Polish booze stampede. In Poland, too, where men in bars were drunk (or were too busy getting drunk to notice), we were invariably well-received, spoken to, shouted at; strangers would shake our hands or clap our shoulders. They didn't much mind what we were like; what swam into focus was the fact that we were foreigners, and we strolled through Poland rather like porn queens, evoking the same sort of bland excitement.

The Hungarians, though, followed our moves without staring, neither avoiding nor soliciting our glances; and they returned our smiles with a nod. They didn't seize on any cue to lumber across; but their reserve wasn't unpleasant.

Kate finished her wine and asked for another.

Mark frowned. He didn't like the atmosphere, the guarded looks. He imagined they concealed Sinister Intentions. He wanted to go. Kate finished her wine quickly and we walked out, along a road that wound through teaseled hummocks and dry grass. Once before the corner I looked around, and a man standing in the doorway of the bar shaded his eyes against the sun that cast our shadows on the road behind us.

Three old men paid for our wine at the next bar: there were bars in every village now. They were the only customers besides ourselves. The bar lady sank a ladle into a tureen of cool red wine that lay under a zinc lid on her counter. 'Enjoy the Bukk,' they said, as we left them; and encouragingly: 'Silvasvarod is only round the corner.'

'The Bukk': regional names were plied freely in Hungary, much more than in Poland or Slovakia, for although Hungary was a tiny country, barely a third of Poland's size, people seemed to like placing themselves, and went into far greater detail than the Poles. The tourist board, I thought later, must have found this a useful way of exaggerating Hungary's size and variety. Certainly in Silvasvarod, had English been spoken, we would have been welcomed into Lippizaner Country.

The whole village was on the hoof. Lippizaners are those austere, dappled grey horses that star at the Viennese Riding School and are famed for dressage, stepping sideways, and not shying when bullets whizz past their ears. They are supplied, now as before, from a stud farm at Silvasvarod.

We were offered a lift over the last mile in, and entered the village by cart, appropriately. There were horses pulling ploughs in the fields. There were horses at a fence who twitched their ears as they watched us tramp about for a hotel. There were horses on the street, in the paddocks, at the plough; horses overhead that pawed the ground in their impatience to see you eating at the Restaurant Lippizaner, horses that gazed at us soupily from menu covers. There were model horses, horsehair switches, riding hats and horse tack in the shops. On the walls you saw winners and hopefuls, horses cute, horses winged, horses wild, cartoon horses and bronze horses. We walked until we found a hotel that was so cheap it couldn't afford much mention of horses, where our key was attached to a varnished shingle and the TV played all night in the deliciously lugubrious little lobby trimmed in black leatherette. And in bed, we sniggered over the pronunciation guide in the Magyar dictionary. ' "A", darker than "a" in card,' it said. ' "E" is the colour of bed.'

We'd eaten wild boar and chips in a restaurant, seriously doubting the boar.

'Boar, my foot.' I said. 'In this town it's more likely to be – '

'Don't say it,' Mark warned. He felt faintly sick, and spoke in his sleep.

A barman's son, a serious boy with the eyes of a girl, showed us a way to escape from the gorge, where the road was hogged by giant trucks making the ground shudder and the steep forest echo to their engine roar. He left us on a ridge after a mile or so, pointing south down a forest path choked with early summer flowers, ramblers dropping from the oaks, dog roses and morning glory, asphodel and foxgloves rising through the long untrodden grass.

Eger looked deceptively close. We caught sight of it at the end of the forest, below the combed vineyards and fields of rape: a cluster of turrets, domes and spires in the valley.

Among them, we knew, was a lonely minaret, the northernmost minaret in Europe: a sentinel on an abandoned border. Eger marked the boundary of Turkey-in-Europe between 1596 and 1687. The minaret was stony proof that in Eger lay the crossroads where northern Catholicism gives out, and peoples and religions take the first of many forks and turns towards the Balkans.

Eger lies on the last faltering hummocks and undulations of the Carpathians. Beyond lie the plains, an irruption of the Asiatic steppe known to Hungarians, since Turkish times, as Alfold, the Desolate. It was said to be flat and barren. Would we find water? Shelter? Food? Then the prospect of making a kind of landfall on the other side, in a weird and rumour-ridden place, as mysterious to us as any uncharted coast or whispered El Dorado: in the last lost place in Europe, Transylvania.

It took two hours, while the sun set, to pass the vineyards and small white summer houses and the yellow stalks of rape. The city walls stood forward as a ring of multicoloured blocks of flats, well-made and laid to lawn at the edge of the main road. Various used car lots stood between them, with a Shell garage incandescent and exotic like a tropical bird. Two pretty girls in fishnets clicked up the pavement ahead of us, swinging tiny handbags. It was Saturday night.

All the beds at the Unicorn had been claimed by a wedding party. The Senator Haz Hotel, resplendent in restoration, had a mirrored lobby, luxuriant with ferns, uplighting on the marble, gold fittings, and a receptionist who rose at our approach from behind a broad white table.

I thought that she welcomed us a trifle coolly under the circumstances. Her gorgeous lobby was overrun with odious tramps who were standing, wherever you looked, in awkward but slightly menacing groups of three. They sagged and bagged. Some carried sticks like wild shepherds. Their clothes were black and dingy and splotched with grease. They wore thick boots and their hair, unwashed for months, stuck out from their dirty faces in great tufts. There were women too, with long black skirts and thick socks and waistcoats slung around their bottoms. The men were depressingly spindly and needed shaves; they held up their trousers with what looked like lengths of filthy ribbon, and as they shuffled about from foot to foot they argued with one another. Even at a distance you could see the black rims of their fingernails. The receptionist patted her hair nervously and said she had no room, and the whole ghastly rabble flitted after us from the marble lobby, smelly, dirty and uncouth.

Eger was so smart that we tried to force our way into the Post Office under the impression that it was a grand hotel where we might get something to eat. As the hoteliers of the town wafted us away with manicured fingers we found ourselves at last before a broad coach gate beside a note in a window which read *Zimmer Frei*. We rang, and our cause was no doubt aided by darkness and a fragrant breeze which coursed from the garden inside, for a moment later we were ensconced in a suite of rooms in a house concealed from the road at the other side of the garden. Majestic beds, a tiny kitchen and a bathroom were ours for a trifle. The landlady was delighted we were English, and showed us a book of photographs her son had taken of Stonehenge, revealed in a dozen lights and angles. Later I examined the same man's handiwork on a calendar in the bathroom, a similar technique used on a bevy of Eger lovelies with nothing on. The landlady gave us the keys, explained about the bath, and crossed the garden to her house.

Houses in Hungary were often concealed from the street: a wooden carriage gate, a couple of high windows with shutters. They were perfectly constructed to resist attack, or prying eyes; the raised guard was more comforting than a slipshod welcome, because it suggested a protective ring.

Seven hundred and thirty miles from Gdansk, 800 from

Istanbul, Eger was the halfway point on our walk. From Eger there were two ways to Istanbul. Slightly more direct was the wobbling hypotenuse that cut across Transylvania and Romania, and then dropped south through Bulgaria; but you could make a case for the road that ran straight to the south, and then turned east through Yugoslavia and Bulgaria, on geographical grounds, because the Transylvanian route cut across the mountains. The right-angled route, on the whole, went with them.

From the outset we had meant to take the Transylvania road, although Andrjez, among others, had done his best to dissuade us. He said that we would be lucky to buy bread, and that the people were hungry and unpredictable. He had heard of Romanians offering corpses as 'butcher's meat'. Friends of his, travelling in a car, had been lucky to escape with their lives when they were waylaid on the road by robbers. Banditry was common in the days of Ceauşescu; how much more dangerous it would be now, when law and order had broken down.

Andrjez was not the only one; people everywhere had argued against us exposing ourselves to the risks of travelling in Romania on foot. Such unanimity, even when accompanied by lurid tales that smacked more of modern myth than likelihood, had unsettled us, and we had long ago resolved to take stock when we reached Eger. From a friend in London we had names of people in Budapest whose views on the subject would be reliable and informed – a trip to the capital seemed to be in order. If the experts advised us to stay away, we would take the southern route; if not, we would return to Eger and press on towards the border.

The fear of finding nothing to eat preyed wolfishly on our imagination. In Poland we had been hungry enough, but the Poles were hospitable; in Romania we might starve. Mark, on the other hand, had been to Yugoslavia, a land he remembered groaning with shashlik and white bread.

Over lunch we plotted our trip to Budapest by the afternoon train.

'I'm not coming,' Mark said.

I stared at him in surprise. 'What do you mean?'

'All these people in Budapest,' he began. He paused, cleared his throat. 'I mean, you stick to your plan. I'm going south to Yugoslavia.'

It seemed a clumsy way of suggesting plan B.

'We could, of course,' I agreed. 'It sounds safer – and we'd be sure of eating, as you say. But we don't really know much about Transylvania yet. Why don't we sort that out in Budapest, and decide from there?'

But I was lagging behind. Mark didn't mean we should all go south; he meant to go on his own.

The waiter brought our food, and it congealed on the plates. I felt utterly bewildered.

'Why this sudden change of plan? The whole point was that we'd all go together, wasn't it?'

It struck me that Mark had spoken to his girlfriend on the phone that morning.

'What does Megan think?' I asked.

Mark pushed out his lip. 'She thinks the same as me. She always thought I should avoid Transylvania.'

'Oh yes?' I was angry now. 'If I'd known you were planning to quit it would have made all the difference.'

Mark had suddenly become a stranger. All the time that we'd walked and talked, and curled up in bed together, Mark had been wondering how to say he was going to leave us.

His jaw was set. Perhaps neither version of Mark's journey included us. Parallel with the commando who was racing to Istanbul in rugged boots there strolled the young artist with a handkerchief at his neck and sketch block in his hand, free as a bird. He wanted to be alone to paint. There was really nothing to be said or done. We couldn't dog his footsteps or ride on his shoulders like Old Men of the Sea.

We said what we could. Then we gave him the relevant maps and Mark stood up. He shouldered his pack, placed a bit of money on the table to cover his share of the bill, and he walked away without looking back, over the bridge and into the avenue. We didn't even say goodbye.

The three plates, the bottle of wine, the third chair set askew looked puny and unreal. I felt overthrown. Kate was in tears.

'We'll go to Budapest,' I said.

And we did. Five hours later we leaned from a balcony and watched the traffic racing on the Gellert Bridge across the Danube.

Budapest

The city roared and heaved. Hoardings shrieked. There were thousands of windows and doors, and behind every window boiled some hope or intention that spilled out into the scurrying crowds that pushed past us without a glance or a greeting. There were herds of people thronging a bus stop, pouring into the metro down holes in the pavement, racing into shops, turning down side streets, dodging their way relentlessly up and down the grand boulevards. For the first time in my life I discovered what it meant to be caught up in the crowd; you needed strong will and a clear goal to start shoving in the opposite direction yourself. I discovered what it was like to be a country bumpkin bewildered in a big city.

And gradually we re-learned the pleasures of anonymity, of convenience, the security of taking well-worn tracks through the city to a favourite restaurant or a good museum. We learned the numbers of useful buses. Sometimes we wandered all day; sometimes we travelled to exactly where we wanted to go: to the races, to the Agricultural Museum, to the top of Gellert Hill from where the whole of Budapest, its bridges and churches, the dome of the synagogue, the nineteenth-century apartment houses on the flat Pest side and the wooded hills, with their villas, on Buda to the west, was laid out for us to recognise. We fled from the Gellert Baths, where the steam rooms dripped with sweat and smelled sourly of feet, and incomprehensible angry masseurs snatched our clothes away. We had lunch with a young MP in a secret restaurant inside the television studios in what had once been the Stock Exchange, and would be again, if the reformers got their way. We sat at Gerbeau's over coffee and strudels, reading books from the foreign bookshops. We went to market, to the Jewish quarter, to the Opera. We made the promenade at evening down the Corso, watching the lights of barges shunting upriver; and had all our clothes washed and pressed, and spent an evening with an elderly couple who lived among Biedermayer furniture and dabbed their eyes when they spoke about the Empress Ersabet; another with a historian waiting for the Prime Minister to ring and offer him a cabinet position.

Hungary came into both world wars on the wrong side. She was punished so severely after the First World War that the Germans were able to enlist her support in the second in return for partial restitution.

The consequence of defeat in 1918 was the collapse of the Austro-Hungarian monarchy along the lines proposed by President Wilson, whose Fourteen Points, giving Americans a cause to fight for in Europe, upheld the right to national self-determination.

A large number of nationalist claims were heard by the victors at Versailles between 1918 and 1921, to whom was entrusted the ticklish job of drawing national boundaries where there had been none. There were always people caught on the 'wrong' side of the line: Germans in the newly Czech Sudetenland; Russians and Ukrainians in Poland; Hungarians in the newly proclaimed Slovakia; Hungarians in Romania; Hungarians in Serbia; Hungarians in Croatia. In the immediate aftermath of war, Poland defeated the Soviet Union, and extended its borders to the east; Bulgaria and Greece enlarged themselves at the expense of Turkey, and Hungary lost four-fifths of its prewar territory, making it the heaviest loser of them all.

Hungary in 1919 experienced the unfortunate combination of a communist revolution, led by Bela Kun, and civil war, won by Admiral Horthy, both of whom used terror to achieve their ends. The revolution particularly alarmed the statesmen at Versailles, and when Romania took advantage of the chaos by annexing Transylvania on behalf of the Romanians living there, the treaty makers accepted the results of a plebiscite in which Transylvania voted for incorporation into Romania.

The loss of Transylvania rankled deeply for a number of reasons. It had not been given up to form a new country, like Slovakia; it was territory lost to an existing foreign power. Levoca, under the Hungarians, was a low-ranking provincial town whose loss was of no major consequence; but the cultural significance of cities such as Nagyvárad, Kolozsvar, Marosvásárhely and the ancient archbishopric of Gulyafehervar surpassed, in the opinion of many, that of Budapest itself. Transylvania had been a Hungarian principality for nearly a thousand years.

The head count in Transylvania suggested that Hungarians were in the minority by a relatively small margin, but that margin widened enormously when the principality was incorporated into a larger country which had barely fifty years experience of independent self-government.

Hungary would seek the return of all or part of its lost province from anyone who could effect it, including Hitler. Hungary, nonetheless, was so lukewarm in its support for Hitler that Germany invaded the country in 1944. At the war's end, with the Red Army advancing, Romania – hitherto a German ally – deftly changed sides, so that Romanian armies invaded Hungary with the Russians, seizing back what Hitler had taken away.

If all the post-war communist regimes were national disasters, the Ceauşescu regime in Romania was a cataclysm in which Transylvania shared.

Romania was in a state of tumult, as far as anyone could judge; the effects of two decades of misrule and terror had left the country crippled. Some of the first reports on the orphanages were emerging. Ethnic tension in Transylvania had led to riots in which several people died. There were even earthquakes, and before long the new president, Iliescu, was to send the miners into the capital to beat up demonstrators and terrorise the opposition. The country's 'transition' from dictatorship to a multi-party capitalist democracy was not going as smoothly as in other countries we'd walked through, and my godfather's advice to sound out the country ahead came to mind; we even wondered how we could sew union jacks onto our packs. We were constantly referred to the Calvinist pastor Nemeth Geza, who worked in Budapest on behalf of the Transylvanian Hungarians, and whose knowledge of that region was extensive. I rang him up, hoping to arrange a meeting.

The first few minutes of our conversation were difficult. Nemeth said that we should go and see what was happening for ourselves, but to every specific question – where should we go? should we carry food? was it reckless to walk? – he suggested we leave ourselves in God's hands.

As far as I knew, no-one ever deliberately put themselves in God's hands until they had totally run out of hands.

'Should we go to Kolozsvar?' I asked, a little desperately. There was a silence before I heard the fruity deep voice again: 'Let God show you the way, my son,' it said.

This was hardly going to reassure Kate: it's alright, we've lost Mark but we've got God. It was made worse by the suspicion that Nemeth was not entirely unaware of the effect his words were having; after my flustered questions there was always a slight pause, and the voice that came back was rich with something very like pleasure. Having let me squirm for a minute or two, he finally agreed that we could meet, if we liked, if we attended evening service at his chapel. He briefly gave the address and hung up.

The first thing he said after seeing us arrive was: 'Do you have a community?' I looked baffled. 'A church of your own?'

'Oh, yes, well, we're Church of England – ' I stammered, sounding Church of England.

'So while you are in Budapest, this will be your community, perhaps.' His smile seemed ironic. I felt a fraud, coming to his church like a rich Christian for a handout.

The chapel was a basement in a block in a modest quarter of the city, just a dozen rows of chairs facing a table and a few chairs against the bare walls.

'This is a very poor congregation,' he continued. He was enormously tall, with jagged black brows and strikingly sensual red lips, on which that ironic smile still hovered. 'Everyone attending tonight is from Transylvania. Perhaps you will be able to learn what you want to know.'

His manner suggested that he thought it unlikely all the same, a challenge which we would probably fail. He seemed to regard

Kate, however, with great interest, and his smile to her said, 'I'm amused to find a girl like you with a clown like this.'

We sat close to the altar-table, from where the congregation could look at us, and we at them. We watched them filing in off the street: men with gigantic seafarers' beards, women in printed frocks and headscarves, and elderly women wearing quilted jackets and skirts of no particular colour. If they looked especially poor it was that they were dressed, on the whole, in rustic clothes. A few of the men were wearing Sunday suits. They all looked tired. Some looked worried. Coming to Budapest had been a shock for us, and I wondered how it felt to them.

When Nemeth Geza stood by the table they all fell silent. His approach was conversational, although for the first ten minutes he did all the talking, perched on a corner of the table, seldom using his hands. He didn't have to raise his voice: it was deep and spread like treacle. He had assigned us an interpreter, but she was both too rapt, and too nervous of speaking, to interpret very much. One moment they were all erect, waiting for him to speak; then they were making themselves comfortable, and they smiled and nodded, or looked serious, just as he wished. He smiled when he made jokes and they laughed easily.

His smile seemed weighed, as though it balanced something very solemn and painful. The atmosphere in the room was very highly charged. An old man stood up to compose a prayer and soon lost his way in tears. At first he wanted to sit down again, but he was encouraged to go on and, occasionally stopping with a hand across his eyes, composed a prayer that was partly a story, partly a lament, and partly a plea. (The interpreter leaned across as he sat down: 'Romanian army shoot on his village with helicopters,' she whispered. Others were crying, too.)

A young man stood and said a short prayer, to which we said Amen. No-one else broke down like the old man, but there were tears in the room, and the voices of several speakers quavered. Had Nemeth been a charismatic preacher in the conventional sense, dragging the congregation to a pitch with his own cries and tears, the thing would have been less impressive. But he had spoken calmly, and used only that deep smile, and the emotion had broken out in a chilly little underground room, in the harsh light of bare electric bulbs.

Later they handed out orange squash and biscuits, and we were introduced, shaking hands; everyone pressed their names and addresses on us, and told us to stay with them when we were in Transylvania. Kate talked to a tall girl in plastic high heels who had decided to stay in Budapest. 'We have been living the life of dogs,' she said, bitterly. 'Worse than dogs.'

Later, Nemeth Geza repeated that we should go to Transylvania. 'See it for yourself. They are a very warm people. When you see a star on a steeple, you are in a Hungarian village. Go to the church, and speak to the pastor. He will tell you what he and you can do.' He wrote out a letter of introduction, addressed to 'Brother pastors'. It explained who we were, and vouched for our honesty, and asked that we should be given help if we needed it.

I asked him, as an afterthought, about the gypsies. We knew that there were a lot of gypsies in Transylvania, and our encounters with them in southern Poland and Częstechowa, although never hostile, had a slight ambiguity, like heavy teasing, which was never predictable and always left me with the feeling that we'd been worsted in some invisible argument.

'I don't think you should try to stay with them,' he said. 'And don't travel at night, of course.' He smiled, and this time his smile was not ironic. 'I think you will be safe. Good luck!'

A few days later we caught the train back to Eger. We stayed again in private rooms, where the landlady gave us a giant bowl of strawberries and in the mornings set a pot of hot espresso on the table. We sat in the garden and devoured all the English books we'd bought in Budapest, knowing we would have to leave them behind.

The room next door was occupied by a young Russian teacher who had just lost her job and was in Eger to sit exams qualifying her to teach English instead. She pointed out that the new job was hers for the asking, because her father was a headmaster. Her English was rudimentary. He was, apparently, using school funds towards the cost of her course, while all the others had to look out for themselves. Before she left she delivered a salvo against democracy on the grounds that Hungary needed a strong leader and elections were expensive to run. To her mind, elections were a form of corrupt practice. The government spent public money printing forms, setting up booths, and contributing, according to the new law, fixed sums to all the parties for election expenses, and for what? To create another government! Her eyes widened in disapproval.

When she had gone we returned to our books. The Hungarian novels, mainly from between the wars, dealt with the *puszta* – the Alfold, which we were about to cross. On the *puszta* nobody spoke much. There was a permanent haze, and strong men who vanished into it observed the coming of Spring in the budding of a scarlet pimpernel. They looked for Winter when the sheep turned their heads north. Almost nothing happened in between except murders, revenge killings, and the flight of the villains who were soon swallowed up in the haze. Cavalry squadrons sometimes pursued them. Occasionally we hunted with the cavalry, but more often we smiled grimly with the fugitive and, if we met the cavalry officer at Hortobagy, a place halfway across the *puszta* with an old bridge and an inn, we sneered at him. Hortobagy was a traditional sanctuary.

One of these novels concerned an ancient shepherd and his son. They sit one evening with the dog and the flock, watching two shepherds approach. After a long time they come up and sit by his fire. They smoke pipes.

Nobody says a word.

Eventually the pipes go out and the men roll into skins and fall asleep.

Night on the *puszta*. Our shepherd, his son and the dog are knifed in their sleep. The sheep go away with their new masters.

A year passes, very slowly, before the murderer comes before the police chief and denies everything. Just as he is about to leave, he catches sight of the victim's embroidered belt hanging on the doorknob. He makes a complete confession.

I pressed this book on our neighbour. It wasn't really Kate's thing.

Poppies had flooded the fields since we'd been away. I thought that Eger would mark a great break in our walk, but as we tramped away the route memory asserted itself. Budapest vanished through a trap, and the walk sealed it up – it seemed like yesterday that we had descended into Eger through the rape and vines. It struck me that Eger was exactly halfway betwen Gdansk and Istanbul: the weakest point in the journey's span.

We reached the town on the edge of the Alfold. There were no more cliffs with caves for storing wine. At night the sky crackled. There was lightning but no rain, but in disordered dreams I saw the sea, great ships, and waves crashing at my heels.

In the morning we had coffee in a bar on the edge of town. A genial old man in a beret capered around our table, slightly cracked. The town librarian led him gently to a nearby table, and beakers of wine soon appeared at our elbow. The librarian smiled and gave us a nod.

When we thanked him he asked a few questions in German about how we liked the country. Then he suddenly held my arm.

'When you leave,' he said, 'say that Hungary is not the Balkans.' He repeated it twice, like a proverb or a spell. *Ungarn ist nicht die Balkan.*

Storks had nested in the telegraph poles along the winding road. We passed villages on streams, and groups of women in flowered headscarves and pinafores tramping to the fields. Only later, when the wine had sunk to our limbs and our mouths felt sticky, the corn and poppies were pushed aside by bulrushes and the hard glitter of still water. A sort of brown sedge lined the road. The air swarmed with midges. All of a sudden the road gave a start of fright and stopped rolling to and fro to call on villages. The water glittered more fiercely, the reeds grew taller, and the road was suddenly running scared. Without pause it shot across a reedy lagoon, bored through a belt of trees and bridged a river, the Tisza, rolling brown and lazy far below, towards the Danube; it didn't stop running until we reached Tiszafured, which showed for hours like a ridge, as though someone had scraped their boot on the horizon.

Nothing in Tiszafured was higher than a bungalow, except the small cinema, and that, too, sloped quickly down from the end that housed the projectionist's box. Everything was shuttered in a weekend silence. Living on the edge of the plain the people of Tiszafured, if there were any, must have found livestock tall.

A bride in white rounded a corner and began marching towards us in wedge heels. She was pursued by the sound of a hysterical fly, and a man blowing a cornet followed her onto the road. Behind him, in clumps, emerged the full wedding party, almost exclusively male, wearing hot suits and polished shoes that were white with dust. As the men went past they clanked and their pockets drooped.

We found a dingy hotel and unmistakable signs of someone else having slept in our sheets. The hotel keeper had a look and deplored the situation, but left without doing anything about it. We gave her time to act and met the wedding procession again on their way back, the bridge hanging onto the groom's arm and all the men waving empty bottles of *palinka*.

When we got back the sheets were unchanged but we were too tired to care.

In the morning, just before we set off, Kate nuzzled something furry in her gulp of coffee. She wiped half a bluebottle from her tongue with the back of her hand. The part with the legs had disappeared.

Periodically throughout the day she announced her intention to be sick.

My pack started to creak. It was like the ship in the ice at the beginning of *Frankenstein*, a doleful *Ancient Mariner* sound. I was an abandoned galleon, marooned on a flat calm sea.

Now and then I stamped hard on the grass just to break the thundering monotony of this tiny squeak. The *puszta* – flat and, bar the occasional honking goose, soundless – was a terrifying place to be pursued by a squeak. I couldn't locate the source. By putting my hands under the straps and pushing the pack off my body I silenced it for a few steps but it found me out, and covered that angle, too. By mile five I was trying a crablike, Quasimodo lurch, one shoulder raised above the other, weight on my right leg, to achieve a few minutes of blessed quiet. It was exhausting, a refined attack of tinnitus. It left me blowing hard.

A train, slithering silently and, for a while, motionlessly out of the haze, hooted in alarm. The geese honked. The train hooted. My pack squeaked.

I presented it to the brain as a concatenation of consciences – all the outlaw consciences that had ever been suppressed on this blind flatland. The heat shimmering up on the horizon was good cover for bad hats and fugitives: I was beginning to see that for concealment you couldn't beat hot wilderness. Nothing was clear until you could practically pat it. A man in a white suit would go on looking like one of the geese until you were close enough to shake his hand. Any goose would look like your man until you could pluck it. Kate, my legs and the squeak were the most tangible things on the plain all day: that, and miles and miles and miles of identical grass track: a conveyor belt of grass track facing a painted backdrop of wavering horizon. I wished I hadn't thought that: it made me slightly sick, like the sudden illusion you can feel in a train at night, that you are travelling in the opposite direction.

Hortobagy's bungalows could have been shipped in kit from the Bournemouth Riviera. There was the wretched inn and the famous bridge. The bridge was the most popular photographic subject in Hungary after breasts and the Houses of Parliament; we'd seen posters of it from Ozd to Eger and knew that it was stone, and off white, and had a record number of seven arches to support it.

In the flesh it was crossing a river that a gander could have forded without getting his knees wet. In Spring the river would be wider, but not deeper; I entertained the cheering thought of mutton-jawed cavalrymen and hairy fugitives shrieking in despair as they minced through the water towards the inn. Tourism had done for the inn, anyway. It was ribbed with stained beams and served dreadful fried dishes to coachloads of Austrians who had been misled by photographs and Hungarian literature into thinking that they were coming to a cross between the OK Corral and Sherwood Forest.

Tucked up in bed in a private room in one of the bungalows I reflected smugly that Hortobagy had turned out rather well. It had kicked the stuffing out of my anxiety. Because we were now approximately halfway across it had shown that the *puszta* was tremendously small. The bungalows were exactly right: compared

– as it constantly was – to the Wild West, the *puszta* was as wild as a putting green. It was nothing but a large goose farm and it was absurd to think that ne'er-do-wells and shepherds had vanished into it for months on end.

Having lost the rump of its dominions to neighbouring countries, Hungary was left so small that the *puszta* seemed like a giant desert. No wonder the tourist board and patriotic *literateurs* conspired over it. The *puszta* was billed as an irruption of the Asiatic steppe into Europe; but it was more like a gentle tug on your sleeve.

The village of Hossupalyi was the first place in Hungary to have neither a hotel nor private rooms. We resolved to try out Geza Nemeth's letter on the pastor but the doors of the church were locked, and the pastor lived in another village, several miles away. A man and his son offered to find us the Catholic priest, and promptly led us to the doctor's wife. She looked uncertain, and patted her hairdo, directing us to a woman who kept the keys of the Catholic church. Liszt, according to a plaque on the wall, had once played the organ here; but it brought us no nearer to finding shelter. Outside we tried to thank our guides for their trouble, but the man would not desert us, and shyly asked us to stay with him.

He lived in a flat in a small block for teachers. His wife Elsa, a schoolteacher like him, spoke fluent German. When we mentioned our plan to cross the border they exchanged glances, and said we ought to be very careful. It was bad enough living next to such unpredictable people, they said; during the December revolution, Romanian army helicopters had clattered over their village and, God knew why, fired at people in the fields. To go among them was crazy.

'I hope to God you know what you're doing.'

Later Kate and I went out for a walk, leaving them to have their supper with the assurance that we had already eaten. We began to nose around the village in search of food, and fell upon a band of gypsies holding a party in the last light. A guitarist was picking out a fast gypsy *csarda*: around him people were singing and starting to dance while a knot of men in waistcoats and black moustaches squatted against the wall, passing round a bottle. A couple started to dance, one hand on the hip like reelers, stamping the ground as they wheeled about each other. Nobody spoke to us; but they watched us curiously until we felt we ought to move on.

Further along stood a bar, where a group of gypsy children dropped their street-game to cluster waist-high around us, bobbing and smiling and reaching out to touch Kate's skirt. A girl of five or six asked to be carried, and Kate hoisted her onto her hip, where she began playing with Kate's hair, and stroking her face carefully with the back of her hand. '*Szep, szep,*' she crooned: beautiful. In a few moments she had discovered a stash of brightly coloured elastic bands in Kate's pocket, and over these she marvelled intently, comparing them to her earrings, exactly like a polite child receiving a Christmas present – an impersonation as beguiling as it was bare-faced.

Kate needed her hairbands to keep her hair off her face as she walked, so she winkled one back. The little girl didn't seem to mind. An older child popped a stream of sunflower seeds from a paper bag, spitting out the husks; and when the troupe poured into the bar after us a gypsy with long moustaches grinned and patted Kate's pockets; we drank a swift brandy and bought sweets for the children.

The sweets vanished and the empty hands shot forward again. Just as the excitement was abating a child would hold up her sweet with a 'thank you', and the scrum would begin all over again. Small hands stole into each of mine; but Kate was explored. Little fingers kneaded her waistcoat, especially curious about the hard square block of our passports and money in her inside pocket. The girl with the seeds took to filling our pockets with them: for weeks afterwards I would find seeds wedged into the seams.

She began to ask questions – where were we from? and why were we here? Struck by the thought that we had walked so far she considered for a moment, and then asked, in perfect mime, whether our mother, perhaps, had died? Our clothes were so dark. We laughed, and shook our heads, amazed by the easy way she showed what she meant, and understood us in return; she laughed back, and asked if we had eaten. A few grown-ups were standing near us now. Scooping up a toddler, the girl pointed out her mother, who approached and asked me for a cigarette. A young man stood close, at a slight angle, not quite joining in as the children pressed us for gifts, or money; but the sweets were all gone and the best we could turn up were a couple of packets of Rizla papers: these seemed as popular as the sweets. The little girl asked if we had anywhere to sleep, because we could always stay with her.

For a moment we regretted that our packs lay at the school-teacher's flat; but one of the men from the bar began fingering the small leather box on my belt where I stuffed my money. I was wary of causing offence, but wary of him coming across a bundle of dollars and forints, too. He didn't smile when he held my arm, and I had to make a show of trying to shake hands before he let go. The children accompanied us almost to the door, where we waved them goodbye. A few shouted, and they all scampered away.

When we came in there was supper laid for us all. Elsa smiled in amused triumph. 'Now you must have something to eat with us,' she said. We ate bread and eggs and salami, and drank black sweetened tea, and mentioned that we had met the gypsies outside.

Elsa frowned and looked embarrassed.

'I am sorry,' she said. 'That is our bad luck.'

About fifteen years ago the village mayor had decided to teach Hungarians and gypsies to love one another, as she put it with heavy irony. Several gypsy families were invited to settle and were allocated new houses. Almost immediately they had burned up the floorboards for firewood. A pattern established itself, with the women working for a few weeks in the fields, while the men waited for money to drink and eat for a few weeks more. When the money was spent, the women returned to the fields. The original settlers, having half-destroyed their homes, had invited others to share them, and the village was all but overrun with strangers.

They made, she said, no attempt to fit into village life. The children came to school, but they were uneducable there. She pulled down her mark book and showed us the class lists: fours and fives for the Hungarians, but twos and ones by the names of gypsy children. We had been astonished by the children's capacity to understand, and their inspired ability to make themselves under-stood, for they presumably had little experience of speaking to foreigners; but they weren't quick in class. We admired their energy: in school they were listless and sullen.

'The children behave like the parents, who burn their own houses because they never think of tomorrow.' Threats and pun-ishments were worse than useless: children turned stubborn, and held adult grudges.

She passed her hand wearily over her forehead. 'We just don't know how things can go on. The other day a neighbour of mine ran over a gypsy girl in her car. The girl was only six. The children are always jumping out onto the road to make people swerve – they think it a good joke to terrify the drivers. This time the woman panicked. She was trying to avoid some children and she hit the girl instead, who died. The gypsies began asking her for money. They threw stones through her windows and her children were sleeping and were hurt by the stones and flying glass. The family moved into the back room, but the trouble got worse and now they have gone away to stay with relatives. It is blackmail.' She shrugged. 'We are all afraid here. We don't know who is in control any more. The gypsy problem in Hungary is a catas-trophe.'

In the morning they saw us to the road. Their daughter was in floods of tears: she presented Kate with a pencil sharpener hidden in a toy dog with a lead weight in its head. The teacher's wife cried and hugged us goodbye, warning us again to be very careful. 'Please write to say that you are safe,' she said. 'And if you change your mind you must come back here, yes?'

Beyond the razzmatazz of inner Hungary, the borders were peace-ful: only Romania snuffled and puffed close by: black chimneys beyond a low hill chain.

The town near the border did a two-way trade, with chocolate, sausage, Tampax, soap, televisions, Hoovers and biscuits for departing travellers, and a market for Hungarians from over the border to sell whatever they could: plastic sandals, glued-together running shoes, cheap shirts and jumpers, and oddments of plastic like soap dishes and fish slices. The old ladies, in black skirts and floral bodices and black headscarves, sold fruit: their wizened, pointed faces bobbed hopefully over nylon bags of cherries and plums.

You could spot Transylvanians by their shoes; their clothes were not ill-made, only less new and more conservative than we were used to seeing in Hungary. The women wore dresses and heels, holiday clothes.

We were obliged to accept the hotelier's offer of a private room because he claimed his hotel was full. We mistrusted him on sight, a sweating bully who poured us beer and vodka in his kitchen and fixed up our supper in his restaurant without asking. The food was disgusting. The room had a huge waterbed and satellite TV, on which we watched *The Towering Inferno* in German. Near the end Kate fiddled with the control box and found the same channel in English.

And just then NEWSFLASH!

NEWSFLASH!!!

The dayglo graphics belched twice and faded to footage of cars askew on a street and people running.

'SkyNews – coming later,' said an excited voice. 'Bucharest – City in Flames.'

NEWSFLASH!

FLASH!

Seldom has anyone been as eager to watch SkyNews as we were at that moment. Rolling uneasily on a waterbed in eastern Hungary we clung to that channel as it swung us relentlessly through the netherworld of late-night satellite viewing. All through the night we started from the bed while a horrible succession of pink sofas, squishy questioning, farts, pies and twanging rakes frothed across the screen in a swirl of absent laughter. Jokes left us twitching with shame and disbelief. We boggled at the screen until light fringed the curtains. But we never found the news.

We tried not to count the bad omens. In the morning our host managed to lose us the World Service just as the news was starting, in the belief that we wanted to make the television work. Later he overcharged. Only the day before I had unaccountably lost my Polish hat, my dumb and predictable memento. I didn't like the border without it.

'Student?'

'Yes.' The anodyne claim. Too loud.

His pen tapped the form. It hovered over Residence in Romania.

'Oradea Hotel?'

'Yes.' Was I nodding too hard? He looked up.

'Pack?'

'Yes. This one.'

He opened the flap, glanced in, and let it go.

'OK.'

I almost stammered thanks but Kate prodded me on and we began to walk the avenue between rusting overground pipes and the giant factory chimneys we'd seen from Hossupalyi.

Transylvania

Shaped like a horseshoe, enclosed on three sides by the Carpathians and to the west by a chain of hills that rise from the Hungarian plain, Transylvania is a little like a flying poop, a deck stanchioned by the mountains.

Transylvania is hard of access, aloof, bypassed by the traditional routes from the Baltic to the Black Sea. The rush of migrant tribes broke round it over the centuries: the Magyars passed it to the south, crossing the Danube plain on their way from the steppe and rounding up into Pannonia; and in the thirteenth century they approached Transylvania from the west, pushing up the Maros valley, to build castles, found towns, and bring the central lowlands into cultivation.

Transylvania became a strand on which people were washed up and silted down over centuries. Most of the nations of Eastern Europe have played a role in the Transylvanian amphitheatre: it has been laid waste by Asian hordes – Cumans, Tartars, Mongols, Turks; it has been settled by Hungarians, Romanians, Poles, Germans and Czechs. Harder to enter than the Polish plain or the straggle-ended steppe of Hungary or Romania, it is easier to defend – a plateau, scored by river valleys, a corrugated landscape of hills and plains. The land is rich and fertile, well-shaped for milling or mining, cropping, grazing, logging or trading. Settlements, allied by circumstance against the world at large, have long been divided by language, lifestyle, wealth and fortune. Over large areas of Eastern Europe the landscape dictates a single way of life, a single form of rule, a single source of disaster, encouraging the formation of empires to bind the regions together into a flexible whole. Transylvania, by contrast, holds everything necessary to life, and many luxuries, within its powerful borders.

*

We walked warily into Oradea like soldiers taking possession of a captured city, street by street. We'd rehearsed the suburbs many times, for models of these low, shuttered stucco houses, with plane trees on the pavement and wide, quiet streets, existed in Eger and Debrecen.

A beggar sat on the pavement, propped up against the railings, rolling his head convulsively from side to side as his eyes skimmed the passers-by at random. He wore a rag of a shirt and tattered shorts, black with filth. His hair was black and stuck out in corkscrews. A begging bowl lay betwen his legs, splayed on the ground like broken paddles. The brown skin was tight over the misshapen bones. People had to step over his legs, or pass to the gutter. The sun was very hot. We didn't have any currency to give. It might have been a day on a Calcutta street: it wasn't like Europe at all.

We tried three hotels. They weren't full: we just backed out when we saw the rooms. One was a tiny box with a fire-escape across the window. In another the curtains were closed, the bed unmade, the air stuffy with dust as if someone had checked out weeks ago, leaving the room locked and untouched. At the third hotel, the receptionist sat by a small black and white TV, and while she hunted for forms we watched it over her shoulder.

A man had tripped on the kerb as he zigzagged to and fro to avoid projectiles. He rolled to his feet but someone was abreast of him already and for a while they ran together, side by side, heads back, pumping their arms. Then they collided, stumbled together, staggered apart.

The receptionist tapped the key on the counter.

The man who had fallen began running again, but his pursuers thronged around, batting his face and shoulders in little soundless movements, drawing tighter and tighter together until their victim vanished in a knot of heads. The camera yawed wildly.

We pointed. The receptionist glanced back. 'Bucharest,' she said, without expression. She didn't seem shocked or afraid. The TV delivered a toneless reportage, quite unlike the strutting ringmaster of SkyNews: City in Flames.

We had a bare inkling of what was going on. A month before, Romania's first free elections in over half a century had returned the Salvation Front and its leader, the interim president Ion Iliescu, to power with a gigantic majority. The landslide result rather bore out criticisms that the election had been called too early, before the opposition parties had had time to present their manifestos and while the people were still blinking from the shock of Ceauşescu's overthrow. As the hero who had vanquished the villain, Iliescu was enjoying his honeymoon with the people.

More sohisticated observers, though, pointed out that Iliescu was the inherent beneficiary of Ceauşescu's fall. For years, as the Conducator's right-hand man, he had waited in the wings; and his appearance on the stage belonged to the same old comedy. Since the December revolution he had been busy making promises, consolidating his position with the army, the factory workers and the miners – the proletarian elite whose jobs were guaranteed and who received more than ten times the average wage. There had been a lightening of the more obvious forms of oppression – no more dawn arrests, freedom of movement restored, the prohibition on speaking to foreigners lifted – but doubters believed he had merely found new ways to manipulate the public. He encouraged, above all, their fears and insecurities. He warned them against the Hungarian minority in Transylvania. He frightened them with images of rapacious foreign capitalism. He fostered jingoism, paranoia, conspiracy theories. Following the example of the students in Tiananmen Square, the doubters had encamped before the parliament in Bucharest, calling for Iliescu's resignation and for an end to 'communism'.

The TV broadcast we were watching marked Iliescu's response. Officially, of course, the arrival of the miners in the capital was spontaneous. Spontaneously, they ran amok, beating and murdering the protestors and anyone else they found in the way, while the forces of law and order looked on. Iliescu did nothing at all, but everyone knew – and he liked them to realise – that the miners were his Varangian Guard.

Some of this we already knew; more we'd learn as we progressed. Until now we'd been hedge-hopping, coming in low across Europe to avoid the blast of rhetoric and political manoeuvring. The Poles, the Slovaks and the Hungarians had seized their opportunity to smash the old system apart, but the Romanians hadn't gone so far: they weren't sure where to go, nor what was being offered them, nor exactly what they wanted. But everyone dreamed, of triumph, or escape; and every dream was driven by fear.

We were given a huge room in the end, *piano nobile*, with two tall windows on the street. The room had long ago been white. Now it was sploshed with greasy smears that marked where the beds had stood. We had two narrow beds, with covers of dingy nylon and mattresses of interlocking wires that sagged to the floor like string bags. There was a small table. The lights didn't work. The concierge wearily removed a bulb from a neighbouring room and eventually it glowed dismally from a flex that hung from the ceiling rose. Our bathroom was huge as well, mosaiced, its hauteur mocked by gimcrack fittings, the lack of loo roll or hot water, the fringe of filth round every join, like flashing.

There were the gypsies under our windows, setting up shop on a concrete tub to sell Gent cigarettes. They were nothing like the short, dark, fox-eyed gypsies who in Cracow had announced our arrival in Central Europe, and who wore blouses and skirts, or shirts and trousers, like anyone else. Instead they were fair and majestically tall and the women's brown-black braids, falling to their waists, were tied off with coloured ribbons. They were handsome women with dark eyes and curving mouths: the gypsies of romantic legend, who belonged in this town like the conical spires of multicoloured tiles. The men wore black – hat, moustache, trousers and waistcoat – over white or striped shirts: very dashing; the women revelled in coloured waistcoats, and floral bodices cut above the elbow like sari tops, and full skirts, layer upon layer of finely pleated, brilliantly flowered cottons (a gypsy girl boasted to Kate later of having thirteen skirts, all on at once, with pockets on the inside). Greens, yellows, blues and oranges flashed as they moved.

They seemed unable to keep still. All day they sketched dance patterns on the ground with their feet. They twirled to make their hems flare out, and spoke to one another with gestures of the whole arm; they fiddled with their hair, or cradled a baby with gently swooping motions. When anyone walked by they would turn the swirl or dance or stroke or swoop into a brief gesture of enquiry, and whether they made a sale or not they resumed their movements and conversation with unconcern, and a remark that made them laugh.

Kate sat on the window-ledge and watched them for hours. I sat on the bed watching Kate watching them, wondering how to find anything to eat.

I was mooning around the room when Kate called me excitedly onto the corridor. From a back window she was looking down on a beer garden in the courtyard. At the back of our own hotel the gypsies were cramming the green tin tables, raising a clamour of greetings and laughter, sweeping the ground with their brilliant skirts, pushing their hats to the backs of their heads, and swigging from tankards of yellow beer.

A chimney sweep wearing a conical fur hat, and covered from its crown to his feet in smuts, leaned his brushes against the wall and pushed in among the drinkers.

'Let's go down,' said Kate.

Great roaring groups were swinging tankards like medieval banqueters. Tight-lipped waitresses aimed precisely between each swaying, amorphous group with another load of beer from a syphon attached to a steel barrel by the entrance. We sat down, expecting to be served. The expressions around us defied interpretation: far from the steady reserve of the men who drank in Hungarian bars, these were uncertain faces. Their mood changed as they caught sight of us – a sudden whisper, a blank drunken stare, a leer. The atmosphere felt faintly thuggish, certainly unsteady: it swung wildly, like lantern light in a high wind.

We figured out that we needed tickets for beer, and I joined a queue near the syphon, where the mugs were coming back in fistfuls to be dunked in a bucket of grey water, refilled, and sent slopping and filthy out again. I reached the front. Someone pushed in ahead of me and was served.

'*Due biera, va rog,*' I said at last.

The man looked at me as if I had emptied a headful of lice onto his desk.

'Uh?' He scowled.

The smell of beer was overpowering.

'*Due!*' I held up two fingers. The man shook his head and looked past me to the next in line, who moved forward without hesitation.

A tankard flecked with dirt swung past my nose. I turned to find Kate. Mouths were opening and closing, people were giving black-toothed grins, pulling one another's arms, cackling. A woman started screaming abuse and a man stood up and punched her in the face. I got back to Kate and suggested we leave, and my heart was racing when we reached the street.

In provincial towns you could read the history of Eastern Europe. Medieval, Renaissance, Imperial-classical, each had its boom a very long time ago. They shared the appearance of having survived as clerking towns for the convenience of the gentry on neighbouring estates – like those provincial towns of O— and P— familiar from Russian novels, with music masters, scandalised widows, and peasant businessmen with pale embarrassed daughters. The remainder were those which were wasted in the war and rebuilt as cheaply as possible. Oradea – Nagyvárad to the Hungarians (who built it), Grosswardein to the Germans – stood out. Its boom had come much later, at the turn of the century, and since nothing of interest had been built afterwards it was a boom coinciding with the last years of Hungarian rule, petering out when the city went Romanian.

As booms go, this one must have been hilarious. Oradea really seemed to have been sculpted out of marzipan. It was a city of coloured brick, mock turrets and lily-like encrustations, a loopy confection of Ruritanian Art Nouveau parading along our street to the square by the river. The square was enforced by the columns of a classical opera house with oval mansards, the work of Helmer and Fellner. While everything was built on a petty scale, it resembled the miniaturisation of Petit Trianon, with a tininess both flirtatious and sophisticated – a place for princesses, dukes, twisted hunchbacks, beaky beggar women, pointed hats; somewhere Doctor Caligari might sit on a crooked stool and child-catchers roam the streets with nets.

The language set my teeth on edge. Romanian is a Mediterranean language and looks familiar at a glance. Yet the more I studied it, the less I understood. It was like one of those code languages children use, with a strand of gibberish woven through every sentence that made it utterly incomprehensible. It was like trying to eat with a rubber fork, or reading through the wrong glasses. It made me feel seasick.

Everywhere, in fact, the gap between first appearances and reality yawned wide like the heaving of a deck against the horizon. They called it '*vinu*', it looked like wine, and they served it in stemmed glasses, but it was a syrup diluted with water that tasted like oily raspberry juice. '*Coniac*' was a brown drink. It reeked of silage and made our heads ache looking at it. Once we had a phony waiter, dressed as a waiter down to the white cloth on his arm for wiping the top of the 'wine' bottle, who wouldn't serve us. After an hour or so he came over to our table and said 'Goodbye' in a nasty voice. It would all have been funny if it hadn't been so relentless, buying pretend cigarettes that shed their tobacco on your lap when tilted, or a newspaper with only one page, or a bar of soap that lathered as readily as flint. The atmosphere wasn't comic. It was tawdry and dispiriting. The dusty shops which sold a ragbag of skinny books, printed on paper that bled type from the next page, or chemicals packed in home-made boxes, or bendy plastic combs – the dullness of suited clerks, the empty concrete pots for absent trees – all suggested a city where witches and crookbacks went unrelieved because princesses, palfreys and grand dukes in opera cloaks had vanished long ago.

At least I didn't have to live here. In dingy suits, their collars undone, people moved with an uneasy privacy. I didn't expect friendliness, especially. I didn't exactly sense hostility. I had a sense of a city sagging, falling apart, not quite adding up. They walked with their heads bowed, as if trying to avoid anyone's eye; or scowled and stared with menacing defiance. People were like gases, vaporous, perhaps vapid, given to random motion.

In the cloakroom of the Restaurant Transylvania I stopped to buy cigarettes. The attendant stood behind a glass-topped cabinet, displaying three or four different brands. I pored over them, trying to detect some useful difference.

'You want cigarette?'

I straightened up, surprised.

'Yes please.'

'What contry are you from, sir.'

'England.'

'Ah, London.'

'Yes, that's right.'

He didn't look me in the eye as he said: 'I was not always a cloakroom clerk, you know. Once I was the boss of a border customs.' He compressed his lips for a second. 'Now I just sell cigarettes.'

I wanted to ask him what happened. On his wrist he wore a digital watch sprouting two plastic-coated wires connected to a large battery taped around his arm.

I asked lightly: 'Are these any good?'

He glanced wearily away. 'Not quite,' he said. 'You want good cigarette?'

He bent under the counter and produced a packet of Marlboro. They were seventy-five lei, about five dollars at the official rate.

'I'll take these,' I said, pointing instead to a squashy packet with pale blue stripes and a red splash of a skier on the front.

'Ski?' he raised his eyebrows. 'Six lei.'

I fumbled for the grimy notes.

'Matches also?' He added with something like irony. He laid a box on the counter.

'Thank you,' I said. 'Please keep the change,' I gabbled, as he pulled out a shoebox of coins.

That night, slung in my drooping bed like a sailor, or a banana, I felt like a frightened twelve-year old. It didn't seem fair. Fifteen miles away lay another world, tangibly European, ordered, clean, well-maintained, reasonably prosperous. Everything here, by a twist of fate, had plunged towards the gimcrack. We could have taken a deep breath and turned our backs on Hungary, hoping to make the most of this fragment of the Third World, with its flies and beggars and disease and heat, except that Hungary would not lie still. The Hungary built here until seventy years before kept the contrast constantly alive, a never-ending might have been. If only the city were still Hungarian! The crookbacked atmosphere would have been dispelled by something hilarious and grown-up.

We went to Mass in the whitewashed Hungarian chapel where the weekday service was conducted for a few old women dressed in black; for there, easing back into a familiar language and Roman ritual, I met God like an old friend strolling across from Hossu-palyi as though the border did not exist.

The Oradea looked like fun. To judge from its ceiling it had been either a high-class brothel or a louche café. The walls, and the pilasters that framed gigantic sarcomatous mirrors, were painted light brown; the heavy hangings that could be drawn across the windows and the doors to exclude the street were of gorgeous faded scarlet velvet. Putti overhead were indulging the pleasures of the grape, the table and love; dice were thrown, glasses tossed off, and Cupid fired his darts in no particular direction. Draw those curtains, strike up the band, fill the tables with opera goers and champagne – it would have made for a mood of naughtiness and playful secrecy. But there wasn't a band of course; no wine, just the muffling drapes and old worn carpet and a sense of menace.

At a neighbouring table two women were being served with unprecedented civility. The older woman wore a soft black sweater and her blonde hair drawn up in a loose bun. The restaurant had begun to fill up. After a while a fight broke out. One of the combatants was heavy and middle-aged: his opponent was young, with sleek black hair and a narrow weasel face. Chairs were kicked aside, the table overturned. The waiters stopped what they were doing and watched. It was quite quick. The older man wrestled his opponent to the floor, got astride him, and smashed his fist rapidly into the face below him until it gushed blood. He wiped the back of his hand on the boy's jacket, and stood up. The young man crawled away. Several people laughed.

The blonde at the next table caught sight of our faces.

'May I speak English? I am so sorry for this.' She leaned across. 'Please do not think this is Oradea. These are peasants, without culture. I hope you understand.'

We muttered something polite. She turned away.

On their way out, however, they stopped by our table.

'I do hope you understand,' she said. 'This is your first visit? Oradea was not always sad like this, believe me. These people fight – well, they are unhappy. They must run, run, run for food. This is the new Oradea. I am sorry you have to see it like this.'

She sat down. 'Once Oradea was called the Little Paris. But different people have been moved in, agricultural people from the south. They work in the lousy factories that are built all around Oradea. They make it a big, ugly city now.'

Her friend nodded. 'You see – Ceauşescu man.' She put her hands to the sides of her face to make blinkers. 'Like this.'

'He has brains in his belly,' said Eva. 'He is not a thinker. Go! and he goes. Come! and he comes.' She paused, balling her fingers at her breast. 'I love my country, but I am not an illusionist. Romania will never get democracy. These people have been told that they had a revolution. They are pleased with themselves. They think it means they can ask for more food. They do not understand what is a revolution. They sure don't want things to change.

'This election – Iliescu frightens the people. They will sell Romania to the foreigners! Your food will go to the Americans and the Hungarians! You will have no jobs! The people cannot imagine anything else. Ceauşescu was a stupid. Iliescu is smart.'

I said: 'With things opening up, won't they soon see that life is better in the West?'

'Why? Why should they see that? They are uneducated and they are too poor. This rich life on television they will believe is propaganda. They think you are super-rich, and that there must be millions of very poor people in the West. Really.'

She looked fed-up. I said: 'Ah, but we aren't wearing top hats and frock coats,' and she smiled for the first time. 'They will think you are in disguise,' she whispered.

In the early seventies, Eva and her husband had emigrated to America. Her husband picked up casual jobs and Eva worked as a cleaner in a school.

'Can you believe? Like a janitor!'

Her husband wanted to stay; Eva came back. They had a son who shuttled between them, an American citizen. In the seventies, she said, it was still possible to lead a reasonable life in Romania.

Ceauşescu filled her now with superstitious dread.

'You think he is dead? How do you know? The film on television? Pah!' She grinned, almost angrily. 'Ceauşescu had seven actors who looked like him. They talk like him, walk like him, and when he was afraid one of these actors went for him. Sometimes, you know, if you read very carefully, you discover that the man is here and there at the same time. It is very stupid.

'But who will shoot Ceauşescu? If he has money in Swiss bank accounts, it is better to learn the numbers and let him go. Perhaps he is in Cuba, who knows? So one of these actors dies, or pretends to die, I don't know.'

Sanda said:

'I think Ceauşescu was tortured. He have money in Switzerland. On the film he lie in a strange way, one foot – so.' She bent her wrist back. 'Also very – beaten.' She put her fingers to her face. 'Not clean.'

Eva left us on the steps of the restaurant, heading off to catch a bus on the other side of the river.

The following day we met Sanda again at a café on the river.

She was a walker herself.

'We walk all day – 40 kilometres in the mountains. It get dark. Ion say we must do 20 more. I say but Ion, I am so tired. But we go on more and more. I cannot walk. I say Ion my legs finish. He says, in the snow you die. Must walk. Then we hear ow! ow! It is wolveses. Ion say hurry. I cannot.

'Then you know? We see light in the trees. Ion say good, Sanda, we arrive. No, you must carry me up, I say to him. But Ion likes me to be strong, not like "weak woman".' She pulled a face. 'So he go on, and I fall down and go with hands and feet. Maybe one hour. He is there and I must help cooking.'

Kate and I stared at her open-mouthed.

'I am proud we share every thing. I am so strong as him. This walk is wonderful to me.'

She and Ion sought out the loneliest and most inaccessible parts of the country and walked them for days on end. This was our nightmare. We asked Sanda who we might meet on the road, and how often we'd be likely to reach a village, and how the people might respond to us, and she kept reassuring us that there were places where we'd be quite alone, bar the odd shepherd. When

On Foot to the Golden Horn

she finally understood that we meant to stick to the road, and go through as many villages as we could, she seemed shocked.

'Every part of Transylvania, different hat,' she said thoughtfully. 'Many old customs.'

She was a claustrophobe. Stifled by the corruption of city life she longed to move to the north, where the mountains touched the Ukrainian border, and teach in a village school. Ideally, she would like to run a little shop, but there was no chance of getting permission.

'It is like passport. Since the revolution we can get passport to travel. You must ask police for the form. The form costs nothing, but for the policeman it is money. They say sorry, no forms. So you must pay, maybe 500 lei. I will not do this.

'You see everything in this country is black market. You must pay for everything. Children pay for good results at school. If a child gets bad results, it is the teacher's fault and the teacher is punished. So teachers cheat.'

'How terrible!' I exclaimed.

Sanda looked puzzled. 'But how else to make teachers work properly?'

'You mean nobody trusts the teachers to work?'

'I told you before, nobody trusts nobody.'

To Cluj

From Oradea, on the plain, it took us a day to reach the hills. On the flat open land beyond the city the crops grew in straggling patches, and the road was badly screened from the sun by a few trees creeping like refugees along the verge, not quite amounting to an avenue. A herd of ponies drank from a watering hole, and two little boys threw stones to drive them away. They were hobbled, and moved like rocking horses.

Against our instincts we had welcomed the forest where the air was cool. The *cabana* was a few miles further on.

It stood in the gorge near a grotto. It was not accessible by road. It mouldered on an apron of dead leaves where the footpath plunged towards the stream, with its shutters closed, brown paint peeling from the woodwork and the concrete green with damp. Half-a-dozen stacking chairs rusted at metal tables on a concrete bib and two sagging wires dropped through the trees from an old winch. Only the padlock on the door was new. We wondered bleakly what to do next. It had been a mistake listening to Sanda. I wasn't Ion, and I didn't relish building a bivouac in the empty forest, lying awake for the padding of wolves.

A whistle screeched down the gorge. A man came through the trees wearing shorts and a loo seat round his neck. He was followed by a boy in an armless denim jacket, a middle-aged woman in black skirts and more men bearing loo seats, paint pots and mysterious boxes. The winch whirred into activity. A pile of bathroom fittings grew at our feet. The man who had first appeared shook hands.

'My brother and I run hotel,' he said, grandly. He was built like a Roman emperor, clean shaven; he spoke with an accent that could have been Italian. It was enough that he spoke English. 'Now we must work,' he said.

It was a command more than anything. A railway line slotted into the foot of the gorge, and a tiny station burst with flowers. Over the whirr of the winch, as I climbed with a box, I heard the proprietor softly call out 'Camel cigarettes' and jerk his thumb towards me; instinctively, I touched my wallet and a man with a moustache leered.

When every box stood outside the *cabana* the chief asked us where we meant to sleep.

'Here, at the *cabana*.'

He cupped his hand around his mouth and breathed heavily through his nose, looking at the ground.

'Problem. Problem. The *cabana* is full.'

A moment ago it had looked derelict. Now, almost as he spoke, it brimmed with youths in leather jackets and dark glasses who seemed to have condensed out of the trees.

'Hungarian childrens, very bad,' he explained. They looked bad. They swigged from bottles and lounged around the balcony, smoking. A devilish scream was followed by a thundering bass chord.

'Perhaps my sister's room.' He was shouting. 'It is not very good.'

It wasn't. It was a concrete cell with a shuttered window and a door that wouldn't lock. A heap of bloodstained sheets lay on a mattress whose springs had long ago sprung and now made a bony squeaking ridge down the length of the bed. We'd slept in better haystacks.

'How much?'

'Fifty lei.'

About $2.50, officially. Officially lei were all we had. I sidled up to my first black-market proposition in the country.

'Would you take a dollar?'

'If you like, it's OK.'

It took us a long time to get our lock fixed, waiting in the cell to guard our packs from the bad hats, increasingly rowdy and curious outside. It was dull in the twilight of the low-watt bulb. Our friend reappeared to introduce his brother, who kissed Kate's hand. Our friend sat down at the end of the bed.

'This *cabana* is not good for foreign visitors.' He frowned; in the half-light he resembled Mussolini. 'In Ceauşescu times, the man here he did not do nothing. Very dirty. And every night many men, bad men – drink, cards, poker, one and twenty. Tourist – bap! Drink, cards – scandal.'

He pulled another face.

'My family is proprietor now. In one year it will be much better.'

We nodded vigorously, secretly hoping it was slightly improved already.

'I have a question. I must go to France or Spain very soon. To join the – *Straine Legion*.'

The Foreign Legion! Why?

'My problem,' he said charmingly, as though he were suggesting a treat.

'It's very hard,' I said.

He laughed. 'I was in Romanian paratroops. For me it's not hard.' He thought for a moment, and his face grew a little anxious. 'Do the Legion fight much?'

We didn't think so. He grinned.

'That is good. And do you know how much money, my friend?'

I guessed for him. 'Twenty thousand dollars, maybe.'

'A month?'

'A year.'

He frowned and smacked his lips.

'It is good work for me. But I must get to France.' The anxious look reappeared. 'For this in Romania we have no money. I buy a little from foreigners. Tell me, can you exchange some dollars for me? Is it possible?'

'We don't have much cash,' I said cautiously, but in the end it was agreed that we could manage $100. He'd hoped for more, and brisk with disappointment he jumped up and told us he'd have to find out the going rate.

He knocked before entering.

'Fifty lei for a dollar, OK?'

We agreed. He explained that he would need time to fetch the money from 'Oradea City', as he called it.

'Have you food? Then you must eat with us.'

We thanked him. He left, promising to send someone in to fix the lock. 'My mother is a – kitchen lady. Very good.'

But we didn't eat with the family as we'd expected. Instead they spread a checkered cloth and laid places for two in the dingy main room, full of cardboard boxes. The food was excellent, the very meal that had been described as the dream of the *puszta* peasant: chicken soup and vermicelli, with golden fat floating on top; then drumsticks, mash and lettuce, and strawberries afterwards.

There was even fresh white bread and a pat of black market butter in its wrapper, on which we read, with a feeling very like triumph, the name of a manufacturer in Istanbul.

Our friend brought the money.

'If I don't go to the Legion,' he explained, 'I will always feel bad.'

Our room had become an amplifier for the Hungarian children's tape machine, and all night the music throbbed around the concrete walls.

On the corner of the main square in Cluj we saw the word Hotel scrawled in dead wiry neon. The receptionist sat behind a sheet of glass with a row of luxuries – wine, perfume, foreign cigarettes – on the shelf behind her.

We were too tired to grasp the point of her insinuating regret. We stood bowed and helpless as she outlined, at length, the problem of finding us a room; at the end we turned listlessly away. This spinelessness so amazed her that she called us back and, with various face-saving trawls through the ledger, discovered one empty room with three beds.

'Three beds is fine,' we said.

'But there is no bath,' she said, in a tone that suggested that a room without a bath was worse than no room at all.

'Fine, fine.'

She played her last card.

'You will have to pay for the third bed.'

We looked at her wearily. She looked back appraisingly. Something stubborn and stupid on our faces persuaded her to give in.

But later from her, rather casually, we learned that the going black-market rate for dollars was at least twice what the Legionnaire had given us, and we went to bed feeling bitter in a poky room with dirty sheets and spidery mat of hairs blocking the basin.

The parish house was located behind a carriage gate on the old main square, facing the church of St Matthew. It was cool in the tiny vestibule, away from the heated clamour of the street, from the leers and stares, the contused faces that had thronged about us all morning as we searched for a priest, Father Zsiriac, who spoke seven languages including Latin. We had been given his name by a historian in London. A fat man with a rim of curly grey hair grinned in a friendly way from behind a desk.

'*Si vous demeurez ici, le prêtre va venir,*' he said in a soft voice, dabbing a handkerchief across his shining pate.

Le prêtre did not come, so Miklos offered us lunch. Behind the vestibule, through several offices laid with red corded carpet, lay an inner courtyard closed on three sides, and a hedged path that led across to the kitchen.

'*Je vous en prie, mangez,*' said Miklos, as we sat at the scrubbed oak table set with two places for us, and plates of good bread and sausage. An old lady cleaned up the kitchen and set a cauldron of water on the iron range to boil. Miklos explained the miracle that Father Zsiriac had performed.

'Securitate had offices in the middle wing of the parish house, overlooking the square and, of course, this courtyard too. After the revolution Father Zsiriac applied for the building to be returned to the Church, and one day, without warning, the army came and took everything away. I'll show you.'

When he was sure we had eaten enough he led us across the courtyard and up a staircase to the repossessed rooms. They were bare, but Miklos described everything as he saw it almost six months earlier, the night after the Securitate fled. The windows overlooked the square and the door of the church, a carved stone doorway that neatly framed the photos taken by the Securitate showing who went in and came out. For attending church once you were likely to lose your job.

'*Le telephoto se trouve ici.*' There had also been a fax machine, a photocopier, telephones, walkie-talkies, video cameras. There was a rail of clothes. A soundproof room containing nothing but a table. Tape recorders. And files. Boxes and boxes of them. Even Miklos's own.

'When you came in, you destroyed the file, I suppose?'

Miklos looked grave.

'*Non. Non. Nous n'avons rien detruit. J'ai regardé le dossier, et le remplace, tout simplement.*'

I tried to imagine it.

'*Mais pourquoi?*'

'*J'avais peur.*' He didn't hesitate.

He held out his hands.

'*Je vous comprends. Vous savez, nous ne sommes pas maintenant ce que nous etions avant – avant –*' he waved a gesture of dismissal. '*La semelle de la peur nous accompagne toujours au coeur. Pour nous, les limites de la courage se diminue.*' His fingers folded around an imaginary object, and opened gradually. '*Nous nous guerirons lentement, lentement.*'

We were all silent, looking around the empty rooms.

'*Les dossiers existent encore?*' I asked.

'*Oui, oui, sans doute.*' He paused. '*Ils sont fuit d'ici, quand même. Ce batiment, dédicacé à l'église, est retabli. C'est extraordinaire. C'est un commencement pour nous.*'

'*Un miracle?*'

Miklos gave a gurgling laugh.

'*Peut-être.*'

Father Zsiriac appeared in a mackintosh outside his office, escorted by two younger priests. He had a strong-boned, broad face and dark hair that needed washing. He was very tall. We introduced ourselves, and mentioned our mutual acquaintance.

'Perhaps you would like to stay with us for a while? Where are you staying in Cluj?'

He told us to quit the hotel. Then he left the room in three huge strides, the flanking priests scurrying to keep pace.

We thought we were to be given a place to sleep in one of the church-house rooms but Zsiriac's secretary, Peter, arrived instead to take us home. He had a long crumpled face and small hands and wore glasses; he spoke in squirrelled bursts of hopeless English. He drove us home by way of a hill from where he pointed out the church of St Matthew, the Protestant church, the remaining city walls, and the long tadpole tail of new blocks which snaked off towards the east. Apart from one greenish stumpy block the old town centre had scarcely altered this century, and the black spire of St Matthew still rose unopposed from the crisscross pattern of low tiled roofs.

Peter and Marika lived in an apartment belonging to the Church which overlooked a park not far from the main square. By East European standards it was a large apartment, with rooms for the children, Marika's parents, Peter and Marika themselves, and us.

Marika's eyes were set in dark rings, but her stolid expression belied an invincible gullibility which was obliged to work overtime in Cluj. For in Cluj the wildest rumours circulated.

That in a network of mountain caves Ceauşescu had reared babies like veal calves, and sought eternal youth with regular injections of their blood.

That the only Romanian cigarettes containing actual tobacco were called Carpathi, one of the cheapest brands available – if they were available.

That Ceauşescu staffed Securitate with orphan children raised to think of him with fear and love as their own father, the Conducator whose life they would protect with their own: for without him, what would their lives be worth?

That the revolution was a coup d'état and that the sixteen demonstrators who died on the steps of the Transylvania hotel in December were shot, not by the Securitate, but by the army to implicate the Securitate.

That the Romanians are descended from Trajan's legionnaires.

That the Romanians are descended from Sicilian bandits cleared off the island by the Vikings in the tenth century.

That Ceauşescu was not dead.

That the gypsies –

'My God!' said Marika. 'Last year the gypsies attacked some

German tourists who stopped for a picnic on the Oradea–Cluj road. Cut the rings from their fingers! A little boy survived by hiding in the woods! Of course it is kept a secret. In daylight!' She mentioned the place, which we remembered well. There had been a concrete trestle by the road, under a canopy of leaves, where we'd sat to change our socks around.

Peter produced a bottle of *palinka* for our first evening, sketching across the patches in his English with a piece of paper and a pencil as the level sank. I have kept that paper, on which mountains and seas, ships and fortifications jostled for room, because gradually through the evening, beneath the scrawls and spellings, it evolved into a kind of map. The seat of the Catholic Church of Transylvania dominates at the centre of the page while the Sicily of bandits is only a spot on the paper's edge. A river of biro flows to the west; the jagged outline of the mountains cradles the page to the south and east. Between the scrawls comes Peter's excited voice, in bursts of rapid half-sense. This map charts an argument: the argument for Hungarian Transylvania.

It plots, as well, the start of a friendship. We stayed a week with Peter and Marika. As a surprise we organised a celebration for their wedding anniversary, and I had my birthday there. They took us into the hills south of Huedin for a picnic and one afternoon we all drove to Alba Iulia and saw the tomb of Hunyadi Janos, the Hammer of the Turks, hammered itself when the Turks took the citadel a century after his death. Driving back in the dark Kate cried out just in time to stop Peter impaling us on an unlit cart. Marika and Peter took to squabbling in dreadful English.

On the map there's Poland, for instance, drawn by me: about the size of a penny. Peter has looped it up to Transylvania with Bethlen Gabor inscribed inside the curve: the Prince of Transylvania who became King of Poland, and of Hungary as well. The Székely, a Hungarian tribe, dwell on the jagged eastern mountains like a row of medals. Up from the south comes a quiverful of Romanians, crossing Dalmatia, vanishing in Bulgaria, and following them up to the mountains where they come to a temporary halt at an arrowhead indicating a small sheep.

'Romanian sheep-people, only sheeps, no architecture, no

writing, no painting,' says Peter, and a date appears on the top left hand corner: 1921. 'Before, no Romanian building. Hungarian, yes! German, yes!'

A crenellated bun appears near the southern range, then another. Segesvár, Schässburg, is a Saxon town near Marosvásárhely: and duly that impenetrable name appears as well, Hungarian for Tirgu Mures. We learn to pronounce it, Marosh-vasher-hay, and feel like novitiates.

Snatches of Petofi, the great poet of nineteenth-century Hungary, who died near Segesvar, decorate the margins of this map. Peter recites a poem, not a word of which we understand, in a *palinka*-timbred voice that almost convinces us we do. He is proud of the beautiful eggy sounds of his language; proud of its inscrutable origins. His voice draws across the soft clogged Hungarian vowels and clatters over the stiff Hungarian consonants. The Romanian language, he explains, is a dim Sicilian descendant, clawing at Slavic vocabulary; Hungarian, on the other hand, is a thoroughbred, an aristocrat of languages. When Hungarian adopts Slavic words it picks and chooses, for particular reasons. A biro bear claws at Brasov-Brassoi. The old Hungarians had a shamanistic awe of certain beasts whose spirits, not at all friendly, were invoked by mentioning them directly by name. To get round the problem, words like 'medve', bear, which we could recognise from Polish, were borrowed from the impotent language of the Slavs.

For Peter, Erdelyi – Transylvania – was as incandescent as one of those hidden words. Hungarian held the spirit of the place, as it held the true traditions of Hungary: its art and letters, history and religion. The highest culture had reigned in the palaces of a lost nobility, a Hungarian culture way beyond anything that Budapest could offer – after all, Buda had answered to the Turk, and Budapest to the Habsburg emperors. Peasant tradition flourished here, too, as it scarcely did in Hungary proper, and the ancient Asiatic symbols – the Persian lion, for example – still constituted the elements of peasant art. To show us, Peter fetched a series of enormous books illustrating the embroidery patterns peculiar to each region of Erdelyi, and tried to explain the variations in form and style between one valley and the next, between villages in a single valley.

Transylvanian history was the record of Hungarian deeds. Hungarians fought the wars, built the churches, the castles, the towns; wrote and made and read the books; founded schools and universities; built houses, palaces, stables; studied agriculture. They even gave Romanians their first education, and as recently as the nineteenth century taught them to use the Latin script. Peter burst into a mainly incomprehensible snort of contempt for those self-proclaimed descendants of Trajan. For the Romanians, whether they lived in Moldavia, Wallachia, or even Transylvania, had none of these historical things: battles, or towns as such, or trade; secular writing; universities, or brick. By the most tragic and baffling stroke of luck, however, they did have Transylvania.

'Romanian victory! Victory of Romanian mothers!!' For the Hungarians took the valleys, the roads, the rivers, and made a civilisation that thought, fought and died, while Romanian shepherds clung to the hilltops to raise sheep and goats – and Romanians. When the Allies ordered a head count in 1918 the breeding paid off. With the fudging possible to victors, the inclusion of Wallachian shepherds traditionally permitted to summer on the mountains, with parts of Hungary momentarily under Bolshevik control and Transylvania in the hands of the Romanian army, the Allies were persuaded that Transylvania contained more Romanians than Hungarians and at Trianon in 1921 the country was handed over to Bucharest.

'To liar people! To no culture!'

When Peter went to Romania proper for any reason, he always took a packed lunch.

Miklos believed in God, opera, tragedy and the Hungarians in that order. He sang around the offices, a sweet tenor, and would have been a professional but for '*un malheur personel*'. Marika speculated freely on the nature of this *malheur*. One evening he took us a box at the opera to hear a diploma performance of *La Bohème* given by students of the Romanian State Opera. After Act I he wore an expression of anticipatory grief, and when Suzette found breath to sing her parting aria he mopped his eyes and forehead with an embroidered handkerchief.

The opera house was built by Helmer and Fellner, who had built operas for the Habsburgs everywhere, including Debrecen and Oradea. It was a pocket affair, a lavish small-scale replica of the great operas, from the gilded swags to the miniature boxes, the little pit and dress circle.

Miklos was not known to have missed any new performance. Each week he left his coat in the cloakroom, bought a programme and took his seat, a minute or two before the lights went dim. A violin sharpens itself from the pit; paper crackles as people stand to let each other past, and a seat knocks upright; a low murmur of greeting spreads through the auditorium; an oboe lows and the piccolo flies up: the sounds of cultivated expectation all over the world. So the lights go down, the voices and instruments fall silent and a dozen people remember to cough, discreetly. Silence; the curtain is gathered up and in the unfamiliar light we find ourselves – not in Cluj. Miklos is transported from the trouble of living alone, from queues and corruption and foul cigarettes, lifted clean away from sordid rigmarole, to the highlands in kilts, to Egypt, fettered, to Paris and tragedy and love.

It was a very good performance, to a full house. Afterwards we escorted Miklos to his bus stop, and waited as one bus after another developed bronchial trouble and froze, inert. The queue lengthened. Miklos apologised for not asking us home, as was his custom, to take a glass of something: but his mother had lately died and he had had no time to tidy up and make the place presentable. At last a bus appeared, and the people crammed aboard, and Miklos was carried off down the dark street, waving shyly from the rear window.

A demonstration was taking place in the square, and we approached one of the protestors to ask about the banners, singling him out because he looked like a flattened version of Harrison Ford. He spoke good English, and asked us to call him John; over the next few days we got to know him. He believed in democracy, in Oriental mysticism, and in the political value of standing all day in the square to bear witness to the terror in Bucharest in

June. When an elderly couple told him, bluntly, to get himself a job, he stuck his hands in his back pockets and looked superior.

Jos Communismus – Communism Out – was written across a banner that had hung along the rooftops on the square for months. The demonstrators caried more recent banners, with more specific accusations and demands. They were after Iliescu's resignation. They wanted the army to stand down, or to step in, whatever would prevent a repetition of the bloody attacks on protesters in Bucharest. They wanted a general election, but with time for parties to prepare and take a platform. A new constitution to introduce a proper balance between executive and legislature. They wanted the names of people responsible. They called themselves *golan* – which means thugs – which was the word Iliescu had used to describe them.

They were immensely confident. Their leader was a harassed-loooking woman called Adreana who was affiliated to Amnesty International. She lisped badly and the spittle flew from her lips as she spoke. Her eyes were frightened, and she pulled us to her as a human shield. Our presence as foreigners, she pointed out, made trouble here less likely, and as a result we felt impelled to visit every day.

Yet as the days went by the *golan*'s vigil increasingly took on the character it was given by an unenthusiastic populace. Attendance dwindled as people drifted back to work. Adreana kept to her bench but the crowd surrounding her had disappeared and in her distraction she seemed more like a bag lady among the pigeons than the leader of a democratic protest rally. John's face increasingly wore an expression of earnest puzzlement.

'Maybe,' he said heavily one afternoon, when we met in a café near the square, 'the Romanian people are just not going to understand. They are not ready.'

'None of them?'

'Perhaps I should say that the Hungarians are more advanced.'

The Hungarians, certainly, showed political acumen: they had demonstrated that they understood the notion of choice perfectly well, by voting *en bloc* for the Hungarian party. This party was now the biggest opposition group in parliament; almost the only group, in fact: the Romanians, faced with a choice, had simply voted back the reigning government of Iliescu and cronies with a majority that Stalin himself might have been pleased to engineer.

After another afternoon of barracking, when the banners had to be leaned against the statue of King Matthias Corvinus because there were too few demonstrators left to hold them upright, John confessed that the group was going to disband. His English had grown almost word-perfect in a few days: he had never spoken English before, only reading constantly, and listening to the dialogue on old American movies. 'Not Oldies but Goldies; Oldies but Rusties,' he explained, with a rare slip of humour. Now he could practise what he'd learned in theory, and it was with the aim of improving his spoken English that he proposed to accompany us to the Turda Gorge on our way out of Cluj.

Peter and Marika were unhappy about John; we had an awkward meeting on the square where they came to see us off. They had prepared us – in the teeth of our opposition – packed lunch, including several tins of Peter's favourite and rarest delicacies, hoarded from a visit to Hungary over a year earlier: fish in tomato sauce, and steak tartar. We all cried and hugged each other.

John was wearing his sawn-off jeans, very short, and a T-shirt and gym shoes, and carried a home-made nylon rucksack. Still snivelling, we led him up the hill past the world-famous Botanical Gardens, and out of Cluj.

Sometimes John seemed just like us; sometimes impenetrably foreign. He solemnly believed in tantric Buddhism, and as we trudged past the hops and strawberry fields of the Maros valley he talked about itinerant sufis in Asia, whose negation of matter left them prone to float, so that they needed heavy weights strapped to their waists to keep their feet moving over the ground at all. At home, John meditated; and having learned to recognise pain as an illusion he could stub out burning cigarettes on his arm without flinching – he alarmed us one evening by offering to set his fingers alight with a candle. Oddly, he complained of blisters; and after a week, when we tended him with every Western salve we possessed, he was hobbling so painfully he agreed that he should return to Cluj.

In other ways he reminded me of Sanda in Oradea. They had

both discovered that intelligence made no headway against the brute instincts of Romanian society. John's eastern religion was a kind of licensed apathy – an apathy prefigured by the failure of the *golans*, and marked in him, too, by dreams of the hermitic life in the northern mountains. Sanda dreamed of her shop and unpeopled walks; John of a hut: both of them leaned instinctively towards withdrawal as the only practical way to stay clean.

John's urge to withdraw contrasted awkwardly with the behaviour of the people who sheltered us in Transylvania; it spilled over into his dealings with them. The Hungarian priests who took us in at night were making a stand that was unimaginable to John. He had the close-set eyes and jutting brow of a southerner, an Oltenian – a look we had recognised among the transposed populations that filled the new suburbs of Transylvanian cities; it was a squint, short-focused. Guilelessly, he would take all hostly offers and protestations at face value.

It would be hard to say Kate and I never imposed on anyone; but from the first night in Poland, when Leon Lis took us into his house, we had done our best – as anyone would – to be grateful for anything we were given, and to protest at generosity.

John was lordly when he asked for more, and complacent in accepting anything that was offered, not from greed or calculation but from self-absorption so complete it blocked any insight into the way others acted or behaved. He had failed to see that hanging around the square in Cluj all day irritated people struggling to make ends meet. Sanda had the same sense of her specialness and the same disdain for her neighbours, and was only the first of many to say that Romanians didn't trust anyone. John's ideals were laudable, but they had been thrashed out in isolation, and what had grown stoutly in the mind of the intellectual graduate looked withered and involved when exposed to the light.

We went into a bookshop one afternoon in a small town where the local vet, a bearded Hungarian, brought us home when he found us looking for the priest. The books, as usual, were stacked behind the counter like groceries – browsing was pointless when books were as predictable as split peas. We asked for maps.

We could see at a glance that our German road map was superior to theirs, which was about two foot square, named only the largest towns and roads, and shaded the whole area uniform pink. Romania all but filled the page, and the overlap was entirely blank, so that it was impossible to tell which countries lay across the borders. Romania floated in limbo, disconnected and withdrawn.

We asked for a local map of the region. It was a long shot, and we were amazed when the shop assistant produced one, entitled *Cluj District*. It looked no larger than the map of Romania, but it was printed to the same scale and we unfolded it almost excitedly. It was exactly the same map, but with Cluj District coloured pink and the rest of Romania white.

John never saw the joke.

Ferenc, the vet, entertained us for two days and nights while we waited for the priest to return from a journey. Like most Hungarian houses, his had a shady pergola around it, and in the evening we'd sit under the vines discussing the problems of Transylvania. John and Ferenc vied to astonish us with horror stories of corruption, beginning with tales of grand graft – Ceauşescu's hunting parties, the perfidy of the Orthodox archbishop – that made our eyes widen; upon which Ferenc began describing smaller and smaller instances of corruption, many of which, I believe, had scarcely struck him before. Of course his wife took *palinka* to the doctor. Of course he had treated the goat that belonged to his child's teacher in return for better marks at the end of the year.

Ferenc was at home all day but both evenings we were there he left the house for a few minutes to attend a friend's cow, which needed pills administered every twenty-four hours. He explained that he was entitled to charge three times the fee for call-outs after six o'clock.

We met the priest on his return. Rather cautiously, because John was there, he mentioned some of the difficulties of his job. He preached knowing that the Securitate had the church tapped; much of his work was to encourage young Hungarians to stay in Transylvania. The political situation had lightened immeasurably in recent months; but there was an ugly tide of nationalism rising from the south, and it was getting stronger in regions like these, where Romanians and Hungarians were in equal proportion. He told us to visit the priests in Tirgu Mures who had, he said, experience of this.

On our way out he drew me aside and asked if we needed any money. Some of the poorest people we'd met had offered us money, not certain how, and if, foreigners could get hold of local currency.

One night we were put up by a priest in a gypsy village. He was the first Szekelyi we had met, a tiny man with delicate small hands and black curls who giggled shyly when he talked. He shared his supper with the three of us – a large supper, since the Hungarian women of the village saw to it that their priest was well-fed, and had brought him a great pot of stuffed cabbage left over from a wedding feast. John waved his fork and explained that this was a typical dish; and went on to say that it wasn't a very good example of it.

We slept on the floor in sleeping bags; and in the morning the priest showed us a ruined country house that mouldered away at the back of a collective farm, on the village outskirts.

It was a Transylvanian Coole Park, rotting relic of the Hungarian Ascendency. Standing among the scabbed colonnades under the porch I could just about recreate the view – weed the crumbling little bridge, gravel the rutted drive, replace a shattered oak in the middle distance across a field of swedes that would once have been grazed like an English park. The great house itself presented fragments of its past; a grey warped panel, festooned with swags that would have been white and gold; a stretch of broken terracotta tiles; a massive hinge attached to a scrap of wood. On an outside wall – undamaged – was a stone scroll with a Latin inscription to the Karolyi family; arms; and the date 1610.

The estate survived until the war. Then the family fled; the house was left to the care of a Romanian janitor who had taken a hammer and cracked the terracotta floortiles one by one; he had worked for days. Gypsies, billeted for years in the stable block and servants' quarters – odd snobbery! – had lit their fires with the panelling and doors. The house had been a pig shed and a grain store; until three years ago the local mayor had some of the massive roof ties, two foot thick, dragged out and used, apparently, to build the local Party headquarters.

Even now, against the sheer relentlessness of the assault, the attics could suggest the building's strength. Large parts were as dry as ever. The tiles were firm, and the solid brick humps where all the flues gathered for a final rush up the chimney stacks were still intact. From here, all the rack and ruin downstairs seemed cosmetic, tatters around the thunderous strength of the building's core.

The future of the house was in doubt. There were rumours that the family would ask for its return (there was an old lady in Tirgu Mures who stood to inherit), countered – as every Transylvanian rumour inevitably was – by the expectation that the local authority would sell it to the highest bidder.

Marosvásárhely

John left us when we reached Tirgu Mures, or Marosvásárhely, and we felt able to approach the church. A small door next to the church steps led us to three priests having coffee. One of them smoked Marlboro. They looked implausibly young.

We stammered our credentials, and asked if there was anywhere we could stay. The youngest and most earnest priest, Gabor, gave us a solemn look and asked if we were married.

I should have said no, but I felt that we'd be putting everyone to a lot of unnecessary trouble if we had to be separated, and once we had been allotted a little room with two beds end to end, it was impossible to back down.

We had barely flopped down on our beds and started to rub our toes when Geza knocked.

'Now you shall eat,' he said, in German. 'Later we will have a swimbath.'

The remains of the priests' supper had been set out in the small refectory. Geza cut bread and proposed a drink.

'This is good wine, don't worry,' he explained. 'From the monks of Alba Iulia. It is made for communion, so it has to be pure. It is white, of course.'

The wine in the candlelight looked yellow and tasted very dry. Bread was heaped on a board, cheese on a wooden platter; a wooden bowl of butter stood by a plate of tomatoes and a plate of cold meat. Inevitably, too, there stood a pat of smoked fat. In Hungary, in all the better restaurants, a cut of meat came with a coronet of fat on top, and we always pushed it off, assuming it to be a decoration which prevented the meat from drying out. In Transylvania opaque pork fat with a faintly grainy texture was a delicacy. Sometimes it was rather tough and you needed to use a sharp knife, but with bread, and best of all a tomato or a gherkin, it was rather delicious. It coated your lips with smoky grease.

I was busy eating when Gabor and Kate started talking. Geza, who spoke only German, asked when we were married.

'When were we married?'

'Yes, yes. When?'

First I told another lie and then I changed the subject. We talked about churches. But over the next few days I found I'd woven a very tangled web. The elderly abbot gazed flatly at our ringless fingers.

Now Geza put in: 'The Orthodox Patriarch Theocritus supported Ceauşescu. After the massacre in Temesvar he sent an open telegram to that wise leader congratulating him for his firm handling of anti-social hooliganism, and so on. Theocritus had to disappear for a while, but now he is back again.'

He drained his glass. 'Now we swim, OK?'

Outside the streets were dimly lit. Geza drove wildly, like any Hungarian. We careered round the back of the Orthodox church and up past the big hotel, which stood on the site of a Franciscan monastery built in 1247 and demolished a couple of years back to make way for the hotel. Before the bridge we swerved and bounded down onto a track along the river.

There was a small wooden jetty. The surface of the water glinted like oil in the starlight. Geza dived in and surfaced with a happy shout. I jumped, sifting the ooze at the bottom with my toes.

'Is the water clean?' I asked.

'Not really,' said Gabor.

'It's OK. Everybody swims here. That's why we must swim at night. In the day it gets dangerous, everyone saluting "hello father". You get no time to swim.'

We swam about for a while. I was the first out, Geza last. He was pretty chubby.

Back at the church, Gabor offered us all a cup of lime tea. Tomorrow he was to conduct the funeral of a girl drowned in the river two days ago. He placed her photograph on the table: a smiling child with two long fair plaits hanging down over her ears, and asked us to pray.

Gabor's room contained a narrow bed, a basin, a wardrobe and

several shelves of books, mostly paperbacks, mostly Hungarian.
After a minute's silence he said:

'Do you have a Bible?'

'Er, no . . .' I blustered, embarrassed.

He went out to fetch an English Bible. 'I want to read to you
both before we sleep. I think this is my favourite part of the
Book.' He cleared his throat.

'When I was a child I spake as a child, I understood as a child,
I thought as a child: but when I became a man, I put away childish
things.

For now we see through a glass, darkly; but then face to face:
now I know in part; but then shall I know even as also as I am
known.

And now abideth faith, hope, charity, these three; but the greatest of these is charity.'

He closed the book. 'Now, sleep,' he said.

Marosvásárhely surrounded a broad avenue leading to the squat
concrete bug of the Orthodox Church, built in triumph after the
Treaty of Trianon in 1921 gave Transylvania to the Romanians.
Steep lanes ran up the hill to the south, while to the north the
ground was flat and stretched to the river. Behind the row fronting
the avenue the town had been razed and in part rebuilt.

At the western end of the avenue stood a magnificent secession-
ist building known as the Palace of Culture, *Palaca Culturul*,
although from the stained glass windows to the inscribed poems
that fluted about the walls it was evidently Hungarian. It contained, among other things, a gallery of paintings by Hungarian
painters given Romanian names, the mandatory collection of
Daco-Roman beads, bangles and arrowheads, and a gallery, firmly
closed, which had hosted the local exhibition of Ceauşescuana.

Opposite you could buy good *langos* at a cubby hole under a
department store that projected a series of enormous plate glass
windows over the pavement. The glass was wavy and corrupt, and
it fell with a splintering crash one afternoon as we walked by on
the other side of the road. No-one was hurt. Round the back was
a beer garden where it was occasionally possible to find a box of
matches.

Compared to Oradea, however, the long trajectory of the town centre gave Marosvaserhelyi an air of formal elegance. Always a garrison town, it was a place not for opera cloaks and archdukes but for stiff gallantry and uniformed parades. One afternoon the circus came to town, and as the players processed by our windows up the avenue, the cockades of the bare-back riders seemed to mimic the pantomime of military life a hundred years before.

Halfway along the avenue the Transylvania Hotel (where once or twice we looked for lunch) strove for the bourgeois solidity of an older era, although it was brand new. There was an enormous weight of scarlet velveteen draped at the windows and smoothed across the chairs. A little sombre daylight trickled through the net curtains and every table was equipped with a silvery wine bucket on a stand. In reception we could only buy Cartier cigarettes in a slim metallic box. The food was disgusting, and the waiters couldn't care less about taking your order, but the dressing-up urge was strong in Eastern Europe. It long ago gobbled up the Revolution in Russia, where the fat armchairs and antimacassars, the monopod ashtrays, the occasional tables covered in glass with doilies underneath fitted oddly with the slogans and exhortations, and in grim contrast to the knock on the door in the middle of the night.

At bottom, this enthusiasm for overstuffed furniture, for giving and receiving flowers, for having your hair perfectly done, suggested a desire to follow a recognised and accepted pattern of behaviour, like the letter-writer boning up on Debrett's correct form of address. The bourgeois style is notoriously preoccupied with externals; and in Romania the externals had long ago peeled away from any reality behind them. So you had silver buckets for wine in restaurants that hadn't got any; tarty cigarettes that no-one could legally afford; pretty receptionists in hotels where none of the sheets had been changed for a month.

There was now wine – of a sort – at the Transylvania.

'I'm sorry you could not drink better now,' our neighbour said, filling our glasses despite our protests. 'We had our good vintages once. But this? Vintage chemical!'

We were sharing a table with the elderly nephew of the last Austrian Oberst of the town. He was a small, frail, blue-veined old man, a *Schwab* – a descendant of the Swabian colonists settled in western Transylvania two centuries ago.

His chemical wine did the trick – the old German began to sing '*Siebenbürgen, Land des Segens* – ' in a cracked voice, until his Hungarian friend silenced him with a frown and a shake of the head.

At the end of the war, the Oberst found himself without an army on the collapse of the empire. He commanded a battalion of Whites in the Russian Civil War. When he fell prisoner to the Bolsheviks his wife, a Polish countess, refused to eat, and she died soon after his return.

The Oberst wanted to kill himself.

'*Er war vor dem Spiegel, so,*' said the German: he stood thus before the mirror. He mimed the razor moving towards his neck. 'My father, his brother, saved his life. He was in the Romanian army until 1939.'

'And then?'

'He became a general on the Russian front. I joined the army then, as well. It was a family thing, and the German Government promised half Transylvania to Hungary, like the old days – *eine neue Karte von Europa*. Hitler did some good things,' he added. The Hungarian said '*Microphon*' and tapped the underside of the table. The German shrugged. 'I can say that. There was no unemployment in Germany. People ate well. The Jews were his mistake. He shouldn't have pressed so hard on the anti-fascists. And of course he underestimated Churchill.' He bowed fractionally.

'But he killed the Jews because they were Jews, not because they opposed him.'

'They opposed him. They had to. Yes. Yes. The Jews were his big mistake.' He seemed after all to think he had said too much: the wine was having its effect. 'It would have been better if Hitler had never existed.'

After a pause, he recalled that he had managed to surrender to the Americans. In 1947 he came back.

'Why come back? Why not stay in Germany?'

He refilled our glasses and stuck the empty bottle in the silver bin.

The family estate had been confiscated and his mother was living in a one-room apartment in the city. The family vineyards were stripped out for planting more appropriate crops. The summer house there was boarded up and fell apart. The terraces were never re-sown, however; scrub and spindly trees grew across them now.

'Why did I come back? *Warum?*' He slapped his hand to his forehead. '*Ich war doch so dumm!*'

By then it was too late to get out. He turned to law and made a living at the bar, whereas his uncle, the Oberst, died on a general's pension in West Germany in 1956.

'I am planning to go to Germany soon. I will have a look around, and if it suits I will take my family there with me. I'm entitled to a real pension.'

They were determined to take us round the town they remembered as gay and smart. We paid our bill after a struggle and followed them rather drunk to recreate the malarkey of young students and officers in the good old days before the war. Here there had been a terrific restaurant; there, on a shady avenue on the hill, stood the Oberst's villa. We saw what was left of the yellow brick road that had once swooped through the town from the Protestant church: the glazed bricks had been recently dug up and taken south to be relaid in Bucharest. Where the Orthodox church now stood there had been a famous café whose owner had once installed a mint, activated by pressure on the staircase – everyone went up and down the steps so no-one could accuse him of forging.

At last we reached a school where the old friends had received a disciplined education in Hungarian and German. The children watched our wobbly tour in surprise. The old men opened doors to vanished dormitories, sighed for the time when you could see your face on the polished foors and running on the stairs was a beating offence; and chortled over the agonies of freezing early morning showers as we stood in the gloomy lavatories.

After a while it seemed they stepped more slowly, took the stairs with less excitement, opened fewer doors. Perhaps it was the wine; or perhaps that every name, excitedly recalled – the fanatical PE instructor, an old school friend, a headmaster, or the

boy who came to school in a chauffeur-driven limousine – led
only to thoughts of death and separation.

We had lunch once again at the Transylvania, and shared the
table with a Hungarian boy taking his Romanian girlfriend out to
celebrate his birthday. They both spoke excellent English.

He was working as an ambulanceman, although his ambition
was to become a dentist. First it was crucial that he reach Hungary,
where he had a family painting that would fetch him a lot of
money.

'It's impossible to arrange from here,' he explained. 'Transylvania isn't an address for business with the West.'

'No,' I agreed. 'Everyone would think of Dracula.'

Our new friend stared into his glass, then looked away.

'Excuse me,' he said with a solemn titter, 'but I am actually –
ah, in village they say so – a vampire. I have the mark.'

He raised his chin and indicated a plum-sized stain on his white
neck the colour of dry blood.

'Also other signs,' he said, with a short laugh, covering his
mouth with his hand.

His girlfriend nodded.

'My parents do not like,' she said. 'They say *strigoi* – is this,
ah, wampyre,' and she made a small taloned lunge across the table.

We arranged their passage to the west with some charitable
Yorkshiremen we had met preparing to drive their empty aid-
lorry home. We never heard from the couple again. Ambulanceman. Dentist. I feel oddly responsible. Immured by the Iron
Curtain for fifty years, travestied in Hammer horror films, now
the Count can come and go, and visit Whitby if he likes.

Created by a Habsburg minister in the eighteenth century, the
Telekyi Library in the city was everything we'd missed – to sniff
old bindings and stick our noses into ancient texts in the long,
cool barrel-vaulted reading room with a gallery and tall glass-
fronted bookcases.

Delving for maps we met Mihaly Spielmann, the head librarian. As a Jewish Hungarian Romanian intellectual, he was in the

minority three times over – twice, if you allowed that Jew and intellectual were practically synonyms in Eastern Europe.

Mihaly had taken us to sit on a bench under a tree in the middle of the courtyard, more out of habit, I think, than caution. It was out of earshot, hard to sneak up on unobserved.

'What makes me uncomfortable is the thought that Petru Roman is a Jew,' he said.

'The Prime Minister?'

'Roman, for God's sake. You don't get a name like that by accident. It was his grandfather who changed it. Lots of Jews in the thirties wanted to seem more Romanian than the Romanians. Roman, as a surname, is as Jewish as my own.'

'You don't like having a Jewish prime minister – '

'Because one slip, and he isn't Iliescu's minister any more. He is the Jew.'

Mihaly invited us home one evening, where we talked about the gypsies. Ever since Cluj, people had done their best to alarm us about the gypsy villages on the road between Tirgu Mures and Segesvar; if we were going to disappear, this looked the likely place for it. (Much later we discovered that our relatives did think we had disappeared in Romania: there were rounds of anxious phone calls, high-level representations to the Foreign Office, and – for reasons I have never properly understood – a Swedish diplomat was roped into the search. There was even plans for a rescue mission – before we spoiled it all by phoning from Bulgaria.) Only Mihaly was quite certain that our worries were out of place.

Fear of the gypsies, he pointed out, was a prejudice the authorities reinforced. Ceauşescu himself had pretended the gypsies did not exist; as a result, no-one had any idea how many of them lived in Romania. Some estimates put their numbers at four million – a fifth of the Romanian population.

For a people who always dodged interference and regulation from above, their exclusion from official records was ironic. The last thing they wanted, Mihaly thought, was to be counted, marshalled, and ordered about. They saw the 'normal' world of bureaucracy and government turn men into puppets, and worked to escape it. Which did not make them cut-throats.

'Most people will trade freedoms for security,' Mihaly said. 'In this part of Europe it is highly traditional. The Habsburg empire is the extreme example of bureaucratic control. The gypsies, who also lived in this empire, stand at the opposite extreme. To many people they look idle, and it is easier to believe that they survive by thieving and deceit than to look to see what they really do.'

Mihaly had come up with a discovery.

'The gypsies are working all the time. They stand in the street and swap information – trading intelligence. Do you see rubbish and litter in the street? The gypsies who seem to be doing nothing are collecting old newspapers, tickets, wrappers.'

He picked up a book – we were sitting in his home now, in a book-lined room.

'Do you know how I can buy this? Because the gypsies take all the paper for processing to the mills. Nobody else would think of doing it, because it would take too long. But the gypsies slip it into their normal activity. They recycle everything.'

'Gypsies are the only merchants and artisans in this country,' he declared. In a gypsy village the smith would be making jewellery; his wife, clothes; his children sorting scraps, rubber, glass, paper. Someone goes into town to sell their produce. While he trades, he is listening out to discover what somebody needs. 'What we call the Romanian economy – steelyards, shipbuilding, mining, and so on – is a joke. The real economy is turned by the gypsies.'

Over the years the gypsies have perfected ways of avoiding the armlock authority puts on most people. By keeping away from the 'clockwork' world, they defy prediction. The government has no leverage over them to speak of. They burn up the houses they are given. They use ten different names. In return the police slam them in jail at the first excuse. The prisons are choked with largely innocent gypsies, whose presence there reinforces the myth.

But for all his careful watching, Mihaly didn't see that the gypsies wore costume.

'They wear ordinary clothes now. The old costumes are for celebrations and festivals,' he assured us, when right under our noses, every day, the gypsies paraded in the iridescent colours and patterns of Asia, in skirts and bodices, waistcoats and hats that were cut on the lines of another century.

From the shelves of books hung ropes of sausage: Mihaly, like every Hungarian we'd met, killed his annual pig, and made pâtés and sausage, smoked fat and salt pork, in the heart of the city.

At nine o'clock his children came in to watch *Das Erbe Von Gulenbergs* on the TV, a sprawling German saga of a brewing family which focused on the cars they drove to boardroom battles and their palatial homes.

'The national programme of Romania,' Mihaly explained. 'This is the life that our president will create for us.'

And with that necessary irony off his chest, he settled down to watch it as eagerly as his children.

In Tirgu Mures, two months earlier, running battles had broken out between Romanians and Hungarians. Although we had heard something about this in Poland – Andrjez citing it as a reason for us to keep away – we now met people who had witnessed the trouble first hand. Nobody believed it had occurred spontaneously, either.

A writer from Budapest, Erno Suto, was to address the Hungarian parliamentary party in a building they shared with various Romanian opposition parties. A crowd of Romanian farmers, armed with pitchforks and scythes, stormed the building. Suto and the others barricaded themselves into the attic by wedging a water tank over the staircase, forcing the attackers to enter one by one.

After two hours an army squadron arrived to offer the besieged Hungarians a safe conduct, and the defenders began to come out. They were jostled and kicked on their way down. They climbed into a lorry with a canvas back stretched tight over steel hoops. When most people were aboard, the canvas blew as a sail might blow in a typhoon. The Hungarians were dragged from the lorry by the mob, and savagely beaten. Suto himself lost an eye. The Telekyi Library was attacked, but its ancient gates proved invulnerable.

Several questions were unresolved. The Romanians were apparently under the impression that the meeting was to culminate in a declaration of Transylvanian independence, to coincide with a military invasion by Hungary. At a time when fuel and transport were scarce, a surprisingly large number of farmers reached the city at one time. And the militia arrived hours after the building was stormed. By inference, the whole event had been planned.

The following day, a Hungarian protest in the avenue was met by a Romanian crowd armed with farm tools. A thin cordon of troops was thrown between them. As the mood grew harsh, the Hungarians sent their wives and children home. The Romanians jeered 'We are the landlords! You are the squatters!' and chanted: '*Vatra*! *Vatra*!', meaning fatherland.

After insults, stones. Hand-to-hand fighting broke out in the afternoon. A truck careered at full speed from the Romanian end of the avenue and the troops wavered and withdrew. The fighting was intense, the street full of the wounded and the dead.

Around six o'clock, a body of men appeared in the failing light. They wore hats and black waistcoats, and they came up a side street onto the avenue. The combatants regarded them with uncertainty. Nobody knew what the gypsies were thinking.

They gave a shout. 'Don't worry, Hungarians! We are the gypsies!'

Their attack was brutal. Romanians who staggered onto buses found the buses torched, and as they tried to jump out they were caught and beaten up. Knives were out; pitchforks and flails; stabbing and beating until darkness fell, and running shadows flickered in the light from the burning buses.

In the barracks the troops were waiting for an order that never came.

One night, unable to sleep, I watched a football match with the caretaker on TV. He sprawled comfortably in an armchair, wearing a vest and a pair of old trousers, commenting on the game.

Eventually we wandered onto the subject of the troubles, when even the church house had been attacked by the Romanian mob. He nodded grimly at the thought, and reached behind him to show me a terrifying club, like a baseball bat, studded with nails. He hefted it once or twice, to show he was ready.

After that we just watched the football; but when I saw him again the next day I found I had made a mistake. He was wearing a cassock, speeding across the courtyard to say Mass.

The son of the Protestant minister struggled not to cry when he recalled the sound made by a man as he was crushed by the careering truck. Andras was a solemn boy, barely eighteen.

His father's church on a rise above the avenue was enclosed by a medieval defensive wall. Above the west door a damaged fresco depicted two Turks in the white headdress of the janissaries. Their Hungarian prisoner had lost his helmet.

Andras's father was arrested as a young man and sent to the Danube Delta, Romania's Gulag, where like most prisoners who dug the canal through the malarial swamp he was expected to die. From the moment of his arrest the authorities maintained a rigid silence about him. His parents could only guess that he had been arrested. Four years later he was released. They barely recognised him.

Andras had been brought up to see silence as the weapon of injustice. The government worked in silence; silence had gradually settled on the people themselves.

'Our telephone is tapped again. It was clear for a while after December, but now you can hear the second click.'

His mother nodded. '*Ils nous écoutent maintenant, probablement.*'

'This time we try to ignore it. If we can all keep talking, making a noise, they will find it hard to make us quiet.'

I thought of the Romanian map with its blank edges. Ceauşescu had tried to put everyone in solitary. Unreported speech with foreigners was forbidden. Possession of a typewriter was forbidden without a licence. Romanians now who spoke of their mistrust for one another would say they could talk to us because we were foreign. Whether one in four, or only one in ten were informing, it didn't matter as long as the people believed it, and censored themselves. In Poland and Czechoslovakia and Hungary, civil society had functioned around the fiction of the state – in church, at scout camp, around literary or artistic meetings. Romania was different. Here the Hungarians, to an extent, were able to clan; the gypsies, too, lived apart, however much bullied; but the Romanians were atomised, paranoid.

Andras sat forward with a concentrated expression, always explaining, moving through this adult territory with childlike logic, childlike seriousness and patience. Watching him I remembered Mihaly's cool joke about using the current freedom to create an association of future political prisoners.

'Iliescu and his people want power. That is all. This is how you connect the events of March with the events of June. First, Romanians against Hungarians. Then workers against intellectuals. Always the masses against the minority. When he sees tension he makes it very tight. He runs this country as leader of the biggest group of frightened people. Democracy is his word for people abroad, so they will give money. Then he pays his supporters.

'The government wants to destroy the Hungarians here. Hungarian leaders, the professional people, leave Transylvania. These people can start again in Hungary. Only the simple people must stay, and with no leaders they will not resist assimilation. In a few generations they will vanish. When everyone in this country is Romanian, nobody will look for the truth.'

He looked up.

'We must have connections to the West – between friends, churches, associations, tourism. It will be harder to cut us off again. We need education. We must build an intellectual class – the intellectuals are against repression, and they understand each other as educated people, not as Hungarian against Romanian.'

Andras made fists in the air. 'I believe in information technology. You see, in this country, technology is for the oppressors. Even not typewriters for the people. But for Securitate – ' he whistled – 'fax machine, computers, radiofones, microphones, cameras, everything. So give this power to the people! Then it don't matter where people live.'

Andras's vision was childlike in its exuberance. The burden of territory – scrabbling for space in a shadowed corner of Europe – was swept away by an electronic version of gypsy life. Censorship would be impossible. Borders would vanish beneath a bramble of wires and digital networks. The blank spaces beyond Romania would clog with friendly modems, and the silence crackle with the beeps and buzzes of unlimited connections, with Liberty scrambling through the system like a beneficent virus.

I wanted to believe it as Andras believed it, excitedly reciting the advances and possibilities open to twenty-first-century

Transylvania. In the right sort of place it could happen, I supposed. But though Dracula might invite Harker by fax, Harker with a laptop was still a frightened guest. The right sort of place was already rich, peaceful and tolerant, not like Romania, where a diploma could be bought, a coup disguised as revolution, and democracy be a name for tyranny.

Later on, Andras showed us around his father's church.

'Not so much a church,' I remarked, climbing steps to an arrow slit in the surrounding wall, 'more a fortress.'

'Of course,' Andras called up. 'It is Transylvanian tradition. Most Székely churches are fortified, even the small ones. You will see more in the Székelyföld.'

I came down the steps.

'And who are the Székely?'

'Original democrats,' said Andras enigmatically.

We left the fort.

Andras had something to show us back at his house: an alphabet.

There were thirty-one runes in the alphabet, each corresponding to a roman letter, or combination of letters found in Hungarian. All the awkward-looking diphthongs that made Hungarian so alarming to read were resolved into neat spikes and circles and triangles. Until the middle of the nineteenth century, said Andras, the Székely had kept to this alphabet, before the pedagogues of Budapest had interfered. We had seen some of these tallies in the provincial musuem in Cluj.

'Now this is original Hungarian writing. Do you know, quite recently some archeologists found the same in western China? It was writing of Turkic nomads. You see, the Székely are Hungarian, but more. Before, they worked together to protect the kingdom. Every man was farmer with a sword or a gun. They live on the borders, and guard against Turks and Tartars.

'Now I said original democrats. Because all their wealth was very equally divided. In the village, no man was so rich, because rich men try to pay for another man to fight. And no poors – poor man cannot keep a good weapon. So always equal. And always, always free men.'

He was keen for us to take a copy of his alphabet.

'Maybe you will show it to Székely people,' he said eagerly. 'I would like the Székely to know it again. They have been strong many centuries. Defend their land, and Hungarian kingdom. Now they need to keep the fight. They have less to defend. Perhaps the alphabet will help them not assimilate.'

'But what about the informatics?'

Andras sighed. 'The informatics maybe – but maybe not for a long, long time.'

We were on the point of leaving Tirgu Mures when the Anthonies arrived. They turned up in the middle of the night and we were roused because no-one in the monastery spoke a word of English and the Anthonies had no foreign languages.

They had driven in three days from England with a consignment of aid for the Church, and they were very tired. They came from Bradford, and they had never been out of England in their lives.

We found Little Anthony wistfully offering to murder a cup of tea. Geza looked puzzled – tea was hard to get. Anthony staunchly took a hot cup of linden water. Neither of them had much idea of anything connected with their journey. Little Anthony had been roped in at the last minute as co-driver; he had no time to get visas and they had been held up a little at the border. The news that the people he was now with were Hungarian and not Romanian came as a surprise.

'What I know about this country might be written with a paintbrush on a postage stamp,' he said, and went to bed.

'You will show them around the town,' Geza declared, and deferred our departure by two days.

Fairly early on we established that the two Anthonies, although driving together, were not friends before they set out; nor after their journey. 'He's a bit of a pillock,' said little Anthony of the other. Little Anthony took everything in, asked a thousand questions, made friends with everybody and was unfailingly kind. A year ago, he said, he'd been a diabetic with one malfunctioning kidney. 'Very delicate,' he admitted, with some disgust. His mother had donated him a kidney and at last he could do things he'd never dreamed of.

He was stoic about the food.

'D'you know what I'd like?' he said, after we'd had another grey and vile meal in a hotel. 'Fish and chips. Sausage, mash, beans, bacon and fried egg. and tomato ketchup.'

He paused. We dreamed a little.

'All together in a bucket,' he added.

He paused again, and said:

'It would make a lovely butty.'

Segesvár – Schässburg

The morning sky was rumpled like an unmade bed. Beyond the Telekyi Library, dirty tower blocks marched abreast of us and wheeled away abruptly as the fields began. About fifty cars formed a queue for petrol along the verge.

An hour later we were attacked by a dog.

Kate saw it, a good half mile off where the trees met a sloping field by a small wired-in hut like an electrical sub-station. The sound of barking meant nothing: we had been barked half across Europe. Dogs were always chained up.

'It's coming for us,' said Kate suddenly. I looked around. A small whitish speck was moving down the hill. But it was still very far away.

'Just rabbiting,' I said.

'I really don't think so.' Kate began to quicken her pace. The dog was almost distinct, coming on at a gallop.

'OK, let's just keep going,' I said superfluously. 'Try for the trees.'

The forest began a couple of hundred yards ahead. Here it was open with a ditch on either side. The fields were empty. The road had been deserted for an hour. The dog was curving across the nearest field towards us, and its bark was full of throat.

Until the dog leaped the ditch and I heard its claws scrabble on the tarmac I hadn't really taken it as a serious threat. It was the ugliest and most ferocious dog I'd ever seen. Yellow fur prickled up its spine. Solid neck tapered to a set of bared teeth and a tawny squint. It splayed its forelegs on the ground and bunched its haunches as we backed along the road. I pointed my stick and said:

'Down sir! Down!'

186

The dog's lips peeled back with a noise that sounded like a saw drawing on hard wood.

'Steady. No sir!'

Simultaneously the dog flicked its head and barked. The bark ended with a sound like water vanishing down a plug hole. Drool began to burble through its teeth.

Very slowly we moved back towards the trees. The dog would snarl, bare its teeth, reveal its black gums, and lower its head as we widened the gap between us by a couple of yards, and then lurch towards us. Sometimes he would come on in a rush, and stop with his eyes an inch from the end of my stick, his lips flanged.

The only advice I've ever had about dogs comes from a book for cyclists (I think a frightened cyclist should outstrip a running dog). There were plenty of things you could do if the dog was very small. Otherwise you should aim to poke your pump down its throat, and choke it to death. Failing a pump, the book had said, you could use your arm. It sounded now like a quick way to lose my arm. If the dog sprang I was of course ready to lunge my stick down his throat, but it seemed unlikely that he would honour his part and spring with open jaws onto its point. He would probably scuttle in round the edge and then swipe sideways. Once he was round the stick he was much better armed than us. The stick would be useless. Already he was growing bolder. He snapped suddenly at the end of the stick and his teeth clicked as I moved it aside – too far – now he'd spring.

I got the stick back in front of his eyes again, trembling faintly. Another thought had crossed my mind. If we were bitten (only bitten!) we'd need rabies injections. We had been advised to carry a stock of needles against the risk of contracting Aids in a Romanian hospital. Naturally we hadn't bothered.

'Back you bugger.' High strained voice.

Cautiously we unbuckled our packs so that they could be used as shields.

And then the whine of a low gear and the noise of an engine.

The dog didn't flinch. I prayed: run it over.

A bus came tilting out of the trees. The dog was nicely in the middle of the road.

'Help!' we screamed as the bus sped past. The dog had sprung back to the opposite verge. The bus drove away. A car followed. We made desperate gestures but it didn't stop.

'Run!'

The passing car covered us for an instant. We belted up the road, all nape; at the trees I spun round with the stick.

Thirty yards back the dog was sniffing at something in the ditch.

Where the road bent back to climb the hill there stood, of all the improbable things, a hotel serving coffee. Our shaking knees jangled the spoons as we mainlined cigarettes. A gypsy leered at us. Another gypsy came in and sat with him. A fat man with piggy eyes complained to the restaurateur and he asked the gypsies to leave.

On the way up the hill we faltered and turned back twice. Crossing an open field to cut a switchback corner we filled our hands with stones. No dog appeared. We stood in the shade of a gnarled tree on the top of the ridge and a riderless horse cantered past us up the road. Below lay a valley on whose broad bottom sown fields padded out one small hamlet after another, scattered like miniature cities on a shrunken plain.

Father Barna, our host in Segesvár, had a theory about the dog.

'When you cummed,' he asked, 'what have you for clothies?'

'Well, er, these.'

'Yea. Black clothies. And hat,' he added, with great emphasis.

'My hat?'

'Chipsy hat, yes? Aha.'

'But the dog was mad.'

'Mad for not like chipsy. Chipsy good mans, but . . .' He shrugged and smiled.

Barna was probably right: the dog was a gypsy hater. So we told him another thing about that hat.

Coming off the hill we had met an old man in a suit of stiff black wool who asked if we had seen his horse. We said it was running towards Marosvásárhely and he grinned.

'I am eighty-five years old!'

At the bottom of the hill we stopped to say hello to the priest whose parish had received all the Anthonies' aid. He was out. His wife asked if we wanted coffee, which we declined. Kate asked if she could use the loo, while I filled my bottle at the well.

'What a bathroom!' said Kate as soon as we were out of earshot. 'Lux soap. Washing machine. Ariel automatic. Deodorant called Fa. Colgate toothpaste.'

'Really?' I was interested.

'Thick matching towels. Oral-B toothbrushes.'

The contents of aid parcels were always eclectic. I wondered why people in the West thought the Romanians needed so much soap.

'Because the Romanians say so. People are always talking about soap.'

'I know. But why? They've got perfectly good soap here.'

'I don't know. But we're always seeing soap on the black market.'

'Flogged off by dishonest aid-receiving priests, do you think?'

'Spoken like a true Romanian,' she said, and we proudly nursed our first home-grown rumour until we were out of the village.

In this way we were far into the fields before we noticed our little gypsy shadows.

A girl of about eight and her little sister, perhaps, both dark and extravagantly pretty, wrapped in cotton shawls like tulips, paddled down the road beside us in bare feet. They stepped erect like Indian women, their feet darting in and out from under their skirts with a tireless fluency that seemed to nibble up the road. They watched us gravely, and sang a tune I recognised. The Lambada.

The old German had shaken his head over the route we'd proposed and warned us to be careful. 'You never know with these gypsies,' he said. 'You are only two, and from the West.' In Cluj we'd been advised that a concentration of notorious gypsies lived beyond Tirgu Mures. 'So they came out for the Hungarians in March,' the Hungarians said. 'Now it's June'. We'd forgotten to ask Mihaly how he could be sure the gypsies were safe.

We anxiously regarded the little gypsies as a foretaste of big gypsies further on. They were beautiful to look at, but they looked back rather boldly and their soft chanting was loaded with menace.

At the foot of the hill a string of low whitewashed cabins lurked behind a fence. The girls met other children, chattered and glanced back and scattered. We plodded on, humming the Lambada inconspicuously. A flock of small children with grubby faces and unpleasantly knowing expressions settled on the fence ahead. A few women shaded their eyes at their doorways and watched.

'Kate,' I whispered shortly. 'My shoelace.'

'Shall we just go on?'

But a few paces further the other lace undid itself and began to flail about on the road.

'I'm sorry. Hang on.'

The swiftest lace-tying operation in world history now could not have forestalled the men gathering on the road ahead. They grinned loosely. As I straightened up one of them moved across and raised a hand.

'*Servus,*' he said.

'*Servus,*' we replied. He was staring. All the men were staring. At my hat.

He touched his head, pointed at mine, and said: 'How much?'

'From Kolosvar,' I tittered evasively.

He nodded. 'How much?'

I hate talking about money under circumstances like these.

'One hundred and ten lei.'

The man looked me in the face.

'One hundred and twenty,' he said.

We stood altogether on the deserted road like cowboys. One half of me said: Give him the hat. The other half shook my head. He turned around and went into a shack, and returned with two hats, one green, one black, a little narrower in the brim than mine and made of fuzzier felt. He held them out and made a gesture of exchange.

When I declined a child thought I'd misunderstood and stepped forward to pantomime a very good deal – two hats for one.

We smiled and said we liked the one we had. Then we shambled forward. The men watched us go without expression. The children laughed.

Much later we reached Sighisoara (in Romanian) – Segesvár (in Hungarian) – Schässburg (in German), and met Father Barna.

'Very not usual,' said Father Barna, when we told him of the incident.

We had been surprised to find him about our own age, because his housekeeper, when we arrived, told us in tones of such anxious reverence to wait for the priest that we imagined him to be at risk of dying of the shock.

When Barna did return he smiled shyly and asked his house-keeper if it was alright for us to stay.

Now he thought about the gypsy hat and said:

'They wants to give you – more moneys?'

'Yes, ten lei more than we paid.'

He shook his head, surprised.

'I never heard it,' he said.

Mihaly, like everyone else in the country, had ignored one obvious fact about the Romanian gypsies. It was so striking to us, and so invisible to the locals, that you could only suppose them victims of a collective hallucination. The gypsies were not all alike. Some were like Rajastanis: pale skinned, with great dark eyes and haughty strong-boned faces. The others were short and dark, more like Gujurathis, round faced, round bellied. It was the Rajastanis who lingered in the streets, selling their jewellery and cigarettes, dressed in costume; who were bold and humorous with passers-by and us. Gypsies like these had asked for my hat. '*Camarad*,' they called, and laughed; and the women watched Kate with interest, as if we'd come to their party.

But the Gujurathis wore hand-me-down sweaters over cheap skirts and trousers, and grew fat, which made their clothes look tight and uncomfortable; rings flashed on the fingers of the women, stout and toothless begums. And they always watched us without expression with jaundiced eyes.

'The watchmakers' tower, the weavers', the tailors' tower,' said the old lady. 'Against the Turks.'

'*Türken*': she formed the umlaut with precise emphasis. It was a schoolgirl's *Hochdeutsch*, not dialect; it was like copperplate, learned years ago, a parlour language for strangers.

She looked between us with an eager smile.

'They were the responsibility of the guilds,' she explained. 'not now, of course! Before. Now all the people are gone away.' *Alle Leute sind weg.* Her hand trembled towards the hills. 'We don't need towers any more, we old people, *wir Bleibenden.*'

She picked her way over the cobbles and down a crooked alley between the top-heavy burgher houses with their gabled roofs. Pink geraniums spilled from a window box, freshly painted green. As the old woman turned the corner three dark barefoot children hollered after her and waved an old hypodermic syringe.

Later that evening, when shadow covered the lower half of the Protestant church, we saluted her again. She sat with three other old women on a bench by the clock tower.

'*Gruss Gott!*' They trilled together, nodding their scarved heads, with their hands folded on their laps.

In Segesvár I banished the last of my doubts over Transylvania and the Romanians. They don't deserve it.

The first German colonists to settle in the province of Transylvania founded the town they called Schässburg in 1265. They were invited in by the Hungarian King to settle his borders, and as more Germans followed they built towns, carried on vigorous trade with the east and north, and fought against invaders for the King, and against the King when he tried to invade their privileges. It would be absurd to suggest that there is any geographical bar to the growth of wealth and culture in this part of Europe for the Germans built towns exactly like towns in Germany. They were able to reproduce the same guild system, the same flow of merchandise, the same splendour of church and town hall, as existed in any town of comparable size in northern Europe. Over seven centuries they maintained a whole culture of their own, based on medieval forms, so that even the Victorians thought them quaint. They resemble a little the Amish of New York; but the Amish are parvenus.

We had walked, in a single day in Romania, from a Hungarian

town to a German one: but we arrived to find the Germans going
at last. They had given up.

'Do you want to go?'

He shuffled slowly from foot to foot. He wore coarse cotton
overalls, a blue cotton jacket, crummy leather shoes and a curious
snip of a hat crammed on his flaxen hair. He stuck out his lower
lip, shrugged.

'*Was kann man tun?*' What can be done? '*Muss gehen.*'

From everyone it was the same refrain: *Was kann man tun?*
After seven centuries the Transylvanian Saxons had exhausted
their ingenuity. Of 800,000 Saxons, half a million had decamped
in the six months since the revolution in December. The more
that went, the harder life became for those who stayed behind.
They'd lost their friends, and lived in half-empty villages, unable
to keep up numbers at their schools – suddenly half-strangers in
familiar country. So they followed.

They left in such a rush that they abandoned anything. Dream-
ing of escape for so many years, all those who ran at the first
opportunity pointed out to their neighbours that it might also be
the last. Until December, the Romanians had sole them piecemeal
to West Germany: the price was $4000 a head. Politics had never
upset them much, while their self-supporting communities
remained intact. So those communities, and the near-medieval
civic sense that supported them, were ruthlessly ground down, to
ensure a steady supply of emigrants – both for hard currency and
the Greater Romanian ideal. If a house in a village or town fell
empty, the authorities billeted there the most cussed and intrac-
table family they could find. A group of gypsies would reduce the
place to cinders and move on in time, after shocking and frightening their *bürgerliche* neighbours. Saxon schools were banned, their
priests and pastors were harassed and the churches closed; Saxon
autarchy – its supply of beer and food and wine – was broken up,
and state rubbish supplied erratically instead.

Schässburg was crammed onto a hill, surrounded by steep walls
and entered by through a tower gateway on either side. Its pointed
roofs, half-timbering, the forward lurch of the upper storeys made

it one of the most perfect medieval towns I'd ever seen, a fairytale illustration. You stooped through a low wooden doorway on the street into a warren of wooden steps, front doors, terraces and corridors. Nothing had changed since the age of the quill. Bluish light came through the old glass and threw a lattice of shadow on wooden floors, waxed and worn smooth by the passage of countless feet.

Five churches were squeezed into the upper town, including Barna's Hungarian Catholic church, the newest of them all, only recently rebuilt after a fire destroyed the nineteenth-century original: the Hungarians were relative newcomers to the Saxon stronghold. As in the German cities of northern Poland, civic buildings rubbed shoulders with the churches; one of the town's marvels was the clock tower, which commanded the approach from the south up a steep cobbled lane lined with cottages and dotted with massive stone stops to prevent carts careering off the road. After farming, the Saxons had turned to industry; they had made the clock and the pageant that emerged from little doors on either side to parade on the hour. It was three hundred years old, but it was by far the most efficient device, well-built and reliable, that we had seen for months, and we stared at it again and again with a sort of barbarian awe.

Its ancient punctuality mocked us, in fact, every time we looked in at the bar. The bar was on the ground floor of a bulging rendered house that had been the birthplace of Vlad Dracul, the Impaler, whose own father had sought refuge in the Saxon town from the Turks. Trestles and benches were laid between the vaults, and the first time we entered, when it was empty, all we could get was a brown furry fruit juice. The following day there was still no beer but an eager clientele had crammed the rooms with cigarette smoke. Later we heard roars and, opportunists that we had become, stormed in for a tankard. Everyone was making up for lost time. We squeezed onto the end of a table with a band of beef-armed Romanian boys, and dipped into the beer. It wasn't bad.

A young German punched the air.

'*Trink auf! Morgen gibt's keine!*' Drink up! There'll be none tomorrow!

*

Local Saxon legend connected Schässburg with Hamelin, a city of the Hanseatic League. If in Danzig the echo of the shifting hinterland had sounded in tales of Arthur, the Wandering Jew and the Flying Dutchman, Hamelin's story of wandering was the famous Pied Piper, taking his train of children into the mountainside. The Saxons used to say that they were those children: and that the paradise glimpsed for a moment by the little cripple boy who went too slow was Transylvania, '*Siebenbürgen*'.

If so, he was getting all his playmates back.

The Hungarians, though equally beleaguered, would struggle on. The Saxons had never had sovereign power in the country as the Hungarians had: there was no going 'back' to Hungary if you believed at bottom that this, in fact, was Hungary. And Hungary had less to offer than Germany. It couldn't have the alluring semifictional appeal of a more distant homeland, where everyone could afford a Mercedes and pensions for the old were a thousand times as big. The cripple boy had made good, after all, and his own pipers piped away to the paradise of Düsseldorf and Essen. The tune they played was instantly recognisable: it had to be the theme music to *Das Erbe von Gulenbergs*.

We were witnessing, I suppose, one of the numberless shifts of the eastern continent. In twenty years, when the last of the old and sick – '*wir Bleibenden*' – are dead, the visitor will find the Saxons of Schässburg as remote as the men who built cathedrals, or the Pilgrim Fathers. Sighisoara will be an old Romanian town, built by German colonists in the thirteenth century: another quaint old place.

The official guidebook to the town, printed in Bucharest, had already effaced the Saxons – rather as the Nazi map had erased the Poles who lived on the Baltic coast. Using silence as a weapon, the guidebook left you with the impression that Romanians had used the help of other nationalities to found the town, and that was all. In twenty years, when the visitor sits at the Café Dracul, ordering *vin rossu* from the Romanian waiter, he will have no notion that the lives of nearly a million people foundered here so recently in despair: *was kann man tun?*

We climbed three hundred wooden steps that led through a wooden tunnel up the hill to the Black Church. Segesvár was on a hill, and the church stood on a final bluff of it above the town. Next to it lay the cemetery, where we spent an afternoon among broken urns and weeping angels. They were trade names on the tombs: Bauer, Eisenhammer, Mahler. In this cemetery, perhaps for the last time, twenty generations lay undisturbed.

Schässburg was a fortress-town. It had guarded the southern approach to the Maros valley against the Turks, and was one of a ring of Saxon towns that grew up to trade over the Carpathians and protect the hinterland of Hungary. Now the hinterland was lost to the south. At the foot of the hill, down the lane that led from the clock tower, beyond the only café in the town serving real coffee – awash with black grounds and sweet, to Turkish taste – stood a sort of hotel-cum-restaurant which beat us back by the strange, sinuous music played loudly over speakers, the hard stares, and the smell of the local brandy, like fertiliser. The same atmosphere of low brutality as at Oradea, the same appearance of being beyond Europe.

Down there the Greater Romanian *Kulturkampf* had been fought, and the gimcrack and ugly triumphed. Where three years ago had stood the warren of streets, *bürgerlich* houses, old inns and courts and carriage gates, cobbled mews and narrow overhung alleys, there now lay only an acre or so of pounded rubble, broken wattling and stones. Ceauşescu had died too late for the lower town, and for miles along the valley rose dirty housing blocks with their empty shop fronts and ramshackle outside loos. Peter had said that the Romanians had not built anything of their own before the First World War; they were making up for lost time.

So we looked for higher ground, like Saxons under siege; and found ourselves in the Black Church.

At the door stood the sexton, tall and thin, with a narrow melancholy face and short black hair. He lived in a tower opposite the church door. He had set a trestle on the grass in the shade of a giant yew.

We talked in the doorway, and he asked us to have a beer. At his table sat an odd couple, farmers from a neighbouring village.

'These people are going to Germany,' said the sexton, placing two rare bottled beers on the table.

'Our neighbours left a few months ago.' The farmer's accent was scarcely penetrable: unlike the Schässburger he had no *Hochdeutsch*. He wore brown felt trousers, gumboots and a checked shirt under his broad leather waistcoat, from which he now pulled a letter. 'We waited to hear what they said. They think we should come after them. The life will be good.'

He tapped the letter with a thick forefinger, and paused, pulling on his beer as if it might persuade him. 'Well, there are too many strangers in the village. Too many gypsies. I've been losing my sheep, and my wife doesn't feel safe at home any more.'

He shook the letter in his hand. 'The Germans have written to me. War-wound allowance and old-age pension. Eight years in Russia. Work camp. I broke my leg and I don't walk well.'

'And your family?' I asked.

'All gone already,' he replied. 'Everything has gone.'

The sexton said: 'Believe me, we had a good life here once. And not long ago. We made our own beer, good stuff. Even in the sixties we had a super restaurant in the hills over there – Klebert's, wasn't it?'

The farmer shrugged and blew out his cheeks.

'The school was ours until the seventies,' continued the sexton. 'Our own teachers, everything in German. Then they sent a few Romanian children there and everything had to change. No more German. They closed this church.'

'The Romanians are thieves,' said the farmer.

'It is like this with them,' said the sexton, slipping his hand behind his back. 'Everything.'

'And now that Ceaușescu has gone? Couldn't it get better, if you stayed?'

'People like that will always make Ceaușescus,' said the sexton, and the farmer gave a short laugh to show it was well put.

'You will eat something?' The sexton was insistent. 'It is done already. We can't eat it all.'

He fetched us a couple of pieces of grilled lamb, and set them on plates with a sauce.

'Mind the sauce. It's hot.'

'Another,' he said, when we'd finished. 'No, don't thank me. Thank my friend here. This is the last of his flock.'

The old farmer grunted, 'Couldn't take them with us.'

This was the tag-end of Germany-in-the-east; this, not the Soviets gobbling up Berlin while Krebs's scratch brigade wheeled round the burning Chancellery in 1945. Right the way from Gdansk we'd been on the track of Germans: the scale of their past seemed immense. Everyone had a different name for them. Every language recorded some dim tribal encounter with a branch of the Germans: they called themselves *Deutsche*: the Poles called them *Niemanski*; they were *Allemands*, or Germans. The English or the French were known by variants of Angles or Franks; but the names for the Germans were legion. After the barons of the Teutonic order, the Margraves and Burgraves, Counts Palatine and the Bans; after the King-Emperor, and the German Caesar; Karl von Hohenzollern-Sigmaringen, King of Romania in 1872; after the Junkers, and the armies – the imperial army of 1881, hunting Petofi; the men who marched in 1914, the Panzer columns running on ersatz fuel, the Sonderkommando, the SS; when these had gone, with the grave elders of Danzig and the sadist Frank of Wawel, the collapse of the *Drang Nach Osten* left only these *Bauer und Bürger* in Transylvania, old inhabitants of one of the farthest flung German outposts of all.

We'd caught up with the vanishing Germans, and at long last they were making in six months the retreat they had resisted for 700 years: these people with weathered faces, chapped spatulate fingers and very clear blue eyes, who withdrew – bewildered, wiping the last of the mutton from their lips – across the Elbe.

One group of legends expresses the bewilderment of no longer belonging: the bewilderment of the Saxons, of the East Germans, even the Hungarians in Transylvania; a bewilderment common in Eastern Europe. These are the legends of the sleepers who wake. They are legends expressing the shock of change.

An early example is the story of the sleepers of Ephesus, persecuted Christians who take refuge in a cave and wake up to find no-one they know in Ephesus, and everyone a Christian. They die of joy.

Another is the story of Rip Van Winkle, a Dutch colonist in America, who wakes to find his children old men in a republic.

Arthur will wake when change threatens, and restore the status quo. But the Wandering Jew may never sleep, and experiences the shock of change till doomsday.

The best-known sleepers who wake are the vampires. In the Habsburg empire they took such a grip on the popular imagination that Maria Theresa sent out a commission to investigate. The commission was unable to lay the vampire legend to rest.

Vampire stories, possibly, work like parables, warning their hearers against clinging beyond reason to what is dead and buried. Village vampires, such as the commission investigated, were by no means suave and titled; they were invariably husbands, wives, parents or children lately deceased. Their return, it has been suggested, whether real or imagined, is in obedience to the survivor's great grieving wish to have them back – a wish that goes so far against nature (for what is dead is gone) it can only be fulfilled unnaturally. The restoration is bloody and destructive.

The message, then, is not to linger in the past, nor by any means to attempt its retrieval. But memory will be restless, nonetheless. In this part of the world, where vampires abound, memories have been gathering for centuries. Injuries seek redress and fear ricochets off fear. The swastika, the iron cross, the arrow are there, waiting to be picked up again; the peoples of Eastern Europe move under a train of baggage, like a column of refugees. Every hope, every triumph, every good is there; and packed away, swiftly unloaded, every evil ever given or received. Each man's redress is another's injury; every restoration is a usurpation; no act is free from guilt. The dead hand of communism lifts: the carts creak back into life, and the columns of refugees jostle for position on the narrow road.

Székelyföld

The route we chose from Schässburg depended on how fast we wanted to reach the plain, Bulgaria and Istanbul. We could have dropped south, crossed the mountains, and arrived in Romania proper in a week; instead we decided to push east, staying among people we felt we knew and liked, treating the mountains as a defensive wall. That way we'd cross the Székelyföld and breach the mountains just south of Brasov, another Saxon city.

Secrets in Transylvania pass as rumours from hill to hill like beacon lights. Transylvania is prismatic with rumours, will'o'the wisps forming, reforming and crumpling up.

No-one knows much about the origins of the Székely, who are the true natives of the place. Of all the people who have settled in Transylvania, only the Szekelyi have nowhere else to go. They are not Hungarian, exactly, although they speak Hungarian. They claim to be the remnants of Attila's horde, stragglers in the Hunnish invasions that swept over Europe in the sixth century. The claim is disputed. They may have been Magyars who filtered through into the Transylvanian plateau instead of sweeping round to the south with their fellows, and so were separated from them for centuries. They may have been a Turkic tribe that met with the Magyars on the steppe as they journeyed west, and rode with them long enough to adopt their language, before heading up into the mountains on their own. Nobody knows.

The Hungarians meeting the Székely in the thirteenth century were quite clear that they had encountered a separate nation. Soon after that meeting, the whole region was devastated by the Mongol invasions. The second Mongol army swept into Transylvania, along the Danube, into Pannonia and beyond, while the first dashed across the northern plain, destroying Cracow. Against the threat of a repeat invasion, the King of Hungary moved the Székely from the Transylvanian interior, where their lands were given to German colonists, and established them on the inner slopes of the Carpathians to defend the passes. With the Saxons and the nobility, the Székely constituted one of the three medieval 'nations' of Transylvania – nation meaning simply a hereditary group with defining privileges. Serfs, unfree, had no privileges to speak of, and were never considered as part of a nation. The Székely fought on horseback, and they maintained the nomadic tradition of light cavalry warfare long after they settled down. They were freemen, and so they were considered noble according to the divisions of the time; but they weren't rich. A Székely farmer had neither time nor money to equip and train as a heavily armoured knight.

This area of eastern Transylvania is known as the land of the Székely, or Székelyföld; and the Székely themselves are known as clever, cunning and independent. In Hungarian jokes the Székely farmer always comes out top. A stranger on foot hails a Székely farmer passing in a cart. 'How far to Udvarhely?' Ten miles, says the Székely. The stranger asks him for a lift, and when the farmer raises no objection he climbs up. After they have been going about an hour, the stranger asks how far Udvarhely is now. 'Sixteen miles,' the farmer replies. The stranger is furious, but the Székely cuts him off. 'You wanted to know how far it was to Udvarhely. You never asked if I was going there myself.'

The Hungarians were proud of the Székely; and in return the Székely took their traditional duties seriously. During the riots in Bucharest, when the rumour arose that the miners were to be sent into Transylvania as well, the Székely apparently set traps to block the railway lines from the south. With tree trunks and landslides they obeyed a medieval king's command to defend the passes. In the eyes of the Hungarians, the Székely were heroes who always held their ground.

Outside Schässburg we passed the spot where Petőfi Sándor disappeared. In 1848, at the age of twenty six, he had joined the revolutionary Hungarian army under the Polish General Bem, who managed to secure almost all Transylvania for Kossuth before the Austrians called in the Russians, campaigning against the Turks in Wallachia. Bem defeated the first army sent against him; but when the Tsar sent 200,000 reinforcements, the Hungarians were trounced on 31 July 1849. Petofi's body was never found; the rumour grew that he vanished alive into the prisons of the Tsar. Returning prisoners claimed to have seen him in Siberia; while all over Hungary a flock of pretenders basked in the nation's refusal to let its hero go. The field now was strewn with rubble, the broken brick and concrete softened by a haze of heat.

I ran my finger down the red line of a road on the map, joining dots; some of the dots were hot. Then the map bit me and I tried to draw my hand back, although my elbow was somehow stuck. I woke up.

At the end of the bed sat a Chinaman with a moustache.

'*Jo reggelt!*' said the Chinaman.

I croaked back automatically: *Jo reggelt kivarnok*. Czech? Polish? German? Romanian? Hungarian? A sort of linguistic porridge seemed to have stuck to the roof of my mouth. And the pink wine? Bottles of it from the fridge. Home-made. Not quite ready for drinking, but Ferenc had insisted. ('Ferenc, this is all your wine!' 'There is more, please. The map . . .')

My eyes hurt. I heeled upright like Lazarus from the duvet. Kate was propped on her elbow, and Ferenc grinned. He mimed a sore head. I nodded.

My feet were hot and sticky. The bath was blocked and Anna Maria had to wash everything in a series of buckets – even duvet covers. They lived in a modern block, in a small flat decorated with Ferenc's carvings. Beside the bed stood the weird stick Ferenc had made me yesterday. After beers and *palinka* in his living room we'd gone across to his workshop in a row of lock-up garages near the railway embankment. Some things in Romania, like the provision of rather smart garages to a car-less citizenry, had ceased to surprise us. Perhaps the architect really had meant to build workshops. Mechanics fingered the sumps of ancient Dacias; a welder examined a join through a mask held on a stick like a Greek tragedian; someone was varnishing furniture and Ferenc had all the equipment to make it. He had a broad workbench, a treadle lathe, a jigsaw and a rack of tools. He selected a thick rod from a stack of dowelling and set to work.

Ferenc was a Székely: he looked truly Chinese, with Chinese colouring, the same flawless smooth skin and dark slanting eyes. His hair was black. He was much shorter than me, but stocky, broad shouldered. His carvings were traditional Székely style: my stick, after an afternoon's work, looked like a cross between Skylab and a totem pole. The stock was covered in cubes and hexagons, in faceted spheres resembling bizarre fruit. The grip was decorated with flowers blooming on the stems that twined up the shaft. It was more a staff than a stick, reaching to my midriff, an inch and a half thick. It seemed an almost eerie coincidence that so soon after I'd lost my old Polish stick we met the man who could make me another. When he had presented me with the stick he set about making something else: a board, to which he attached wooden pegs. He carved the whole thing freehand with twining flowers. On the back he gouged his name, and the date, and wrote: For Kate.

Afterwards he had tucked his baby daughter behind his ears and showed us round the Catholic cemetery.

The Székely do not have gravestones: they have wilder, fatter versions of my stick. We wandered through a forest of tall and spiky totem poles. They were irredeemably pagan – despite the inscriptions, the small black and white photographs, and the representations of the Cross. These were mere overlay on something that must have travelled in the baggage of the great migrations, centuries ago. The wooden stelae were creations of the steppe, loaded with shamanistic symbols and graven representations of purely eastern things: chrysanthemums, and the Persian lion.

Ferenc's wife was delicately made, with high cheek bones and fair hair. She worked as a nurse in the local hospital. With scant warning of our arrival she produced a delicious goulash. Ferenc had said she spoke French, and very shyly she said a few simple words, but that was all she knew and we conversed in basic Hungarian with the aid of our dictionary – the Hungarian flowering as the pink wine appeared, and using the dictionary less and less until Anna Maria and Kate were dozing and Ferenc and I were consulting the maps to no purpose whatever.

Using the stick as a crutch I hobbled after Kate, Ferenc and Anna Maria, who was going to work after a little sleep and a marathon of early-morning laundry. Three small faces appeared at a window as she went into the hospital.

Ferenc had an idea that we might find batteries in the free market, to get our camera working again. The black marketeers were trading thinly in the very poorest contraband: Lux soap, a battered box of Omo, spark plugs, German stock cubes, biscuits and some tinned food. Someone had a cumbersome Russian camera and a Bulgarian watch, but nobody seemed to be buying and there were no batteries.

Ferenc spoke to a group of gypsy men standing nearby. They wore the usual black hats and waistcoats, and one of them had a long grey beard. They shook their heads and suggested trying in Csikszereda.

'I have to go there today,' claimed Ferenc. 'I'll look for your batteries.'

We suspected that he was ready to make the trip for our benefit alone, and tried to dissuade him. He remained adamant, though, and when he suggested accompanying us for a while we all set out northeast towards Homorod.

The next village boasted three attractions: a Unitarian church, recognisable from the three balls that shinned up its spire; Szekelyi gates, and a terrific bar.

Without Ferenc we would have missed the bar in a roughly converted wooden barn, down a maze of village lanes. We bought six beers at once, just in case they ran out before we'd finished the first three, and sat outside on a trestle in a cleaned-out byre built of wood. We showed Ferenc the runic alphabet, and he became terribly excited. He had never seen it explained before. He copied it out carefully.

The gates the Székely erect at the entrance to their farms are perhaps relics of the palisade which once protected each farm in a region prey to raids and robbers. They stand around 15 feet tall and rather more broad, high and wide enough for a fully laden cart of hay to lumber through the double gates. A small door to one side is for everyday use. The whole edifice is carved, and often painted. The lintel is generally hollow to make a dovecote: the birds come and go through heart-shaped holes. But what make these gates particularly striking are their roofs which, tiled or shingled, are narrow and steep with ends that fly off in fanciful curls that remind you immediately of Chinese gables.

Coming away from the bar, Ferenc tried to teach us a song. It was impossibly difficult to catch the rhythm and gauge the moment that the notes dropped. Ferenc strode along, conducting, and at last hailed a passing lorry and sped off down the road, waving cheerfully from the cab.

The road gently ascended the valley up an avenue of walnut trees. Small orchards shed blossom, the branches in full leaf and the fruits tight and sour, the tree-trunks limed white against ants, like the bandaged fetlocks of thoroughbreds. On the slope the orchards were separated by handkerchiefs of wheat, ready for harvest, and here and there the harvesters themselves appeared – a man and his boy, lying on the grass with their scythes leaning against a nearby tree, a satchel open at their feet, a loaf of bread, a lump of fat or cheese standing on its paper wrapper. Whole families were reaping. Further down the slope a wagon leaned on its shafts in tall grass, and a horse was tethered in the shade of a tree, and everything was so still that you could hear the grass being torn by its teeth.

As the reapers moved towards the middle of a field a buzzard would appear, forming a tiny dot against a cloud, whose shadow meandered idly on the opposite slope.

A man snored on the grassy verge with a hat over his face. The road dropped through the trees, a sign announced Homorod, and for twenty minutes we went downhill without any sign of habitation until at the bottom we found a big chalet hotel and sat on a verandah overlooking a car park and a swimming pool made by damming a stream.

Baile Homorod thrived on the Central European passion for spring water. The famous spring burbled greasily from a rusty pipe, slightly warm and stinking of bad eggs; the disgusting combination had perversely secured its reputation. You could sluice yourself with it in the man-made pool below the terrace, and in the hotel itself you could buy the water in bottles. There was no beer or wine; it made peculiar coffee. There was a drunk about, all the same: he came by cart and spent a long time trying to force his horse to drag him up the hotel steps, roaring and brandishing a long whip.

Ferenc met us there several hours later – so much later, in fact, that we thought we'd misunderstood him, and enquired for rooms in the hotel. They were not available. Little was: only grizzled sheep's tendons from a barbecue on the terrace served with dry bread and a sweet grey mustard. We chomped thoughtfully on that and watched the beer lorry arrive below. Not a single bottle made it to the restaurant: the moment the lorry pulled in, the clientele fell upon it and picked it clean, backhanding the driver. (He made a tidy profit and would no doubt return to his depot with some story about losing his load on a hairpin bend.) It took me a while to understand the system, and by the time I reached the lorry there was nothing left.

A lorry slowed and a familiar figure in a white T-shirt dropped from the cab.

Ferenc apologised that he hadn't managed to find any batteries. On this evidence that he had spent his day searching for them on our behalf we berated him with our stock of Hungarian reproaches. He waited until we had exhausted the possibilities of the dictionary and then fished out four batteries, after all. They were of unknown manufacture, but they were just the right size.

He suggested we take a lift with him and spend the night in Udvarhely, and we were tempted to agree. There were no rooms in the hotel; a twilight chill had settled on the valley, and the fires of a youth camp already glittered through the trees. But behind the hotel lay a hamlet and we resolved to ask there for shelter first.

The Székelyföld is brown-bear country, and in winter lean wolves descend from the Bukovina to enjoy the fruits of Székely husbandry. Naturally bears and wolves appreciate the warm spring at Baile Homorod. It doesn't freeze, and there may be pickings in the village. The villagers had done what they could in self-defence. With Ferenc's help we found a barn, attached to a farm that was half fortified, fenced in by a tangled hedge and approached by a plank over a stream that led to a wooden door.

Wolves may be shot in winter, when they are considered vermin; but the penalties for shooting a bear without permission are draconian. In recent years, permission was almost never given, because Ceauşescu reserved the sport to himself. The Great Huntsman would order up the chopper and head for the hills, invariably accompanied by Securitate marksmen and a camera crew.

Ceauşescu's pretensions as a hunter seemed to irritate the Transylvanians more than almost anything else he did. Confiscating typewriters, forcing women to undergo internal examinations, knocking down towns and villages, squandering resources: these things made him hated. But it was the hunting trips that everyone mentioned, in tones of deepest scorn.

The hunts were pathetic. Boar, bear and wolves were driven onto the Conducator's gun while the real marksmen hung from trees, ready to support his fabled prowess as a shot. Sometimes, to credit the stories, the bear was hobbled first.

Perhaps it was that Ceauşescu's hunts appeared on TV, so dreadfully edited that even a child could spot the pretence. Every evening, during the two to three hours of television broadcasts, The Leader Goes Hunting jostled in the ratings with Ceauşescu Meets a Head of State, Elena Receives an Honorary Degree, or The Conducator Flies Abroad. Some of this material was fresh, but most was a rehash of old footage. When Ceauşescu popped up with the President of Burkina-Faso, or foreign dons were shown clapping as Elena was rewarded for her contributions to science, nobody could tell if this had happened yesterday, or years ago, or, indeed, at all. Everyone loathed the meagre evening broadcast so much that I couldn't understand why they bothered to queue for a television. But then they bought the papers, too, and the papers were choked with the same patent tosh.

At a glance, the farm where we settled for the night seemed unimaginably remote from the world of televisions and papers. It was built around a yard, of beams, and wide, uneven planks, and pegs; but the wood was smooth from age, and the roof-line undulated where over the years the buildings had settled and sunk. Our hay loft rose in three tiers over the rooms below; it was reached by a ladder from the cart-shed. We spread out our sleeping bags on the fresh prickly hay, and marked them with our packs, and I took my torch with me when the family called us out; the sky was almost dark through the chinks in the shingle roof. Outside it seemed paler.

The farmer had a wooden leg; his wife had a nose like a finger and wore trousers tucked into her gumboots. She was taller than him. They led us out of the yard at the back and up a rise to a wooden bungalow, grander than the house in the yard, which was wattle and daub and opened directly onto the yard. This was the winter house: it had a glazed hallway and in the room beyond a television was set up high on a dresser which contained a small museum of luxuries: an untouched bar of Lux, a bottle of Fa, an unopened bottle of Russian vodka, displayed in a cabinet as though it were a dollar shop. The farmer stamped over to the telly and switched it on. An indistinct murmur of voices broke from the speaker. The whole family were watching us: the farmer on a high hard chair for his leg, two little girls sitting on a settle to one side, the mother and grandmother at the table behind us. They insisted we took the armchairs.

All of a sudden a clipped British voice said:

'A light, your majesty. Look! Through the trees.'

There was a noise of thrashing about, the jingle of a harness, and before our astonished eyes Errol Flynn materialised, swinging from his horse.

The farmer touched my arm.

'*Angol*,' he explained.

The film creaked on. Caught in a storm out hunting, the King of England was obliged to seek refuge in a humble Saxon woodsman's hut. He sneered at the filth, the primitive furnishings, and the thin gruel that the woodsman offered. He swaggered about, booted the woodsman, groped the woodsman's daughter, and declared himself disgusted with the whole place. I cringed for him. Our hosts were silent.

We wanted to go to bed, but thought we should wait for the film to end. In the end we decided to move – upon which they all leaped up so eagerly it was obvious they had been waiting politely for us. They saw us up the ladder into the hay before shutting us in with a wooden catch. We performed the trick of undressing and getting into our bags without bringing in tufts of scratchy hay as well. The new hay was spongy and soft underneath; in Poland we'd bedded down on what was left after winter, hay which was thinner, of course, and more dusty. The last we heard was the soft thump of the barn cat as it arrived in search of things to eat.

Ferenc had assured us that the walk from Homorod to Csikszereda would be the most beautiful in all Transylvania. Experience should have taught us that when anyone in Eastern Europe advertises beautiful scenery he invariably means pine forest. We hated pine forest. But the day began well. A few miles up the hill that led from Homorod we saw the spiky ball on a spire that means the reformed church, and in the village square a small boy was selling bottled beer at a kiosk. Nor were we the only walkers; for while we glugged our beer in the kiosk's shade an old mountaineer came through the village. He was wearing much the same outfit as Tatra shepherds wore, far to the north up the Carpathian sickle. We had been told that whether they spoke Polish, Hungarian, Slovak, Ukrainian, Russian or Romanian, the Carpathian highlanders were related more closely to one another than to any of their linguistic fellows and rulers on the plains: that they constituted a nation in the medieval sense, not bound together by objective criterion of race or language, but by lifestyle and common traditions.

The old man's beard was short, rough, snow-white; and he walked with a staff. A green felt hat, like the traditional Tyrolean mountain hat, with a yellow braid above the narrow brim, perched on his head: it looked several sizes too small. (Not to wear a hat used to be considered a sign of mourning and remembrance among the Szekelyi.) His shirt and trousers were made of brilliant white wool, and were tucked into a buckler of hard oiled leather, about a hand's width, worn under a black waistcoat. He was carrying a small leather knapsack over one shoulder, and with the other he hefted himself onwards with his staff, slanting it across his chest and punting from right to left. I tried to adopt this style myself later on but I soon gave it up, it only slowed me down when the stick got tangled in my legs. In the square he rested for a few minutes on a whitewashed step, and then passed on; the beer boy thought that he was here for the harvest.

He would have to hurry: haymaking was almost done. The wagons jounced empty out of a village, and creaked back bulging with hay like enormous cottage loaves. The design of the carts was much the same as in Poland: they were a little broader, measuring three feet or so in the beam, but about nine feet long with sloping-out sides and a plank laid across at the front to make a seat. Once all the hay had been forked aboard they lumbered along the road, about ten foot wide and as high as a house, scattering only the tiniest wisps of hay across the road.

One of these carts was heading for the fields and the driver and his wife offered us a lift. Between them sat a grandchild who gobbled up the popcorn we'd bought that morning in Homorod. Forks and scythes bounced at our feet on the bottom of the cart. The old couple were friendly and amused; they posed for a photograph and told us to visit when we next came, writing out their address with solemn care as we stood at the start of the track leading down to their field.

We waved until we'd passed the brow of the hill and rounded the corner. The brow frowned. A few twisted trees were hobbling across a heath of scorched grass and gorse. Ahead of us we recognised a thick belt of pines. Our hearts sank, and then picked up again with a sudden catch as a grey animal slunk from a thorn bush and crossed the road ahead. All of a sudden it stood stock still, its head hanging on a level with its belly. I fingered my new stick. The thorny trees looked too brittle to be climbed; they weren't very tall, either. While we were dithering the dog slunk out of sight. We filled our hands and pockets with stones, and went on.

The road was steep, ascending in an endless series of switchback curves; there was no view on the way up, or from the top, only a press of blueish firs. But at last we came out over a wide valley. A river wriggled through the fields and a railway line cut a huge arc close to the opposite hills.

At the top the road was up, a surface prepared with sharp white stones. The works attendant, supervising nobody we could see from a small cabin, came out and asked for cigarettes. I handed him two Ski cigarettes from my crumpled pack, though I was anxious to conserve stocks until I could be sure of buying more. The cigarettes crackled like dry leaves. The tobacco, if it was tobacco, was old and dusty. Half of it always shot out of the cigarette unless you twisted the end. Romanian cigarettes were a parody of the real thing, like Romanian democracy; revolutions; restaurants, hunting expeditions. From a considerable distance you could be fooled. If they were *filtru* they had filter wrappers properly speckled brown to resemble cork, just like anywhere else: but this attention to the wrong detail was typical. To stick it together they used a soluble gum, so that even if you screwed the paper to stop the cigarette collapsing at one end, it invariably disintegrated from the other. The wrapper unwound, gummed itself to your lip, and let the filter fall out. You could try to smoke very drily, but after a few puffs the filter went completely flat. Without the filter – *fara filtru* – the tobacco naturally cascaded from the filterless end. Either way the burning end kept running up against woody lumps which put it out. You pulled the lump free in a shower of powder and relit the cigarette.

If you had a match. And if the match would light. When you could find a place selling matches they were invariably restricted to one box per person. When I discovered the last of my Purfleet Bryant and Mays wedged into a side pocket of my pack it was like looking at a box of joists. In Eastern European match factories, nimble-fingered workers pick out the duds and box them up for domestic consumption. Most matches in Romania incorporated the knotty parts of the wood, and splintered when you struck them. No two matches looked alike, but they all had the same kind of hard-to-ignite heads, made of liquefied asbestos. Nonetheless they were not safety matches: you could spend half an hour fiddling with matches only to have the whole box go up in flames after you'd put them in your pocket. The strike paper became tattered and useless and before the box was empty you were reduced to wittling the head against a square millimetre of intact strike paper.

Like the television or the newspapers, it made you wonder why anyone bothered.

So I gave the man two cigarettes and watched his face sag in disappointment. I suppose he wanted a foreign make. Failing this, he went for bulk.

'Two, for my friend,' he explained. It was lucky that Romanian was such a baby language, because otherwise I wouldn't have understood a word.

I gave him two more.

'*Mulcumesc*,' thank you, he said, and graciously put out his hand. I took a step back to grab it and disappeared over the edge of the road.

The broken surface of the road flashed past my eyes and I crunched heavily onto a pile of gravel. The pack crunched down on top of me. Since I wasn't seriously hurt – I had only torn my knees, broken my watch and somehow bruised my ear, Kate and the cigarette thief broke into peals of laughter.

The base of the valley spread broad and flat: in the lee of the opposite hills rose the twin grey towers of the Franciscan monastery Father Barna had told us to visit, the centre of Catholicism in the Székelyföld. We'd made a detour to the northeast to reach it, but we could follow this valley south towards Brasov and the Carpathian pass above Bran.

Going down into the valley I had that familiar feeling of exultation and safety, sinking towards orchards, warmth, crops and habitation. Storks in the telegraph poles clattered their bills as we passed. At the bottom we picnicked on the grass, drinking a little sulphurous water from our pigskins and sharing a hard bread roll. Having lost our view we ducked and dodged across the valley. Roads veered off, gave out, or edged so subtly out of true that the towers kept springing up on an unexpected quarter and bewilderingly far away. In the heat I grew irritable and contrary. I nagged at Kate when we backed from a pack of snarling dogs. Shame made me furious, and before long, goaded by weariness, thirst, and disappointment, we had the row I'd perversely engineered. Kate stoned me with flints she gathered from the road. We stopped at a derelict house and sat on opposite sides of the verandah trying to recover a better mood for approaching the monastery.

Victorian travellers in Transylvania (there were not very many) were astonished by the local propensity for divorce. The Unitarians were easy on the question, with the result that Cluj became the Reno of its time: anyone could procure a divorce in the town provided they were a householder. There was a derelict row of houses constantly changing hands in order to fulfil the condition.

But it was not only Unitarians who countenanced divorce. The Saxons were keen. Scanning the records for three villages betwen 1861 and 1863, Dr Boner discovered that at least thirty divorces had been registered each year. Of the reasons given *Abneigung*, antipathy, was the most common. But others were not nearly so vague. Compulsion to marry was cited. Drunkenness, insuperable disgust, ill treatment, staying out at night, groundless complaining, were all legitimate cause. So was ill-smelling breath. Boner was particularly struck by the party who filed successfully for a divorce on the grounds of *Augenverdrehen*: rolling the eyes about.

Boner, who was no prude, noticed that divorces were more frequent after the grape harvest, but all in all he could do no better than the Hungarian he spoke to who confessed that divorce had simply become a habit.

It was about five when we reached the monastery gates. Through the main doors we were met on the stairs by a man in overalls who suggested we come back at nine. The church was white and gold; I recalled my better mood on the hillside. The unhurried rhythm of columns and pilasters progressed towards a statue of the Virgin on a balcony behind the altar – the largest miraculous statue in Europe – before which a young couple were praying.

My temper improved still further when I read on a notice that the monastery had been established by Janos Hunyades in 1442 to celebrate a victory over the Turks in southern Transylvania. The Turkish general, and 20,000 of his men, had been killed; prisoners were dispatched while the Hungarians feasted; and the following year Hunyades crushed an army 80,000-strong that came for vengeance.

Hunyades died at Belgrade in 1456, having successfully repulsed

the Turks under the command of Mahomet, the conqueror of
Istanbul; and his memory was so feared that his tomb in Alba
Iulia, which Peter and Marika had shown us, had been hacked
about by Turkish raiders more than a hundred years after his
death. He lived at that fluid moment before the settling of empires
on Eastern Europe: Ladislaus, King of Poland and Lithuania, sat
on the Hungarian throne, and Ivan the Terrible was yet to wrest
Muscovy from the Golden Horde; the Habsburgs were cadet
Electors still; and Hunyades himself aspired to be made King of
Bulgaria, through which he twice led a Hungarian army, nearly
to the walls of Edirne. But in 1444 his army of Hungarians and
Poles was defeated at Varna on the Black Sea – King Ladislaus
among the dead. The failure of the campaign, which had come
close to driving the Turks from Europe altogether, sealed Constantinople's fate. Nine years later the city fell, securing the Turkish presence in Europe for centuries to come.

We went into the village. Close to the hillside a stone gazebo
sheltered a sulphurous spring where people were queuing to fill
their bottles in the dusk. A gypsy boy had been at the tap first,
but he gave way to a farmer who had arrived on a cart rattling
with empty bottles in their crates. The queue murmured against
a woman who filled her bottles too slowly. The farmer left his
nag on a rein so short she couldn't reach the grass, and then lashed
her thin flanks mercilessly when he set off. It was a careless way
to treat a useful asset. The gypsy boy, with only a few bottles to
fill, sat patiently in the shadows until everyone had gone.

The clock struck as we reached the monastery again. Without
explanation an old woman showed us to a room with two beds
made up with hospital corners. We thanked her gratefully, and
were about to undress when a man we had met earlier on the
stairs knocked and suggested that if we were not too tired we
might follow him upstairs. On the way he explained that we would
find the monastery a sorry place, for its numbers had dwindled
since the confiscation of its lands, leaving just three monks, of
whom he was one.

He led us into a kitchen where an elderly man in a beret and
workman's dungarees cooked us a six-egg omelette, with bread
and butter and a glass of Alba Iulia wine. He watched us eat

with a quiet smile, and only when he had asked gently after our nationality and our religion did we realise that he was the abbot himself.

Next morning I put my hat over the chamber pot and crept about the corridors looking for somewhere to dispose of it. The place seemed deserted, but on my way back I passed the monk in his habit who wanted to know if I had looked out of the window. The courtyard was blocked by a lorry. The monk seemed as surprised by it as I was, and hurried off to investigate.

When Kate and I came outside the monks were buzzing around the lorry as if it were a vast sculpture someone had idly winched into the courtyard overnight before running away. It was huge and shiny and had German plates. The monks peeped now and again through the driver's window, looking for life, but they seemed thoroughly perplexed. I climbed on the footplate and rapped on the glass until a face appeared through a curtain at the back.

He was a young man with a faint blond moustache. He rubbed his face blearily.

'They don't seem to know what this is about,' I said.

He opened the curtains and swung out.

'*Ja*. I dunno.' He said.

I glanced enviously into the cab. The glossy wrapper of a chocolate bar and several bright packets of Knorr cup-a-soup snuggled between the windscreen and the giant dashboard, fitted with a twinkling computer. There were plush adjustable seats upholstered in velour.

The driver rubbed his hands with aftershave and ran them over his head. He yawned.

'There's a press in the back. Here's the address.'

It was correct. The monks looked bemused, but not unhappy. We helped them unload and set off across the valley to Csikszereda.

We had seen the city from the corner of our eyes the day before, when we stood on the summit of the Harghita; we had seen lights twinkle in the distance last night. We would have been tempted to avoid the place altogether, even after coming so far, if we hadn't found that our visas were on the point of expiry. Csikszereda, or Mercuria Ciuc, is a county city, and we hoped to get visa extensions from the police headquarters.

The city began abruptly at the edge of the fields. We stood on the brink of a silent lake of chequered paving. The surface of the lake heaved. Here and there small concrete islands sprouted a low tundra of steel wire. A broad avenue rolled away into the distance. Soaring out of the square and the avenue was an escarpment of enormous blocks, with balconies, circular windows, gigantic pediments, enormous tiled mansards. Millions of square feet of office space, thousands of miniature flats – and the tiles were slipping. Jagged cracks ran up precast concrete sections. The glass was spotted with blobs of cement, and the concrete tubs down the middle of the avenue were empty. Boarded shop-fronts pondered the absence of passing trade.

A bus trundled into view, creeping down the giant avenue like the survivor of some ecological disaster. It still bore the rack that until recently had been fitted with a lethal tank of natural gas, in lieu of petrol.

To make empty offices, shops that want trade, roads that would swallow London's rush hour and still look bare, the people of the town had been forked out of their cottages and gardens into ninth-floor flatlets with outside loos. And this was only a county town; few people outside the province have even heard of it. Perhaps it should remain obscure, and its inhabitants simply slip away one day and leave it to the weeds and cracks and slipping tiles.

We crept into the vast and crapulous hotel and hunkered down in the restaurant, to battle with the Romanian waitress for a cup of coffee. We thought we had a better chance of getting visas if we made a hotel our base. A foreigner in a hotel is a known quantity: a foreigner reeling in from the hedgerows with irregularities in his visa is a natural object of suspicion.

I telephoned the British Embassy in Bucharest to take advice. It was Saturday, and whoever picked up the phone didn't speak English. The hotel receptionist, though, directed us to the police station which lay, ironically, beyond the normalised city. The rooms were choked with petitioners filing for passports, and we would have been lost in the mayhem if someone hadn't recognised us from the spring at Homorod and pushed us forward to the window. We filled in a form, and handed over our passports. The extension visa had to be paid for at another office more than a mile away; I walked over while Kate stayed to guard the packs.

We visited the museum, housed in a modest old palace, and watched a group of demolition workers tear into the ancient clock tower outside. We had to dodge an Austrian Space Waggon backing out through the carriage gates and called hello in German. Then we saw that he was leaving the *Reformatus haz* (the minister's house). Fingering our introduction from the minister in Budapest, we went inside.

Csikszereda

Fraulein Eva Schumann champed so briskly on the bread that her glasses hopped to the end of her nose and with a practised jab of her finger she pushed them back. Each time the candlelight bent in the breeze her face slipped into the blue light of the dusk.

She taught English at a school in Vienna and everything she heard about Romania had frightened her. She was scared of being ambushed, of getting caught in a civil war, afraid of thieves and gypsy children. She was always nervous, anywhere: frightened of dogs, and of being alone; but she was never weak. Willpower determined her not to be the slave of fear; made her, instead, its victim. She had driven over the border with only her pet Alsatian for company. Maxi was half-mad already: he could sense the uncertainty in her commands and always had to be locked in her Golf.

'I shink he vill be good for my protection,' she said. I thought he might eat her eventually.

Georgy, translating into German for the minister, said that the labour had been local.

'The plans and orders came from Bucharest, but the people had to destroy their own houses. The city was levelled in two parts, in 1980. *Befehl ist Befehl,*' he added, '*und Geld bedeutet.*' Orders are orders, and there was no money.

We had heard differently, that Hungarians and Romanians were used to demolish one another's towns and villages. The minister shrugged. Maybe elsewhere.

Eva had driven from Vienna in a small convoy Georgy led. He was a Hungarian who'd worked the last fifteen years for a Catholic charity in Austria and he had been visiting Romanian orphanages once a fortnight since the revolution. Karl and Barbara were sitting beyond the feverish perimeter of light, a warm presence like cows beneath a hayloft when we slept. Karl tipped the double bottle of French plonk to every glass: we thought it was delicious. Barbara laughed easily. Karl looked like Captain Haddock and spoke four languages perfectly: English with barely an accept. He was the youngest of thirteen children born on a farm: his mother bore her first when she was thirty-three. It had left him with a faith in abundance. He and Barbara radiated a healthy, unquestioning open-handedness. Barbara had two girls by a previous marriage; together they had three more children. Then they started to adopt. The child of an underage junkie was followed by another from a Viennese orphanage; finally, as their eldest daughter started at university, they adopted a baby from the hospital. Across the courtyard their Space Waggon was blocked with clothes collected from friends in Vienna, with teddy bears and toys, paper nappies, babies' bottles, crayons and shoes. It was Viennese bourgeois jumble and looked brand new.

They ran a paper-recycling business and planned to quit Vienna for a farmhouse on the Croatian border – a farmhouse with a stork's nest, where their children would grow up speaking German and Croat, learning not to be afraid of languages.

Fraulein Schumann was afraid of them. She sparred with the English she taught, reducing it by argument and citation to something barbarian and rudimentary. She delved back into the faint Germanic past to discover a string of weird, glottal cries that formed, as she said, an awkward system of early vowels.

'Oooaaa, iiiooo, aaaeheheh.' Her thin lips pressed them into shape. 'These were too difficult, of course. They had to be simplified by the Early Germanic Vowel Shift.'

Early English, she explained, had benefited from this process, but later the High German Sound Shift passed it by. It was excluded from occlusive development, barred from the sophistication of the aspirant. In her eyes, the inability of the English to drop 'th' sounds was linguistic Ludditism.

'German is more modern dan English,' she said.

Only at supper she may have noticed that Karl managed his 'th' better than her, and so kept silent, picking at the loaf of bread.

Karl and Barbara had come to organise an adoption for a childless couple in Vienna.

'Once the mother signs the release form the adoption can go ahead,' Karl said. 'The trouble is that the mother has often disappeared. Most children in orphanages have parents alive, often gypsies, who can be very hard to find.

'Find them – then you must persuade them to sign the form. A lot of these women have never seen an official document before and they can't see what good it will do. They don't want to leave any legal record. They are frightened that they will be in trouble for it one day.'

Would it seem politic some day to excoriate the gypsies for 'selling babies' and humiliating the nation? Or might they as easily be blamed for seizing benefits which could otherwise have gone to 'Romanian' children? The relationship between rulers and the ruled in this country seemed governed by a popular tradition that went back beyond the days of Iliescu or Ceauşescu, beyond the fascists, perhaps to the time of the Turks, of bowing to demagogues; the governmental tradition was of rewarding the strong and intimidating the weak. The reluctant mothers might be wiser than Karl supposed.

Karl would believe that the world treated you as you treated the world: if you believed in a better future for us all, and acted as if the future were here already, it would rise up around you.

Anyone who thinks that the Austro-Hungarian empire was too large to succeed should eat a tomato from a Viennese supermarket in the eastern marches of Transylvania. Mine was so firm, red, and tasteless that I felt a momentary pang of homesickness. We made an Austrian breakfast – pumpernickel, cheese, salami – and purred out of the gates of the Protestant House in a convoy bound for an orphanage 70 miles to the south.

Later it would take us three days to cover the same distance, burdened with presents of pumpernickel and a weighty parcel that had to be delivered to Szent-György, but now for an hour we sat up high in the passenger seats of György's van and waved at the gypsy children who grinned and waved as we sped through their villages.

At Baile Tusnad, near the spring, a gypsy woman selling popcorn snuffed about the vans and set up a doleful clamour as soon
as she realised what was in them. The popcorn business appeared
to be brisk, and she was taking in – at 100 lei a bag – considerably
more than Peter earned at the church in Cluj, or Mihaly from his
Library. When Karl handed her a sack of baby things she stood
in a stunned hush, and suddenly moved off, positively cackling at
his simplicity, at a speed that suggested she feared he might change
his mind.

I said she would be sure to sell them on the black market.

'It's not a problem,' said Karl. 'Some child will get to wear
them.'

'Hmmph,' I said, but too quietly for him to hear. After drinking
from the spring we drove on.

These children had always lived in a twilight that was broken only
when they ate. Those who were old enough still could not speak.
They didn't cry – nobody listened to them. Nobody touched them
much. They lay breathing in the half-dark and when the door was
opened on their room we blinked in the sudden shadow and
supposed it to be empty.

It took an effort of the senses to clear the gloom and to catch
a soft suspiration, inchoate and unexpectant, as the babies lay in
their cots and heard sounds beyond the sounds of their own
breathing.

Karl and Barbara opened the curtains. Some of the older babies
stood and held up their arms so rigidly that they bent inwards at
the elbows.

The room was bare and smelled sour. It was painted brownish-
yellow, with forty cots lined up in three rows, two cots deep, and
a chair and table near the door. A single bulb hung from a flex in
the ceiling. The babies left this room only to be bathed.

It appeared that the townspeople barely knew of their existence:
we'd had to ask several times in the town for directions to the
orphanage before we were set right. On the steps the director, her
subordinate, and a couple of nurses were waiting for us.

We carried bag after bag of clothing and box after box of
disposable nappies up the steps into the hall. György himself had

visited once before. He had brought advice and encouragement, baby foods and nappies and toys. Bewilderingly, the cots were completely bare, and the toys stood ranged about the hall on a high shelf, like prizes. The nurses were slow to move, slow to react, finding it scarcely worth changing a nappy that would be soiled again in minutes. The nappies and vests were marked with red splashes that looked disturbingly like blood.

Karl and Barbara took the toys from cot to cot. Few children knew what they were for. We crouched by the bars, dandled a toy, and the babies looked at us instead. They did everything to keep our interest – turning away, wriggling or holding up an arm; only as they realised that we were not about to vanish, would they turn to the toy and then with so many anxious looks at our faces, and blank looks at the toy, that it seemed that they did this only to please us. Such children, at least, formed the majority, clinging on; but many were submerged beyond any mark of interest; they seemed catatonic.

Our task was to teach each child to play. Literally and figuratively, the children were wrapped in upon themselves, curled into balls of loneliness where they sought sensation by thumping their heads against the cot, or hitting themselves with splayed hands, over and over again. They might watch with frightened interest, as you made the bear jump, the doll walk, the bell ring; but as soon as you left it to them they would sit immobile, watching the toy with an expression of great intensity, as though they were trying to commit to memory its wonderful performance. The idea that they could create one for themselves was absent.

The nurses' expressions were as bemused as the children's.

György returned from a discussion with the director, his face sagging.

'She's asked for news from the secondary orphanage, where a lot of the children are sent when they reach three. At that age they are given tests to establish their ability, physical as well as mental. Marks out of ten. The tests themselves were abandoned years ago in the West. The lowest-scoring twenty per cent, or thirty, or whatever number are required to leave, are then sent on to the secondary orphanages.'

He pulled a hand down his face.

'*Vernichtungslager*,' he said. Camps of destruction: the term for Birkenau and Treblinka.

'When the children arrive they are put into a large room. Many of them have physical or mental handicaps. They are all disturbed. They receive no medications, no more clothes, only food and water is put in, as for animals.

'Since the revolution the place has become more secret. They send someone now to collect the children, and it is impossible to visit.

'So I asked the director here to find out how the children are – she has sent ten there since our last visit. They just said: "Oh, quite well. Four still alive." '

There were Down's Syndrome babies among the forty in the room: in some ways they seemed the least withdrawn. They smiled easily. One, with black curls and a round, cheerful face, fastened on to Kate and would not let go: with her he laughed contentedly, but in his cot again he made a strange repetitive cry like a bird and started to knock his head against the cot. There was a baby with Aids, who lay utterly still and silent. He was thin, his skin was covered with small pink scabs like chicken pox, and his eyes remained half-closed. The nurses said that he was both blind and deaf; his thin blueish arms twitched convulsively.

I tried hard to draw life from a little girl and hung a board full of noisy gimmicks on the bars of her cot – a squashy ball that rang a bell, a dial that ratcheted, a telephone dial which tinkled when you turned it, and various plastic animals on a stick. She had begun, after a long reserve, to put a hand towards the board herself, when I touched her arm. She shrank instantly, without a sound, kicking herself into the further corner of her cot and pulling her arms over her face. It took longer to win her back, and I was careful not to touch her again.

Two nurses began to feed the children. Karl was shocked.

'I feed one baby in the time it takes them to feed eight or ten. They don't give it time even to swallow!' The babies' mouths were crammed, spoonful after spoonful, and the food rolled out of their mouths. When the bowl was empty they were returned to their cots. A child suddenly stood rigidly to attention, his arms upraised, waiting to be lifted out and fed. Oblivious to everything and anyone, he stood for minutes with a look like terror on his face.

Outside the sun shone, there was grass and trees and birds. There was even a fence which would have stopped a straying child. 'Couldn't they have found people in the town who'd enjoy watching over the children?' I asked. 'Even if they only went out in little groups?'

But the orphanage had no links with the town, except that some people worked here and lived there. György was sorting through the piles of disposable nappies, and explaining the food jars to the director. A thousand disposables would vanish long before György returned with any more. Anyway they had reasonable washing facilities: we'd been shown the laundry, with its enormous boiling vats and its spaghetti of hot pipework, and if it was primitive at least it was a going concern.

The Austrians saw their task as raising morale, showing the staff that the world valued this kind of work and would try to help. A thousand nappies were evidence of commitment, encouraging the nurses not only to take greater care at work, but to discuss it proudly at home, with their friends, until larger numbers of people were involved. A thousand nappies were a step towards charity drives and volunteer help.

The Austrians had energy and commitment. My reaction was to loathe the staff and despise the townsmen: charity began at home. The Austrians refused to judge.

As we were leaving, György asked casually to see the next room. The director pushed the door. Twenty older children, between three and seven – those without obvious handicaps who weren't 'sent on' – were sitting on blankets on the floor. We tossed the children in the air and let them touch the ceiling from our shoulders. We pulled toy carts on string, made dolls walk and animals roar again, counted fingers, smoothed foreheads: but they could not be put in a cot and left to watch with big eyes as we left. A child put her arms around my leg and squeezed, while two little boys gripped my hands. Another tried to climb up, so that I had to catch him up and sit him on my hip. We staggered with children, ballooned with them, were barnacled with little bodies. A nurse began a clumsy ring-around with those who were still loose, but they didn't want that game: they wanted to push and jostle for a grip, silently pleading with us to stay.

György had pointed out that these children grew up 'unsocialised', beyond the capacity for giving or receiving love. Orphans composed the core of Ceauşescu's Securitate, but it needed no sinister design to raise them.

I felt the Austrians were treating a disease as though it were a wound. They ascribed children developing into suspicious, antisocial characters to faults and deficiencies in the orphanage organisation: but you might have answered that Romania thrived on suspicion and that children who fell, as it were, into the nation's care, steadily grew to resemble their parents.

Karl and Barbara surprised themselves by adopting a child that weekend. She was a little gypsy girl, had trouble breathing, scowled and shied away from strangers – from everyone, that is – but her papers were already made out, and she was, they said, dangerously thin. They drove her home in the empty Space Waggon.

A few months later we visited them in Vienna. It was late afternoon; only Barbara was at home. She was, naturally, surrounded by children. The smallest was as brown as a berry and round as a pumpkin, giving little grunts of satisfaction as she showed off her ability to climb the stairs. When Karl walked in she squealed and ran with bow-legged, nappied steps towards him, arms outstretched, and he caught her up and held her high like a trophy.

To Brasov

Georgy's lust for giving was close to an obsession. With an aid parcel he adopted the earnest and slightly hasty air of an enthusiast who is anxious not to lose your interest.

'Is there anything you need?' he asked hopefully, the morning we were to leave.

We confessed that we lacked batteries for the camera, as well as a way of telling the time.

'Ah, I am sure . . .' he began, delving into his van, 'somewhere . . . yes . . . yes . . . batteries, um . . . a clock . . . a clock?'

He rummaged on, desperation mounting in his voice.

'Don't worry, please. It's not important.'

Georgy was mortified. In shame he flung himself on his food boxes.

'Aha!' he cried, handing us a couple of packets of pumpernickel and a tube of cheese spread.

'Thank you very much.'

'You need this, too,' he said, pushing a stack of tinned fish in tomato sauce into our hands.

'Thank you. Perhaps just one – '

'And you must have . . .' A ham in a can; a fistful of packet soups; two salamis, a packet of cornflakes, a jar of olives, a circle of cheese wedges, individually wrapped, three packets of pastrami, a carton of Ryvita –

'Georgy, stop!'

'Ryvita is good,' he said, disappointed.

'But we have to make room for things.'

'So you need them to be small,' he countered, slipping a handful of stock cubes onto the pile.

'It will be too heavy.'

Georgy looked at us sadly.

'You must eat. You must take them.'

'We just can't manage so much. Thank you all the same.'

He shook his head, convinced we were lying.

'Take whatever you want from these boxes. Please.'

'Well alright, thank you.' I made a rummaging motion and came up with a packet soup. 'Thank you.'

'Please. Now, do you have money? Traveller's cheques?'

When we had shaken hands, or hugged, as appropriate, our friends and hosts he stepped forward with a large parcel like an outsize shoebox.

'If you are going to Szent-György, please take this with you.'

'What is it?'

'I don't know, actually. Someone in Vienna asked me to deliver it. It's not too heavy?'

It was very heavy. Smiling bravely I laid it on top of the tins of fish and packets of soup and pumpernickel loaves and salamis and pulled the flap of my pack down hard. Its square edges towered over my head as we clanked out onto the main road.

The white towers of Mercurea Ciuc were swallowed up behind the hill.

We scanned the road ahead for spires. Nothing was more comforting to us than the sight of a spire pricking the horizon, advertising a settlement and a sanctuary. We'd grown to cherish the presence of the Church in unknown country. From the moment we saw a spire in the distance we began trying to decipher its denomination: a cross for the Catholics; a spiky iron ball like a mace for the Calvinists; three spheres transfixed on a spike for the Unitarians. Catholics and Calvinists were about equally dispersed; there were fewer Unitarians, grouped in particular regions. We saw no Orthodox churches in the countryside.

The Romanian Orthodox churches were to be found squatting in larger towns, where their domes seemed to weigh heavily on the ground. Seeing them as bastions of state orthodoxy, I found my own tolerance strained. Inside, candles started from the deepest shadow. There was something herd-like in the way the congregation were never allowed to sit down within the ring of guttering candlelight. When there was no service you could sit in some niche against the walls and watch the devout stoop to kiss the image of the Virgin, which stood on a low lectern.

On the road the churches themselves were changing, adopting more openly the role of sanctuary as we approached the borders of Orthodoxy. Cemetery walls began to thicken and rise, and wicket gates were losing ground to gateways. What we'd glimpsed in the fleeting landscape from the window of György's van was a world in imminent expectation of attack.

And yet the road to Szent-György was easy and delightful. We felt secure, as though those high defensive church walls protected us; perhaps comforted by the impression that people had something to protect. From a caravan of gypsy carts the gypsy who swung towards us merely proffered a bottle and roared '*Servustok!*', gripping our hands; and one afternoon, as we cooled our feet in the little river that ran behind a Protestant chapel and the minister's vegetable garden, Kate wondered if we should book a room in Istanbul. Then we went back to the house and ate stuffed cabbage with the minister's wife and waited for the return of the minister, roaring drunk, from a fishing expedition. He brought a barbel for his granddaughter, and declared, with charming modesty, but speaking in Hungarian, that he spoke five languages as well.

A gypsy cart gave us a lift over the last two miles into Baile Tusnad, with the gypsy family aboard assiduously bumming cigarettes the whole way, a couple for each member of the family including the children. The popcorn lady was nowhere to be seen: she had probably retired on her windfall. The café had run out of gas and was unable to produce a cup of coffee until the waitress ran home and brought back hot coffee in a pan, thick and sweet and reviving, and we lumbered out without so much as touching the water of the sulphurous spring.

As soon as we were settled at the church in Szent-György, we went out to deliver the mystery parcel. The address brought us to a small apartment where a grandmotherly woman asked us to wait in a tiny sitting room stuffed to the gills with cushions embroidered in Transylvanian folk style. The furniture was ebony inlaid with mother of pearl; the room looked a little like a gypsy caravan. Everything was spotless and well-ordered.

The old man to whom the parcel was addressed was a former Calvinist pastor; his wife offered us tea and cake. He took the parcel with gratitude and unwrapped it on the spot, politely, so that we might know what we'd been carrying. We had, of course, shaken it and weighed it already: but it was too well wrapped. The cardboard fell away to reveal a bottle of *schnapps*. I ground my teeth. With it came a letter: the old couple glanced at it briefly and put it away for later.

The old lady put a handkerchief to her face and went out of the room. The pastor smiled gently and speaking in German explained that their daughter had gone the previous year to Germany for work and a holiday. She was their only child, the apple of their eye. She was killed in a car crash.

He rubbed his mouth with the palm of his hand and blinked. 'She had so many friends. Everyone loved her. This letter comes from one of her friends in Austria.'

He showed us a photograph of their daughter. The old lady came back into the room. 'I'm sorry,' she said.

They pressed us to stay for supper: we had to refuse, because Tibor had already set supper for eight o'clock. The pastor's wife was adamant that we should have something: if not supper complete, then a little taste. We went with them into the tiny, pin-bright kitchen, and ate the best food we had tasted all year: a cherry soup, a small dish of pasta and cabbage, and a sort of sweet risotto made with sausage and tomatoes. She watched us eat with pleasure; the pastor poured us tots of *palinka* and glasses of his home-made wine.

'You are not strangers, and you are not guests,' said his wife, smiling: *nie Fremde nie Gaste*. 'You are our children.'

Raising our glasses, looking from the smiling pastor to his wife, we burst into tears.

Supper with Father Tibor was formal. He ate well. An old Székely woman cooked and kept house for him. Taciturn and devoted, she looked extraordinarily Chinese: tiny and crinkled, with yellow skin, a dark plait down her back and a shuffling gait. He held firm opinions on every subject. He was plump; his soutane resembled the costume of a country gentleman at home, perhaps unwigged, and he plied us generously with *palinka* and yellow Alba Iulia wine.

Szent-György was a kind of banishment after a term in a difficult church in Kolozsvar. His career there had been overshadowed by the spectaculars of Monsignor Zsiriac; but Tibor missed the intellectual life. He had taken the news of his transfer to the provinces with stoic resignation; hoping, perhaps, that his suffering would be rewarded.

He believed in the early origin of the Székely. Székely meant seat: there had been seven 'seats' in the Székelyföld, each a seat of authority, a chieftain's throne, and each corresponding with a tribe. The Csik, of Csikszereda, were one tribe. Tibor believed that the seven tribes had settled together in the region very early on.

He shared the claustrophobia of many Hungarians in Transylvania, who felt they were living in a country dominated by people of lower cultural and intellectual standards. He spoke of 'Balkanism', as a hopeless, suffocating blend of deference and corruption: to explain the behaviour and attitudes of the Romanians he looked for clues in the philosophy and logic system of ancient China. The mono-culturalism of Romania, the fusion of spiritual and temporal loyalty expressed in the Byzantine concept of Caesaropapism, was an echo of Eastern society: he read Lao Tse.

'Lao Tse explains to me the Romanian concept of law. Every law, he says, has a door. Many laws mean many doors. Nothing is absolute, no-one expects rigidity or firmness. So everyone is looking over his shoulder at the next man, looking to his own advantage. There is no ground for trust. Everyone pushes to find the doors he knows exist. It is a kind of moral anarchy.'

It was this which had allowed the Romanians to suffer a Ceauşescu for so long; it was in allegiance to Western traditions – the tradition that justice was natural and ubiquitous – that a handful of Hungarians had finally defied his power, and brought him down.

Cronyism, corruption and deference were hallmarks of the

Orthodox Church, whose clergy were prepared to work hand-in-glove with the Securitate. These attitudes were bound up with the history of Orthodoxy itself: but they were deeply embedded in the Romanian nature. The Romanian, Roman Catholic bishop of Bucharest, observed Tibor, had also congratulated Ceauşescu on his suppression of vandalism in Temesvar, just like Theocritus.

Szent-György had perked up, though, since the arrival of the Sisters of Mercy. The Sisters of Mercy, for whom he regularly performed Mass and confession, and who regularly sought his advice, afforded him a considerable amount of dry amusement. 'They have taken a vow of poverty,' he remarked, 'but they never expected to find the shops so empty.' It was the sisters themselves who amused him: in matters of religion he was quite sincere. The sisters, whose leader was Mother Theresa in Calcutta, had arrived barely two months before, to establish a mission for the gypsies.

On the second day we took a bus out to the railway station, where the mission house was established: a bungalow, standing among railway sheds and crumbling tenements. Two dazzling purple and white saris hung on the line. The lawn was clipped and neat, the wooden verandah freshly painted up. The sisters had thrown the frenzied nomadism of life outside into stark relief. The tooting, crashing, puffing, shouting atmosphere of the railway yards, the constant turmoil, movement, collision and racing about, all the smuts and sweat and muck and disorder, came to a full stop at their tidy picket fence.

In charge of three other sisters was a Calcuttan, very fat and jolly. There was a slim, pale Irish girl and a tall Mauritian, who was stately and serious and wore big spectacles, and a dark young nun from Kerala.

We asked them how they were getting on.

'Oh-ho!' chuckled the mother superior. 'Such a difficult language to be learning! I am afraid we are very foolish!'

They were studying Hungarian at breakneck speed, every morning. They rose at five; prayed; cleaned the mission; ate breakfast, and had communion from Father Tibor. He conducted the service in English, but they recite the Lord's Prayer in Hungarian, and attended regular services in the church as well. At eight o'clock their teacher arrived, and until twelve they bent their tongues round the bristling language. After lunch they studied on their own. There were more prayers, some reading, and a great deal of cleaning up before bed. They were not due to begin pastoral work until they had made proper advances in the language; until then they were to lead exemplary lives, and try to speak to anyone who visited.

The mission house was practically bare inside; their chapel had wall-to-wall carpet and a small crucifix. The keynote was this awesome cleanliness.

'We are told most of the gypsies are Catholics. But they feel awkward in the church. This is why we are making our chapel for them here.'

But there was this insuperable language.

'Do you know what you can do?' said the mother superior. 'Your footsteps can be a prayer: each time you are taking a step you must think about the three little sisters in Szent-György, trying so hard to speak this language, and offer up your steps to God for our sake.'

Later that afternoon we visited the Székely museum. Traditional cottages had been reconstructed in the grounds: unfortunately they were shut up and the tradition is to have small windows. By squinting we glimpsed pale-blue tiled stoves, and painted furniture: flowery dressers and blanket chests; the beds were high sided and piled a yard deep in embroidered quilts and bed linen, and the chairs were very low, their seats scarcely a foot above the ground, with tall thin solid backs. In the museum itself the only other visitors, a couple like ourselves, shrugged the curator onto us with a half-smile of apology and vanished down a corridor. It was a shrewd move: the curator followed us from room to room, breathing fumes and babbling incessantly. In a room devoted to coloured Easter eggs he fell into a picnic basket, set up with two hollow tubes of bread (wrapped in plastic) and two bottles of wine (empty). We chose the moment to escape. As we fled down the steps he weaved after us, hollering 'Linneker' at the top of his voice.

Tibor thought we had been lucky to get into the museum at all,

since the curator was a notorious misanthrope who kept visitors
at bay by releasing a pack of ferocious dogs to roam the grounds
while he lay in a Székely bed, getting drunk.

Tibor had assigned us rooms in an empty part of the church
complex, opposite a school which the church had erected in a
single night to evade a prohibition. The authorities had got wind
of the ruse and ordered it to be pulled down, and while the
workers agonised between their fear of the authorities and their
religious scruples, the revolution had intervened. Our bedroom
was being used as a store house for Western aid, very little of
which seemed to be leaving the premises. We asked Tibor about
this.

'What should we do? I have nearly 6000 parishioners and in
that room 300 bars of soap,' he explained.

Transylvania, so frequently ravaged in the past, has suffered little
from war in the last two centuries, compared to the rest of Eastern
Europe. As the Turkish menace receded, and the Danube was
opened, the country stood more or less free of external threat,
and gained its reputation as a backwater, a half-forgotten corner
of Europe in which it was possible to imagine bat-like counts
scrambling down ruined castle walls. Beached by the shifting
course of trade and war, under the dull hand of the Habsburgs,
little disturbed its chequerboard diversity.

The village of Hermann lay off the main road – a bleak upland
road lined with trees that led south into the Burzenland. We
wanted to see the church, which we had been told was typically
Saxon.

It had rained all morning. The village was quiet, unusually
strung out. Ahead rose the great walls of the church and a large
tower or gatehouse with small windows and a sharply sloping
roof. Behind the gate, like Malbork, an arcaded covered bridge
crossed the moat on arched piers to the church wall. The gatehouse
and walls were covered in sandy render, and the whole place
looked exactly as it might have done to any traveller in the last
400 years.

The gate was opened by a child: a flaxen-haired, snub-nosed
little Saxon who invited us inside in perfect *Hochdeutsch*. A flight

of steps rose on the left, and we followed our small guide upstairs through the body of the tower. At the top a heavy oak door stood ajar, revealing a room that itself had barely changed in centuries. On the broad floorboards stood a sturdy trestle, and a number of plain wooden chests were placed against the smoke-dimmed walls. A little daylight came through a narrow casement window and illuminated a high-backed chair on which a woman sat and sewed.

She looked up, without evident interest. We introduced ourselves and asked if we might see the *Pfarrer*, and look over the church.

She grunted, bit the end of her thread, and stood up. She was extremely tall, broad, wearing a dark bodice and full black skirt to her calves.

'*Gibt's noch hier kein Pfarrer*,' she said: there's no pastor here any more. She paused, as though deciding. '*Aber, kommen Sie bitte.*'

She took a headscarf from a peg behind the door and tied it under her chin. We followed her downstairs and across the bridge, where she pulled a giant iron key from her pocket to unlock the inner gate. The walls were massively thick. They contained a large number of chambers, reached through low doorways.

'The people used to store food in there for times of trouble. If Tartars came, or Romanians, there was food for the whole village, and safety. It was a duty, "*eine Pflege*", for each family to give something: *Speck, Korn*, cheese.'

We had read about the Saxon storehouses. The bacon or grain that went in never came out: it was added to, year after year, a protective tithe that no-one ever thought to question. Nineteenth-century travellers smirked at the sight of hundred-year-old hams hanging from the rafters, and at the Saxon's bull-headed observance of traditions that had long since outlived their purpose. The storehouses were stocked up all through the Second World War.

'Is there anything in them now?'

'Rats, probably,' she snorted.

It was economics that had finished off the Saxon nation of Transylvania, in her eyes.

'We Saxons are hard workers,' she said. 'Everyone understands that you work hard to make money. Then you live well.' She led us into the church. 'Only the Romanians don't understand that. They think they can have money without work. Iliescu promises them that, too. So we all stay poor.

'Do you know what they make in Kronstadt (that is Brasov)? Tractors. Alright. They sold a lot of them abroad, for valuta. The workers were congratulated. But do you know what happened to these tractors? My husband was in Constanza, on the Black Sea. There was a Japanese ship loading tractors from Kronstadt. It picked them up like this.'

She made a crane of her arm and crushed her fingers into a fist.

'They wanted only the metal. I tell you, the Romanians will never understand economics. And freedom? They want it, but they don't understand it, either. They think they have freedom, but they do not realise that they must work also.'

We poked about the church. The backs of the pews were cantilevered, to face one way for divine service, the other for community meetings.

'How many families are left in the village?'

'About five. This used to be a very good community. Can you believe that this church was full every Sunday?' It was a big church with room for several hundred people. 'They came from this village and some farms around. And who do you think was the first to go to Germany? The pastor! What an example! To my mind a pastor should remain with his people until the end. He should have been the last but no, he was first.'

She folded her arms, exasperated.

'We're trying to stay as long as we can. This is our home. My family has lived in the village for hundreds of years. But it gets more difficult, with everyone going off. Now I am worried about the children. The nearest German school is in Kronstadt. It's too far. Nobody's money has any weight. You can't sell anything, because they can't pay. You can't buy anything, because you can't pay. It's ridiculous, this Romanian economy.'

I suggested that the West Germans were responsible for the exodus as much as the Romanians. Any German could claim pensions and benefits, but only if they settled in Germany. If they remained in their ancestral homeland they got nothing. The German government should be glad for them to stay where they were, rather than clogging up the refugee camps; and they could even pay out smaller pensions than they would in Germany, provided they paid in German marks. It would save them trouble and money and preserve a unique community. Instead they did nothing.

'Well, there have been schemes,' explained the woman. 'But they get worked out between governments. The German government gives the Romanian government money for the German community. But the things they do are big, unnecessary works, real Romanian economy. They build a factory or something in the village. It makes Kronstadt tractors, or something like this. You are right: they should give the money directly, to each family. Then the people would have something to start a business of their own.'

She held up her hands in a gesture of helpless resignation. '*Es ist doch zu spät, glaub' ich*,' she said: I think it's too late.

Across from the gatehouse stood the village inn. Men were sitting with their beers on trestle tables on the grass, and when they saw us they asked us to join them. We had a beer. They asked if we were married and when we said no they chuckled lewdly, and one of them declared Kate to be my '*Nachtsfreundin*', or night-time friend, which they thought was very funny. We described our route for them, but found that they had only a hazy notion of the countries we'd visited. They were better informed about the country ahead, and Istanbul, they declared, was a fine and prosperous place.

Something was about to happen in Kronstadt. It was not stated openly, but everyone held their own opinion and prepared accordingly. The authorities tarted up the town, repaved the market place and rebuilt the shop fronts. Plate glass and gold plate were flung about, travertine and pot plants. The shops hung out ironwork signs – three balls, a bear with cubs, pseudo-medieval motifs – but they were as empty as ever. When they paved the square they had not bothered to dig down first, so that the level was raised by a foot, rising around the old town hall in the centre of the square like a menacing tide.

In the citadel overlooking the town the battlements sheltered
bars and discos and a crowd of young Romanians in jeans and
Puffa jackets. The atmosphere was heavy and aggressive. It was
impossible to buy beer, but the Romanians talked loudly and
laughed without moving their heads, and flicked their hair back
like well-heeled youngsters anywhere; and we thought sourly of
the many doors to many laws, for they had beer bottles sitting in
front of them.

The Lutheran minister was tall and smooth and fair and had no
time for us. He told us curtly that we might sleep in the Kapitelzimmer after evening prayers, this night only. Afterwards we
would have to find somewhere else.

We removed ourselves in the morning, after the minister had
ushered in two workmen who commenced the installation of what
must have been a satellite TV. Our brief presumption on Saxon
hospitality had been a damp squib. Instead a sexton outside the
Black Church told us about the great library that had once existed
in the town, an how the Romanians had come in 1945 and
destroyed it.

'Very old books, hundreds of years old,' he said, shaking his
head. 'Out of the window. They made bonfires. In those books
was a real European culture. They tore them up and used them
in the toilet. Barbarians.'

We found our way to the Hungarian Calvinist church. The
minister was out but his wife suggested we leave our packs and
have a look round the town until he got back.

Towards evening a crowd gathered in the square around a display of child dancers. There were perhaps forty of them, between
eight and fourteen, performing in little leotards, in shorts and T-
shirts, simple choreographed routines: forming a cross, fanning
into a circle, weaving between one another in figures of eight,
cartwheeling. They were mostly French, from an international
convent school in Switzerland.

The object of the dance was to attract the people: it was a great
success. When the dancing was over, a young man began to address
the crowd over a microphone with the help of a Romanian
interpreter.

'The churches tell us many lies,' he began. 'Yes, they argue. Their priests say, "We will tell you about God", but they hide the face of God. Do you need them? I tell you, no. You need Christ. Who will look after us? Christ. When we are alone, afraid, unhappy, Christ comes to us. For he loves us. We are his children.'

His smile never wavered. It was a healthy white-teethed good-time smile. His voice was deep and reverberative. It melted, and oozed across the square.

'How can we know that Jesus Christ our Lord loves us? Because it is written in that marvellous book by ordinary men and women, like you and me, who actually saw the Saviour. They heard the good news he brought. Such news! If you had been there you would have wanted to tell it to your friends and neighbours. Well, they were there, and they wanted to tell us all about it.'

He had crossed the square and climbed on to a platform. The children surrounded him, carrying parcels.

'We want to share that good news with you!' He leaned towards the crowd, throwing his arms forward. 'We want you to read it for yourself, just as it was written nearly two thousand years ago by a man who was there. John. A plain man with a plain name.' He bent down and straightened up to hold something over his head.

'This book is for you!' he cried, waving it ecstatically over his head. Then his voice dropped with intimacy. 'Read it.' The crowd began to wedge in closer around him. 'Think about it.' His voice was so full of bass sincerity that the speakers woofed. 'Show it to your friends and family.'

There were the beginnings of a scrum. People scuffled from the crowd clutching a slim blue book; by-standers began to edge inwards. They saw people running from the other side of the square and began to run, too. The good news of something for nothing was racing round the town. Those who had their copy sauntered away, flicking through it; those without barged in, trying to leapfrog the crowds in front.

'Please, my friends, you can all get to read this wonderful story.' He had vanished in a scrum of heads; only his voice echoed through the square. 'If you have one, show it to your friends.

Pass it around. Engrave these words on your heart, and pass it on.'

The books ran out. The crowd milled about. A few latecomers raced to the scene and began to ask each other what had happened. Anyone holding a copy of the gospel was surrounded by the empty handed. They saw what it was, joked and turned away.

Dusk was falling as the children and the minister climbed aboard a coach waiting in a side street. The coach was stuffed with their luggage. They had sleepy faces, dozing over their duffel bags.

'Pas si mal, ce soir,' explained a little girl. 'Il y a des endroits ou nous sommes bouleversés. On m'attaquait vraiment au sud. Nous étions dans un théâtre, et la foule a envahi pour déchirer les livres.'

We ended up eating in the restaurant of a new hotel just beyond the city walls. It was incredibly pretentious, serving the usual *antracot* and boiled potatoes on a stack of matching plates, with linen napkins and silver-plated cutlery. There was a no-smoking rule, and when I slipped out for a cigarette I found myself squatting with all the waiters in the lobby, puffing on Carpati.

The hotel had an information desk. We explained that we were walking, and asked the woman what she could tell us about the plains.

The woman stared.

'You want information? This is Babylon, mister,' she said. 'This country is not ready for tourists. We start from zero.

'I think it would be easier for you to go to Biafra. Look, the man in the street has no money, and his mentality is like this.' She made a tunnel with her hands and lurched upwards. 'What you want for tourism? Mister, you had better take a train to Bucharest.'

A quiet group of Dutch Christians had arrived with Hungarian Bibles in their camper van. On Sunday we met them at the Calvinist minister's church, a basement prayer-room in a new part of town. The minister explained that for their benefit he would speak in German: the Hungarian congregation smiled their approval. They all knew German, of course. The sermon was too elevated for me to understand very much. Afterwards the Dutch contributed a hymn, sung in English to a guitar. It was a very professional performance, sung in the round, though the words were stunningly simple.

'Jesus, Prince of Peace!
Hallelujah!'

They were all tall without seeming overbearing, plump without being fat; their skin was firm and glowing. The girls' hair fascinated me, it was so thick; they tied it up in big bows. They had come the previous year, and the border guards had asked if they had any Bibles. They said no: but one belonging to the group leader was discovered and the guards had ripped the van apart. This year the same guard posed with them for a photograph.

In Kronstadt everybody was waiting. Expectancy may be a condition of the town. The founders, the Teutonic Knights, waited twenty-six years to hear that they weren't welcome and went north to conquer Prussia instead. The Black Church was apparently not well built; nobody thought it worth the expense. Wit Stosz the Younger, whose father worked in Cracow, didn't finish his work in time and was fined. The first experiment at printing in Romanian was made here.

Now everyone was waiting to see how things fell out. The Saxon villagers watched to see if the Saxons of Kronstadt left. Others had theories and prepared to meet events. The authorities tarted up the town. The evangelists sensed the knife-edge that ran through Brasov and turned up to tip the population towards a revelation of God. The Lutheran minister had something up his sleeve, making us sleep on a table in the Kapitelzimmer and avoiding our questions, and we guessed that he was preparing to fly. The whole town was involved in a game of brinkmanship: as perhaps it always has been on the brink.

After Brasov, the Carpathians, and then everything tilted towards the Bosporus. The Romanians had their religion from there, their first script; their tax demands for centuries; they were quarantined, literally, with the inhabitants of the Golden Horn. They shared the same traditions of statecraft. The Carpathians were a wall: beyond that wall, I wasn't sure that Eastern Europe meant much, except that geographers had triumphed over sociologists, historians and politicians. If not Western Asia, better to say the Balkans. I remembered the librarian we met on the *Puszta*: 'When you go there,' he'd said, 'say that Hungary is not the Balkans.'

On our way back from church we visited the market. I needed batteries, camera film and a new watch to replace the one that had shattered on the road to Csikszereda. A few gypsies sat cross-legged on the pavement, wearing their black hats and working jewellery. Each had a tiny anvil and hammer, and a spindle in front of him looped with thin silver rings. '*Collega!*' they called, beckoning us.

Each man had a bundle of silver coins, from which they clipped the silver to beat into a ring. Many of the coins were antique. There were forints from Horthy's regency, and old Habsburg schillings; they had Yugoslavian dinars with the head of King Peter, and Prussian marks. We sifted the hoard in astonishment, wondering if it could be read as a map of gypsy wanderings. The gypsies, as soon as they saw what interested us, gathered round in competition, undoing their bundles and spreading them on the ground. One of them had a huge silver coin with the head of Maria Theresa (Imp. Aust. et Reg. Hung) and the date 1784. We viewed this as a souvenir of the Habsburg country we'd been walking through all the way from Cracow. The seller asked thirty dollars, but he took eighteen. We thought we had a bargain and everyone grinned their satisfaction.

Much later, when we got the coin home to England, a knowledgeable friend sniggered and said that 1784 Maria Theresas were still issued by the Austrian mint. They were worth, he thought, about £10 for their silver content.

We sat with the minister and his father-in-law, an old communist who worked as an adviser on labour relations to a factory in the town and viewed the changes in Eastern Europe with guarded concern. The minister had a high-boned, hollow face, the face of an ascetic saddened by the world's ways, but he drank *palinka* cheerfully enough.

'Forty-four per cent!' he declared. 'Home-made.'

We asked them about the gypsies, though it was clearly not something they considered very important. The minister's views were surprising. There existed, he agreed, two kinds of gypsy. It was the first time anyone had admitted the fact to us.

'They are hot or cold, black or white, *flessig oder faul*,' he explained. 'There were two routes for them into Europe, after they had left Constantinople. One – the major route – through the Balkans and up the Danube, into Hungary. The other along the Black Sea, to the Dnieper, and into Russia. The Russian gypsies were in Scandinavia in the seventeenth or eighteenth century.

'But I think things for them were hard in these countries. Perhaps the Scandinavian wives complained,' he added, laughing.

'So they returned to the south. Two races.' He knocked back his glass of *palinka*. 'Some of the gypsies work gold. They are organised, with three princes – *vovoides*, with *boulibashas* under them. One of these *voivoides* lives outside Cluj and he has a Mercedes bigger than the Queen of England's. They say he is so rich that he bought protection for his people under Ceauşescu by delivering a whole kilo of gold to the police every week. I don't know if that's true. But I did hear that he once made a bid for a chalice – he has a collection of rare old silver and gold – of 100,000 lei, in cash, and when he had got the chalice he admitted that he would have paid 500,000, if necessary.

'You know, many gypsies wore gold coins as jewellery. Most of these things were taken by the state, but now they must return them.'

That, I reflected, sounded too good to be true.

Koestler suggested that the Jews of Eastern Europe, the Ashkenazi, are the scattered Kazhars of the tenth and eleventh century. He based his thesis on the known conversion of the Khazar King to Judaism, and to the apparent scarcity of Jews in medieval Germany to support the notion that the Jews migrated towards the east.

In pressing his thesis he tends to ignore the apparent diversity of Khazaria. If the King adopted Judaism, as a matter of state policy and high diplomacy, his 'people' were not necessarily all Jews. Gypsiologists maintain that the early gypsies, migrating from India in the fifth century, divided on the further shores of the Black Sea, some coming towards Constantinople, some turning north into the Caucasus – into Khazaria. A Muslim traveller states that the Khazars themselves were not all alike, and he divides them into black and white, just as we divided the gypsies.

Beyond the Carpathians

Four miles below Brasov the road forked and flickered towards the Romanian heartlands like a serpent's tongue. The main road ran up to a ski resort that in Summer, without a modest covering of snow, sounded so horrendous that we took the lesser road to Bran, where the pass was also slightly lower.

Bran's castle, peddled to the skiers as Dracula's stronghold, was of course a sham – Dracula may have passed through, but it never belonged to him; it was merely a ruined keep that Queen Marie had rebuilt and enlarged as her Petit Trianon in the 1920s. (It was at Trianon that Queen Marie had made her name. Romania needs a face, she had said, and I have come to show mine. Naturally, being partisan, I begrudged Queen Marie her diplomatic triumph – doubling her realm at a go – but Bran was charming.)

We slipped into the castle under scaffolding poles and dust sheets. Except for the occasional visit from the Ceauşescus, who made the castle one of their private hideaways, the place had been neglected. Dodging workmen who might order us off, we skeltered through little alcoved rooms, and turret staircases, and spindly winding corridors; we peered through lattice casements, and ducked in doorways, and imagined Marie's house parties without any difficulty at all. The place was made for cosy champagne dinners, corridor creeping, mustachioed equerries at the piano, and sardines. The only Dracula in the place would have worn wobbly fangs of sugared almonds, and won at charades.

Bran reunited us with the Carpathians, which we'd left behind in Slovakia on the day Spring revolved into Summer like an automatic. We recognised the same rounded hillocks of beech, and when we stopped in front of the small hotel below the castle, the evening air was cool again. The hotel was full, so we slept at private rooms, practising Romanian on our patient host. The old man ran his finger down his map and made a grimace when it reached Oltenia, saying 'bad, bad,' with surprising fervency. Peter took his packed lunch onto the plains, but Peter was Hungarian; this old man suggested Romanian mountaineers, too, held plainsmen in contempt.

The forests dwindled away, leaving the Summer pastures exposed, a few crippled trees, the occasional patch of firs in a hollow, while the road wound slowly to the lip of the Transylvanian bowl, to drop so abruptly our ears would pop. The grass was thin as though the last snows had only just melted, and between the scattered villages roamed shepherds, with their dogs and flocks, placed for the night in circular sheepfolds of stacked thorn. We walked shy of the shepherds, sharing the same great solitude; when we met them on the road they seemed (even without their dogs) frightening and wild, in leather breeches, shaggy cloaks and strange conical hats. I suppose they were romantic figures, but their romance rather escaped us at the time; to us they looked just as they had meant to look in the dim past when they chose a costume that made them seem taller, wider, bigger and more ferocious than ordinary men.

But the shepherds did suggest a sort of quiet dignity as well: there is something dignified in the sight of a human being alone. Each lonely action seems in a way divine: why that impulse to stoop, or to shepherd? The single man draws his energy from a mysterious source, and this seems to an onlooker to be the mark of humanity, just as crowd behaviour seems touched by bestiality. Crowds are notoriously like the pack, picking up the scent; and like the herd, each borrowing his impulse from his neighbour. As soon as someone merges with a crowd he gains brute strength at the expense of his own dignity.

By now, Romanians formed the crowd in my mind. In Transylvania we'd met Hungarians singly, and Hungarians were not the mob. All the crowds had been Romanian, always brutish, from the leering beer-garden swillers in Oradea, through the peasant farmers who had rioted in Tirgu Mures, to the shipped-in proletariat of Sighisoara. My feelings towards Romanians were suspicious and harsh, partly because I tended to see them en masse.

But this was how many viewed themselves. In Cluj we had watched the *golan* – intelligent, articulate, hopeful people, with liberal attitudes and impeccable aspirations – founder upon the gang mentality of ordinary Romanians.

The *golans* stood against a system that worked the Romanians as a crowd; and worked them successfully, which is the point. When he sent the miners into Bucharest, or the rioters into Tirgu Mures, Iliescu had given proof that he could and would rule by the mob. The atmosphere of intimidation and victimisation, of stirring up resentments and establishing false idols, was the same atmosphere that prevailed all over Eastern Europe after the First World War, when countries were meeting democracy for the first time; but we hadn't encountered it upon democracy's second coming in Poland or Slovakia or Hungary. It was only Romania that still lagged behind.

More than any other nation, Romanians had never been treated as anything but the mob, and they hadn't advanced as a result. In other centuries they had been serfs; the twentieth century was hardly the best time to catch up. Romania came to independence under a powerful aristocracy; the first stirrings of democracy or 'people power' bent towards fascism in the 1930s; fascism defeated was replaced by authoritarian communism, which had finally evolved into the most repressive totalitarian autocracy in Europe. It had evolved because the Romanian nation behaved like a panic-stricken crowd; everyone had been too busy looking over his shoulder; no-one had stopped or stood forward. The average Romanian had no opportunity to learn civic virtue, because obedience and not responsibility was all he was ever asked for. Either he knuckled under, or – like John or Sanda with their dreams of the mountains – he ran away.

The old man's grimace was a reminder that we fear and dislike most what we don't really know; but it is one thing to accept the reminder, and quite another to exorcise the fear and dislike. For three days over the Carpathians I felt unmitigated dread. On the summit we stayed in a *cabana* weathering the stares of the truckers in the restaurant; they had stared at us earlier on the road, leaning from their cabs and twisting for a better look as they ground uphill in clouds of burnt-out gearbox smoke. We went to bed

early, pushed a table weighted with our packs against the flimsy
door, and listened through the night to the sound of lorries, to
footsteps, and the wail of weird, Oriental music that sounded
sometimes like an incitement, and sometimes like a keening dirge.

We struck the gorge around noon, terrified by the possibility that
we had chosen a ravine leading miles in the wrong direction, or
reaching an abrupt end at a cliff. The stream had undercut the
rock, and we scrambled over banks of scree, following the twists
in the gorge until we imagined shepherds lurking round every
corner, and at dusk, battling with panic, we mistook the welcome
glint of a holiday *cabana* for a sinister cabal of cut-throat mountaineers, and approached rather as though we were crossing scree
again, on our hands and feet.

Further down the gorge next morning Kate left me to go into
a cave with a small boy who guided me into the darkest recess
and there asked, with tiny menace, for chewing gum. From what
he intelligently explained, the cave had been used constantly as a
hideaway by bandits and by rebels fighting the Turks or the
Habsburgs. (At times the volume of traffic in the cave must have
strained its claims to be a very secret lair.) I gave the boy 100 lei
and we trudged away.

A dog was chained to a post where the gorge made a final turn
and opened out. He had a shaggy, knotted coat and a thick fringe
that must have blinded him completely. The roar of the stream
where it bolted against the cliff almost drowned his bark; it was
surely enough to drown the sound of footsteps, and so the
wretched animal detected a threat by scent alone, and met it as
something invisible and soundless.

In Rucar we established ourselves in a small hotel on the main
road; the hotelier was beside himself with excitement at our visit
which held out the promise of an infinite number of black-market
transactions, if only he could come up with a few suggestions.
Every few minutes he came into our room, sat on the bed, and
proposed a wheeze he'd just thought of that would net him an
extra dollar, and at the word 'dollar' he would lower his voice
and glare around the room, patting his palms with a balled
handkerchief. For a dollar he promised us breakfast in bed;

although it was I who earned the dollar, running up and down the stairs the next morning to see that his promise was fulfilled.

Rucar was an overgrown village that lay in a bowl beneath the mountains. There were looms in the houses up the hillside, and a knife grinder toured the streets with his trolley. We'd run out of liquor, but the only bar in town was pure mayhem, and when we managed to wring a beer from the serving hatch the glass as usual was chipped and filthy, and the beer tasted of carbon dioxide and swam with little black grains.

Later that evening, though, we leaned over a fence to admire a prewar villa and were invited in for supper by a middle-aged couple who ran a restaurant in Brasov. The villa belonged to the woman's mother, who was frail and needed her children to come by several times a week to cook and clean. The restaurateurs had made her lunch, they had made her – and us – supper, and in a moment they were going back to Brasov for the evening sitting.

I found this notion indigestible. Not because it had taken us four days to achieve what they meant to do in an hour, which was obvious, but because they treated the mountains as though they were meaningless. For weeks I'd been raising barricades on them. Language, religion, political tradition, history and geography made, to my mind, a formidable barrier which I'd crouched behind like a bunkered revolutionary. Now here they were, simply popping to and fro.

That wasn't what we talked about. We talked about the tourist trade in clumsy German. Ceauşescu had a depressive effect akin to an airline disaster or a salmonella outbreak at the resort. Transylvania particularly had had beautiful old towns, grand scenery, hunting, fishing, skiing and handicrafts – I saw her eyes light up at the word – *Handwerken* – but Ceauşescu had dumped a slag heap or a tower block on everything.

In this version Transylvania wasn't at issue any more. From where this woman stood, Transylvania was simply the northern extension of the country and I'd got it wrong – Romania wasn't shaped by mountains but by rivers: the Danube, which made its southern border, and the Olt, which rose in Transylvania, flowed along the Carpathians and dropped into Oltenia to the Danube. Then I saw something new about John as well. He had simply never realised that feelings in the province ran so high. He had been surprised, if anything, to discover so many Hungarian speakers in his country, but he lent it no particular significance. John wasn't Transylvanian. He came from Oltenia, the region that produced all the '-escus' in the ruling mafia and whose people were the butt of jokes. He hadn't really noticed the bitterness, because it was in Transylvania itself, between rival Transylvanians, that it lay; where Vatra could boast of its strongest support; from where the mountains did represent some kind of barrier, either to be strengthened or battered down, depending on your loyalties.

For a moment, sitting in the gaudy garden room beneath the villa, like a converted garage, under an icon between chaises longues containing these calm and pragmatic business people, I saw the way clear to making a passionless exit from an argument that had filled me physically with an exhausting fist-clenching fury. Enough people around me in Romania would say that barriers did not exist, and that things you heard in Transylvania could be ignored. Ignorance could be feigned, and become a protective salve.

The moment passed. I was not detached, but had I been it still wouldn't have justified denial. Ignorance was the primitive horror, the food of evil. In the town where the orphanage we'd visited lay, evil was done to children while the townsmen played the card of ignorance. Iliescu played on ignorance to retain government. Ceaușescu had tried to inculate ignorance by destroying trust and information.

It wasn't late, but we were very tired. We thanked our hosts, and explained to the old lady, who sweetly asked us to stay, that we had made too many arrangements at the hotel. On the way back no dark clouds slid from the mountains. The sunset was rosy, and there wasn't the whisper of a wind. But I shrank from Romania as if it were a storm.

The landscape wanted to go to Romania as little as I did. It scrambled desperately up cliffs, catching on clumps of gorse and sliding on broken rock and dry earth; the trees whined and stooped and the road itself was cringing, doubled up. A stream bed cracked in the hot sun. There was one last ridge, where the road cut through a defile marked by a gigantic memorial to the Soviet and Romanian armies, and then fell listlessly upon a sloping plain down to the city of Cimpunglung, home of the Romanian jeep industry, where we spent the night in a hotel on the small tree-lined square.

The next day, descending gradually into the plain, we walked in the shade of trees from one village to the next. The buildings, as Peter had predicted, were astonishingly primitive: each house was dug into the earth, and low walls were built from cubes of shallow mud supporting vast thatched roofs. People emerged upwards from the low doorways, like burrowing animals, to watch us walking by, and I was reminded of Indian villages, where you might find the same muddy water hole, the same yellow sandy soil beaten to dust in the sun, the same lack of 'pukka' housing, housing of brick or stone. Each village had been dredged from the soil – and back to soil it could return in a moment. Buffalo stood patient at the roadside, or hauled a creaking cart slowly along the verge, lowering their massive horns. We had seen buffalo working in Translyvania, but there they were exceptional; here they had replaced the horse. People said that the gypsies had brought the buffalo from India, centuries before.

Children chased after us; adults stood with folded arms and watched us trudging by. In Rucar I'd played with the idea that Transylvania was part of Romania, after all; but the border we'd crossed was as sharp as a leap from Switzerland to Rajastan.

The city of Pitesti belonged to the impermanent landscape. It had been scratched up towards the end of the last century, and laid out in a grid like a military cantonment or a new town in the desert. We'd been told that there was a Hungarian church mission there, and went to find it, looking for friends; but either the address was wrong or passers-by didn't really know the names of the streets, which were identical and unsigned, and ran in wide, treeless avenues of villas to the edge of town. Eventually we grew tired of pounding the pavements, and returned to the apparent centre of town, the normalised heart, where a big hotel loomed over an empty pedestrian quarter without shops or streetlife.

The hotel was shockingly expensive, and the receptionist

commiserated. 'Television in the room,' she reminded us, as a palliative. We climbed to the third floor, room 304; the lock was already worn and loose and it took no effort to turn the key. The room was a cheap imitation of a million cheap hotel rooms around the world: purple carpet, formica headboard, one of those peculiar slatted stools for placing your suitcase on, and a television on a stand. There were dusty net curtains and a view on to unfinished buildings waving concrete rods at the sky like insects. It seemed ironic that here, in the poorest part of Europe, we had encountered our first 'international' hotel. Gloomily we switched on the television. Petru Roman, the Prime Minister, was being interviewed by an Italian reporter who was giving him an easy time in explaining that difficulties were bound to arise in any period of transition and readjustment. At nine o'clock we watched *Das Erbe Von Gulenbergs*, and thought how our friends in the north – Peter and Marika, Barna and Mihaly – would be glued to the set.

After Pitesti the villages dried up, or lay some distance off the road, down dusty tracks that made the only break in a landscape uniformly flat. The metalled road fused with the crops on the horizon, running through a prairie of sunflowers and cob corn; the shimmer of heat on the road in the distance was the only thing moving and it moved as we moved, keeping the same monotonous distance. Yet it was all we could look at: the still stalks of corn, and the slim stalks of the sunflowers, presented a ragged wall on either side of the road, too high to see over. Now and again a shape would stir on the horizon, flare in the sunlight, and gradually detach itself like an amoeba, growing larger with infinitesimal speed; you could hear the sound of the truck engine long before the truck itself grew distinct; then it would roar past in a swirling cloud of dust while we turned to the fields and covered our faces with our hats.

We smoked out of boredom, but the smoke was invisible in the sunshine and the cigarettes kept going out; it was so hot that the feeling of a flame near my fingers was unbearable. Eventually we stopped and drank some water while I ate one of the smoked sausages we'd bought in the mountains. We wondered how much longer we could go on.

The answer came quite soon. Before noon I felt strange, as if I were made of a grainy paste. I blamed first the monotony, then the sunflowers. There were too many of them. The thought of millions and millions of sunflowers quietly growing beside me was making me feel sick. I thought I could smell them, and the saliva ran in my mouth. I plodded on, but I felt very weak, and my legs shook; I had two words, 'succulent seedlings', turning and turning in my head, which I must have spoken aloud, because Kate looked at me sharply and asked if I was alright.

In response I slid my pack to the ground and reeled backwards into the sunflowers, tearing at my trousers. At the third or fourth cramp I was brightly aware of insects pattering up the sunflower stalks close to my nose; through the stalks I could see bits of Kate, standing in the road. My bowels were blowing hot but my skin felt icy and my teeth were chattering while nausea volleyed over me in bouts.

Kate helped me back onto the road. I badly needed to sit down, and to turn out the sun.

'It must have been that sausage,' she murmured sympathetically. I know it was the sausage, because when she said the word I turned to the much-abused sunflowers and was sick.

'Can we go away?' I asked feebly.

There was the sound of a truck coming up the road from Pitesti. I stood up, as steadily as I could, and we waved. The truck slowed, seemed to accelerate, and then came to a stop. Kate pulled open the passenger door but I poked my head over her shoulder.

'Giorghiu?' I croaked.

The driver remained motionless for a long moment and then suddenly leant forward, his face straining as if he hadn't understood.

'Giorghiu?' he bellowed.

'South?' asked Kate, by way of compromise.

But the man was going to Giorghiu. He shouted the name again, and nodded, and helped us toss our packs into the back of the truck. Then we climbed aboard, settled ourselves on the scorching seats, and started off.

I dozed fitfully, knocking my head carelessly against Kate's shoulder. The driver pointed at me, and made a sleeping motion with his hands against his cheek, releasing the wheel. Kate nodded. The truck drove on.

We lost perhaps three days in as many hours. The landscape didn't seem to vary: the same unrumpled expanse of yellow corn and heliotropes, mile after mile. Once or twice we slowed to pass through towns where we would perhaps have slept: industrial jungles worse than anything we had seen, where all the buildings were black with soot, though all of them were new. On their outskirts lay the aftermath of battles: torn earth, black glistening pools, mounds of leaking rusty drums; over which hulked factories that seemed to have been eviscerated in the struggle, leaving nothing but smoking entrails, a circuit of bandaged pipework, funnels and tubes. I recalled Middlesborough, or Częstochowa, drily enough. This was pure barbarism, bloody and benighted; the groping tendrils of some hideous industrial insect. I closed my eyes, and when I opened them again the monsters had disappeared, and we were bumping down a potted road across a plain of reddish earth, sown with root crops on an enormous scale.

I stopped the driver twice, so that I could climb out and find a bush. But I felt better. Probably I'd thrown out the poison; but perhaps, as I thought then, the poison wasn't found in smoked pork, after all. Romania, Crippen-like, had been administering it from the moment we crossed its border, varying the dose with spidery intelligence. In Oradea, where the first black depression had settled on me, the dose had been incautiously large, and so it was reduced; but every day it was building up, lodging in my system. If I felt better now it was because we were on our way to Giorghiu; to the Danube; to Bulgaria. We were getting out of Romania, and capping the blue bottle once and for all.

The driver set us down at a crossroads in Giorghiu. Kate had talked to him on the way, and he didn't want to be paid. But we thrust our lei into the pocket on his dashboard, and shook hands, and I was grinning like a monkey when we waved goodbye.

Bulgaria

The queue leading onto the Friendship Bridge began more than a mile inside Giorghiu. Giorghiu was concrete and inert, with wide cracked pavements, patches of hard burnt grass and stubby blocks without curtains, but the queue was a lively township, an immobile caravanserai of traders and truckers, holidaymakers, shoppers and a baffled angry Pakistani without an exit visa.

It took us half an hour to reach the Romanian customs post, but the queue hadn't budged. The bumpers of overloaded Dacias sunk onto the tarmac. The pavement had become a fragrant galley where people cooked up on primus stoves. Cars sprouted make-shift awnings; chairs appeared; doors and boots and bonnets were left open to circulate the air and radios played competitively down the street. The improvised air of patience and settlement was typically Eastern, and the further up the queue you got the more everyone and everything spilled onto the road. The sole exception was a black Golf with German plates and tinted windows, whose owners sat invisibly inside, primly disconnected from the rabble around them.

The Romanian customs officer had drunk himself into an oper-atic mood. Cans of beer stood in the shade beneath his desk, and his small son appeared to be helping him in some capacity. The officer held the Pakistani's passport between finger and thumb and waved it from side to side.

'This goddamn country,' said the Pakistani, reaching for the passport.

'Ah ah ah,' cautioned the customs man, pulling his hand away and holding the passport over his head. He blinked several times, slowly.

'Visa, no.' He swayed visibly and the Pakistani made a sudden furious jump and grabbed the passport.

'This, this, here, this, look!' He spluttered, riffling the pages. 'Bulgarian visa! Bulgaria, OK! European country, OK!' he practically biffed the man's nose with the splayed pages.

'No.' The customs officer swelled to his full height and avoided the passport with his eyes.

'Aaaaagh!' The Pakistani screamed in disgust. Then he clapped the document onto his open bag, grabbed the zip and pulled it shut. 'Goodbye,' he snapped, and walked away towards Bulgaria, unchallenged. The customs officer turned to us with a charming smile, caressed our passports, and waved us on.

The Danube winked and showed us its broad brown belly. Of course we'd met before, on the sly in Budapest. I dropped a coin from the rail and we watched it spin until we felt giddy and it disappeared.

The river here was almost a mile wide, and the Friendship Bridge was three miles long. It took us ages to cross because the lorry drivers were so curious: I suppose it was rare for foreigners to cross the bridge on foot. They were almost all Hungarian or Turks: old friends, or promising acquaintances, who one by one invited us to lunch. Under every trailer hung a metal box I'd always believed to be a tank of some sort; in fact it was a kitchen and larder, packed with delicacies, pots and little stoves. Potted meats, fruit, raw vegetables and beers were arranged neatly on the shelves, for no-one thought highly of Romanian food. Bulgarian food, they said, was not so bad, but Istanbul! The Turks grinned and kissed their fingers, and all but promised us paradise on earth.

At the Bulgarian border we changed money and received *cartes statistiques* and currency exchange forms and directions to a hotel.

The day was turning into evening; workers and shoppers trudged homeward in the sun. The murmur of an unfamiliar language floated soothingly on the light breeze that cooled the nape of my well-scrubbed neck. The wine arrived chilled, with water beading on the glass, and the label read Bulgarian Country Wine, just as it did at home.

The last commuters slipping from the street now mingled with the evening promenade. The promenaders came fresh and pressed in suits, pleated skirts, ironed jeans and gleaming T-shirts; their hair shone as though it have never been washed. At seven o'clock, Ruse was dressed to the nines, a solid, civilised affair that hard-pressed, weary, gimcrack Romania couldn't have begun to emulate. Promenades were made in Hungary; in Romania they had vanished like the yellow brick road in Tirgu Mures. In Romania people loitered at street corners like toughs, throwing suspicious glances, avoiding your eye. (Kate waggled her index and little finger at them to ward off the evil eye.)

A man leaned his bicycle against a pillar and asked us something in Bulgarian. We apologised. He said he spoke a little English: would we mind his bike for a moment?

On his return he thanked us gravely and seemed to hesitate. Naturally we asked him to join us. He said, 'Thank you,' and we thought we bought him a beer; in fact he arranged to pay for our wine.

His name was Christoph. He was a sailor. He had short grizzled grey hair and wrinkles around his blue eyes.

Christoph's life was a sequence of voyages, punctuated by time ashore: Ruse was a port, the Danube was a highway and the sea wasn't really far away. He'd been to Falmouth, fished in the Alantic, and worked the river from Budapest to Odessa. Only Hungarian eluded him; otherwise he could speak every Danubian language – German, Russian, Romanian and Serbo-Croat – as well as English and Turkish.

He asked us home for lunch next day.

The next day, under wall-sized photographs of forests in Christoph's sitting room, we pored over albums of postcards from every Mediterranean port I had heard of, and ports on the Black Sea; near the front there was Falmouth looking sunny and Mediterranean, too. Christoph's daughter, Albena, spoke English, and was married to a sailor who commanded a Danube patrol boat. While he was away she stayed at home and ate – the first fat person we had seen in months.

Her mother had made us lunch, and it was a feast – peppers,

yoghurt, meat balls, pitta bread – an elixir for palates grown old on mealy Romanian *mamaliga*, smoked fat and gherkins, rye bread, steamed cabbage and frazzled leathery schnitzels.

Albena said between mouthfuls that anyone with brains felt Bulgaria was a dead-end. As soon as you received your diploma you worked out how to get abroad; only ignorance, sloth or insuperable ties of kinship kept anyone in the country at all.

'Do you know that an official gets 2.7 kilos of meat a month, and we only get two? It is shocking.'

Albena looked forward greedily to the Party's overthrow; but we felt cautious. Against our recent experience in Romania, Bulgaria's current problems looked like luxuries.

'Do you know what is chocolate?' she asked. 'In Bulgaria, little children do not know. I cannot buy chocolates for my children in this country.'

It sounded ideal.

'I think it is very sad. I see their little faces . . . hoping . . .'

'Not hoping, if they don't know what chocolate is.'

'Ah, but I tell them,' Albena said.

Ruse is surprisingly cosmopolitan. Trees line the boulevards of nineteenth-century houses with shutters and false balconies of wrought iron, silt from the Danube, flowing from Vienna. But the Danube opened the Black Sea, too, and brought welcome treats like thick black coffee. Perhaps it was the contribution of Ruse's Jews, as well. Elias Canetti was a Ruse Jew; Bulgaria had protected her Jews from the Nazis. Bulgarian Jews were Sephardim, from Spain via Istanbul. We were going to hear, all through Bulgaria, the echo of Istanbul like a summoning gong.

If I thought I had got the measure of Bulgaria from Ruse I was quite wrong. The atmosphere of cosmopolitan intelligence petered out rapidly into a dry scrub dotted with leafless thorns and a few sheep, and clumps of gorse like pilling on a jersey. It was the landscape that follows the Mediterranean from Provence to the Peloponnese, and always before I'd seen it from a moving window.

It wasn't really the place for walking in midsummer. Mediterranean civilisation worked along the valleys or the coast, wherever it was close to water. Our route south cut against the grain; all the rivers ran like the Danube, west to east, between the corrugated mountain ranges that ribbed the country. Bulgaria is a larger country than Hungary, with a smaller population, unevenly spread. Millions dwell on the Black Sea coast; a million in Sofia. The rest live in small towns and villages. But in central Bulgaria there are almost no villages at all.

It was several hours before either of us spoke: a motorbike driven very fast had shaved us on a corner. It wasn't the first speeding vehicle: the roadside was alien with disintegrating wreckage. It was a landscape of creeping roots and tough, wiry plants, of lizards, and stones, and adders, and the sun. A gauze of dust settled on my boots.

Twice that day we passed through villages. The first village looked like the outskirts of a town, but there wasn't a town and we had to accept that the village had turned itself into a tip without outside help. The Romanian villages on the plain had seemed primitive, with their low mud walls and long sloping roofs, dug into the silt; but they were smarter than this.

Each allotment held a squat dwelling like a bunker that bristled with thorny rubbish: bottomless buckets, torn and rusted scraps of corrugated iron, a half-smothered thorn tree twisting from a ruin of pots, discarded bumpers, tatters and piles of rock. The villages were ushered in by a fanfare of rusting junk and flapping plastic, and trailed away in a fugue of half-buried metal and odd shoes; and there was no-one beyond the boundary at all. The emptiness of the landscape; the wild unfriendliness of the last village; our naivety towards the new country, sent the old horror of pursuit prickling on our napes. A single man trudged after us in the shade of the fruit trees that lined the road, gaining on us all the time.

We stopped, to have at least the advantage of watching our pursuer approach, and let our packs sink to the ground. The man seemed to hesitate, and then came on. He was carrying a small bundle in one hand, swinging it easily as he strode up the hill towards us. Kate suddenly noticed his blue jeans and glasses, and my breathing eased. No country bandit would wear blue jeans and glasses. Whoever he was, he had dropped from the sky: jeans belonged to the town, and glasses, milder still, were the badge of the Intellectual.

The man with the bag was astonished to meet two English travellers on this lonely road. 'You know, I speak English!' he cried happily, making it sound like a famous coincidence. He made us explain ourselves twice, and then shrugged and laughed at the absurdity of it. We fell into step and trudged on up the hill.

We had thought he might be a bandit, we explained, with relieved smiles; he shrugged rather disconcertingly. He had come by bus from Ruse, and cut across country from the highway that shadowed the old road and avoided villages. It had been built in the 1870s by the Ottoman pasha governing Ruse, as a military highway: the young man was an engineer, and knew the history of the road in detail. It was the first road in Bulgaria built in a Western manner. Not that the Turks could have built it themselves; even its bridges had been designed by a Bulgarian engineer. The pasha, astonished by their long, low spans and apparent flimsiness, had ordered him to stand under each bridge while he tried it out with a column of marching soldiers. Privately the Bulgarian had pointed out that the road would prove as useful to an army of liberation as to the Turks themselves.

'That is true,' added the engineer. 'The Russian army use the road to push the Turkish away.'

I realised what bothered me about the villages. It was an odd atmosphere of concealment. There were any number of innocent reasons to explain why both villages had seemed deserted at that hour, and it wasn't the fact that we hadn't seen any people. If the villagers were hidden they weren't hiding themselves consciously; yet they were concealing everything else: what they did, how they lived. I had taken away the impression of people living in bestial poverty; yet, while the impression was strong, it didn't seem quite right. For rural poverty seldom advertised itself. All through Eastern Europe the dwellings of the rural poor were spick and span, surrounded by evidence of laborious thrift: chickens in a run, a pig, a tended vegetable garden. In Poland a broken fence was a curious sight. In Transylvania houses were not merely clean and well-maintained, but elaborately and beautifully decorated. Right now there was a more crucial subject to discuss. I was wondering how it could be broached, when the engineeer asked where we meant to sleep.

In a moment it was arranged. We could have kissed his boots.

We set out the remains of Albena's picnic on the table where it joined the engineer's own bread and cheese. He'd smiled at the bottle of wine.

'Heavy for you, no?' I pointed out that packing was a question of priorities.

When the light faded the engineer lit a paraffin lamp, and the house grew in the shadows. It had belonged to his grandfather, but had stood empty since his death because the family were all in Ruse or Sofia, provided now with steady jobs, and unwilling to take over the little house with its orchard of fruit and its rose garden. This village, the engineer explained, grew rich on fruit and roses. His grandfather's house, which lay, like all the others, invisible from the highway, was a small bungalow of brick with a tiled roof and three rooms. There was no electricity, and no running water; there was an earth closet in the garden, made of corrugated iron, and a well with a stone lid. The engineer would come up here when he had the time, 'to stir the water'. Tomorrow he was checking on the roses: the crop of petals was nearly ready for harvesting.

The village was unlike either of the villages we had passed that day, except in one respect: it was, from the outside, as sealed and forbidding. Instead of rubbish and choked ditches, every dwelling was protected by a high brick wall, with no entrance from the road itself: you had to skirt the wall to find a gateway at the back.

Earlier the engineer had shrugged when we joked about bandits; over supper he expanded his shrug into a series of unnerving horror stories, mostly directed against the Turks we were likely to meet on the road to Istanbul. They were, he said, cut-throats to a man. Bulgarian Turks had unwisely fled across the border when the Zhivkov government, in an effort to retain some popular ity with the people, and divert attention from the state of the economy, had forced them, for example, to adopt 'Bulgarian' names. The Bulgarian Turks had expected kindness and assistance from their fellow-Turks; instead they had returned, dazed, unable to comprehend what had happened to them: beatings, rapes, murders, castrations.

'In Turkey they say, why you stay in Bulgaria?' It seemed that the Bulgarian Turks had nowhere to go: to the Turks they would always be Bulgarians, and to the Bulgarians, Turks; more vampires from the shadow-world between oblivion and reality, more wanderers from another age.

Turkisn rule explained the curious appearance of the villages, the engineer thought. In the face of centuries-long occupation, the Bulgars had gathered together for protection and mutual defence; screening your home from passing eyes was a safeguard. Every village had been under the eye of a Turkish landlord, to whom any sign of wealth was an invitation.

The Turkish menace was still there, a century after the Turks were driven out and Bulgaria proclaimed – after six centuries – an independent state. It was as durable as the traditions established under the occupation – the defensive villages, the show of poverty, the eccentric habit of Bulgarians to nod when they meant no, and shake their head in agreement – traditions designed to confuse and evade. Turkey, thought the engineer, still harboured designs on Bulgaria, and would seize it back if ever the opportunity arose. Six hundred thousand Turkish soldiers were stationed on the Bulgarian border. Until that menace was lifted, it was the duty of every Bulgarian to do his military service for the security of the country – Bulgaria was the only country that wanted to retain the Warsaw Pact. Now that the Pact was dead, only Turkey's desire to join the EEC could guarantee its good behaviour.

As we laid out our sleeping bags on the iron bedsteads, I asked our friend if religion had offered the Bulgars a focus for resisting the Turks. The engineer considered. 'No,' he said. 'Our religion is not very strong.' He thought how he should explain. 'Our Church developed in a different way,' he said, and left it at that.

The road which had risen so abruptly from the Danube sank next day, and the next, falling in slow waves against the yellow fields. Cultivation appeared at last, and trees at the roadside; but the landscape had the loneliness of a dream. Occasionally we were passed by a donkey cart – it was always painted yellow, with shy decoration in green and blue: cornflowers, leaves and tendrils. Once we got a lift, but our weight brought the donkey almost to a standstill, and although the driver insisted we stay aboard he must have been relieved when, sparing the donkey, we slipped off and sadly watched them trotting out of sight.

At Pavlikeni the hotel keeper was at first incredulous, then suspicious, and was on the point of turning us away when he abruptly showed us to a bald concrete cell with a naked bulb and charged us, with an unfettered leer, a large sum of money. We were too tired to argue. Outside the gypsies watched us with a naked gleam in their eyes that beat us back into our cell early for the night.

We rose triumphantly with the dawn, eager to get on the road before the sun did. The town was completely deserted, and we were miles down the road before a speeding Lada told us that Bulgaria was at last awake. We had taken the military road, which ran like a die to Veliko Turnovo, intent on reaching the city before nightfall: almost 30 miles through the heat.

It was a grim day. Around noon we stopped at a roadside kiosk to clear the fogginess and headaches that invariably set in if we started without coffee in the morning. The kiosk woman must have come from some village out of sight, away from the road, because we had passed no habitation yet, and for the rest of the afternoon we tramped an uninterrupted avenue of trees: perhaps the Turks had simply planned well, but it seemed significant that you could drive a straight road through the heart of Bulgaria without touching a village.

The road at last began to slip around, slewing from side to side like a dozing driver suddenly encountering an obstacle. Still skidding, the road careered into a gorge and then braked, with a flourish, before the city.

'City' is a courteous nod towards the glorious past and the underpopulation of central Bulgaria. 'Ruse is the only Bulgarian city,' the engineer had said: even Sofia was something else, an administrative dormitory, perhaps. By that token, Veliko Turnovo was an ancient capital (but there are, in fact, ancient capitals aplenty in Bulgaria, reflecting only the pattern of successive decline and advance from that queen of cities, Byzantium, Constantinople, Istanbul). It had lingered into the modern age as a middle-sized town, dabbling in a little industry, shoring up a row or two of housing blocks in the valley.

The castle had been built beneath the town, instead of the other way round. From the verandah restaurant of the Veliko Hotel you stared straight down at a rock-strewn ridge on which, it was alleged, the castle had once stood. It seemed like an act of faith to discern so much as a single ruin. The view from the verandah encompassed an impressive amphitheatre of mountainside, harsh and forbidding; we naturally sought the castle everywhere except at the bottom of the bowl. We would probably never have noticed it had it not been dramatically brought to our attention that night.

We were halfway through our supper when the lights failed. A few candles winked feebly from indoors. Slowly a thin, reedy flute-note spun out across the dark valley. A sudden puff of pink light exploded somewhere down below. We craned our necks, and the eerie note changed, and was followed by another blink of light, and then another, until the whole valley floor was puffing and blinking like a frenzied switchboard to the quavering note of the mysterious pipes.

A drum rolled. A blue wall, gap-toothed, rose suddenly from the valley floor. Another roll, and this time a pink tower reared out of the darkness on the other side.

The show was immense. Looking over the parapet the following day I could at least see a few scraps of stonework, the line of the fort, and the occasional ruined turret: but for twenty minutes the son et lumière had conjured up an enormous castle out of this unpromising litter from the past. Battles of light had raged from the citadel to the outer fosse; the clash of arms and glint of steel had been visisble along crenellated walls from east to west. Having accepted for so long things that didn't quite work – bulbs that blew and keys that wouldn't turn and telephones that died – we were astonished by the display of technical virtuosity. Our food was cold when the lights came on, but we were impressed.

In other respects Veliko Turnovo lacked warmth. The tourist office issued us with a private room in a flat in one of the blocks, where we flitted through the lives of our hosts without leaving a mark, seldom meeting. The flat was panelled from top to toe in dark wood, and stuffed with a heavy, bourgeois type of furniture that looked more comfortable than it was. There were the ruins of a cathedral, and several shops, and cafés; there were the remains of the castle, of course, and little lanes lined with secret houses leading up to the summit of the town, where the citadel should have been. But there was no reason why we should not push on; no reason but a strange reluctance, a sort of unconscious shrinking from the road.

You could see from a glance that there was something fishy about Arbanasi. The village had street lamps. Here on the mountain top you expected dry stone walls, but not careful, ugly pointing in cement; nor to find the roads tarred.

The official attraction was an ancient church that looked from the outside like a stone byre or a long pig shed. The Ottomans were tolerant of other religions provided they knew their place: it was forbidden, for instance, to build any church that might overshadow a mosque; but the Arbanasi church belonged to the tradition of safeguards and secrecy. Inside were several low vaulted aisles, leading through low doorways into chapels: it was rather like visiting a submarine, except that every inch of walls and ceilings were painted on a background of deep blue: stars, heaven and hell, tiny townscapes, curiously Islamic flower patterns repeated around the tiny windows that admitted no light. The churches I had recoiled from in Romania were bombastic: in them, darkness was amplified to create a mood of fear, an oppressive darkness. The Arbanasi church was mysterious without being sinister, and did not force you to the ground: it met you there.

Two houses in the village were open to the public – all the houses in Arbanasi were huge, and mushroomed out on the first floor so that the upper storey overhung the lower, extended by three-sided window bays. Inside, the ground floor was paved in stone; here were the kitchens and counting rooms, perhaps; for upstairs great divans occupied half a room; stoves were built into the walls, and all the plasterwork was simply moulded, into ferns and flowers. The windows were protected by sliding wooden shutters, and the doors were broad and wooden. It wasn't hard to imagine some odalisque reclining on velvet cushions, her feet close to the stove.

In Arbanasi an enterprising couple had opened a hotel, and we promptly moved in. There were four rooms, and we were given the worst, although a better room was empty. Nevertheless the hotel reached a standard of luxury which we found unimaginable: hot baths, enormous soft towels, drinks on the verandah and good evening meals. We managed, after one night, to inveigle ourselves into the better room, and pretended that we were having a holiday.

A French couple had advised us to move into the hotel: they were staying in an annexe, possibly the house of the hoteliers themselves. After supper we spent the evening in their garden. They were determinedly intellectual and cynical.

'Democracy is a product, products are what we have in the West, and products are what we sell. So Eastern Europe is going to buy our product, the democratic image. In their hearts no-one cares if it works or not, whether it is actually better for them. That is not the issue with products.'

Zhivkov, the last of the old communist leaders in Eastern Europe, had fallen just a few days before. A video showing him ordering in the tanks in December had proved more than parliament could bear; our hoteliers were quite pleased.

On the lip of the amphitheatre overlooking Veliko Turnovo stood a huge white box. I had asumed it to be a water tower or a radar beacon or something; in fact it was a presidential palace and the hoteliers had friends who had the key.

I had rubbed my hands in anticipation. This is surely the peculiar sport of revolutions: staring into the homes of deposed presidents. The Parisian mob had done it in 1790 and 1830; the Romanians did it; even the Filipinos had done it; and now, courtsey of the Bulgarians, I'd do it, too. Was there a Mrs Zhivkov? I could see her shoes stacked up already. A collection of hunting trophies. Gold taps, maybe, rhinestone heels, a jacuzzi polished from a lump of solid quartz.

The approach to the palace was quite good: the tarred road sank and pulled up beneath a flight of broad white steps, leading up to a pair of massive iron doors. Just inside there was a plain formica desk with a reading lamp and a swivel chair. The hallway was carpeted in a sort of cheap office-grade twill, colour plum. There were no pictures or decorations, just bare white walls, pierced with shiny brass uplights.

For the benefit of our guides we trailed through the entire building. Here the Zhivkovs had dinner; here was their bedroom; here was the conference room. We nodded, but there was absolutely nothing to see. The furniture was solid and new: leather sofas, varnished tables, a set of functional wooden chairs with plain covers. There was a normal-looking telephone on a telephone table in every room. There were green or red curtains on a Swish system. There was a fireplace of modest proportions that had recently been swept, and in front of it a rug. Not a Turkish carpet, just a plain wool rug, white. The president and his wife had a white candlewick bedspread. The place looked like a rather spartan dreary international hotel.

'They are going to make it into an international hotel, I believe,' said our guide.

The great heat reordered our packing. Kate finally rebelled against her boots, which was just too hot and heavy, and bought herself a pair of desert boots in Veliko Turnovo in which, to my chagrin, she walked as comfortably as I did in my bulging clodhoppers. There were articles we could not possibly need any more – jumpers and woollen shirts and long johns; books we'd read but were loath to throw away; and Ferenc's carving, and several pieces of embroidery from Poland and Transylvania (presents from people). We sorted them out and made a big parcel, and went into Veliko Turnovo in the French car to send them home.

In the post office the woman nodded and said that the parcel could not be sent. It took us hours to discover why: she kept shelving us by dealing with the customer over our shoulder. At last we got her to ourselves. She folded her arms. She poked at the garments with a pencil as if they were crawling and said that old clothes had to be sent from a customs point. It was a stupid argument: the nearest customs point was Ruse. I didn't believe her. I didn't believe that the Bulgarian regulations made specific reference to old clothes. And I couldn't believe that the customs could not inspect the parcel, if they so desired, wherever it was shipped out. At last, in high dudgeon, we demanded to see the manager.

She did not suddenly remember that old clothes could be sent, after all. She just sat back and gestured to a staircase. Please yourself. See what good that will do you.

The chef had a distinguished quiff of wavy white hair. He sat with his feet up on the table, reading a sporting paper and listening to pop music on the radio. He put his feet down, shook hands, and invited us to sit. We started to explain, as best we could. He turned down the volume on the radio, and faced us again. He was polite, but would not catch our eye, and eye contact is vital if you are to make yourself understood in a foreign language. We repeated our mime when he had folded his newspaper and smoothed it out on the desk, which was otherwise empty. At last he nodded and said, 'No, no, no.'

It took us a moment to work this out. No, after all, means yes in Slovak; but nodding, of course, means no in Bulgaria. His reply seemed to mean nothing at all.

'*Sprechen Sie Deutsch*?' He said at last. I leaned forward eagerly. Now we'd get somewhere.

'*Ja, ja,*' I said happily.

He looked at us sadly and blew out his cheeks. 'Me,' he said in Bulgarian. 'No *Deutsch*.'

The French, in the end, relieved us of our burden, offering to take it with them 'to the West'. We handed it to them gratefully. From the moment it had been refused at the post office it had been heavy as lead.

Kate caught me muttering under my breath while I pored over the map: I was calculating the distance to the border, measuring out the days like a schoolboy crossing out the lessons one by one as the holidays approach. We walked our quotient each day and worried as usual where we'd sleep, fretting over dogs and axemen, sweating uncomfortably in the noonday sun. In the afternoons we walked more cautiously. The afternoons were sleazy now. It wasn't just the casual heat, or the wild driving; it was the thick, concealing foliage of August, the heaviness of the day, the indolent

Mediterranean afternoons that seemed dangerous. Who went abroad when the sun was hottest? We should have been sleeping now. We tramped on, slippery in the heat, pulling our brims low to shade our eyes.

And when we found our bed for the night – in a grey giant hotel in Gabrovo, a hut on a camping site by the monastery at Tryavna, a package holiday resort in the town of Dryanovo – we curled up almost silently, our minds full of the monotony of the road that day, and of the sure monotony of the road tomorow, of forested hilltops, and yellow fields, and the thick green borders of the road.

In reply, almost as if sensing our detachment, Bulgaria made strident efforts to signal its presence. Having spent centuries learning to conceal itself, the country was in a frenzy that it might get overlooked. It spoke, in semaphoric language, about its history, which began little more than a hundred years ago with the period known as the National Revival. Before National Revival, the country was Turkey-in-Europe; and the Bulgars had learned to live in obscurity, digging their churches into the ground, and piling rubbish on their doorsteps. Then, they had been very quiet; but now they were positively bellowing, like children at the end of class; or people coming out of a library; or an awkward party after a glass is broken.

Bulgaria dwelt with insistence on its martyrs and great men. Sometimes it seemed that anyone who had died during the period of National Revival had been tipped for one title or the other. We rambled in every town through a rogue's gallery of tarnished portraits: men with beards, with cartridge belts, with bright-studio lit eyes, with ruffian features, bandoleros. The statues rose almost apologetically at street corners, touching your sleeve. It was a shadow army that Bulgaria enlisted; then rendered physically, a terracotta army like the one dug up in China.

Dryanovo's hero was a young man called George. Son of a local tradesman, a very intelligent youth, the Bulgarian merchants of Ruse had clubbed together to send him to agricultural college. Learn the ways of the West, the path of prosperity, power to the Bulgarians, out with the Turk. So intelligent was this youth that after two years he abandoned his course and the merchants found themselves contributing again to a fund designed to tide him over in Vienna, where he picked up revolutionary ideas and studied agriculture for a while. In his heart, of course, he was burning with patriotic zeal, eager to strike a blow for his oppressed country. He wrote furious articles and returned to Ruse, hidden in a passenger ship. His brilliant incognito, though, was challenged by the slovenly Turkish oppressors as he stepped ashore: drawing a pistol, he fired and killed one of the startled officers before he was hacked down, crying Long Live Bulgaria! There was an etching of the event, a puff of smoke from the pistol, a towering, angry youth, a bevy of shrinking Turks creeping towards him. George was the Bulgarian Petofi, I suppose; with two flunked degrees instead of poetry, and an aimless lonely death at Customs and Immigration instead of battle honours. Yet his name is not likely to be forgotten in Dryanovo; the museum guide was very nearly in tears as she related the story.

'So young. It is what our country had to suffer.'

We were told, too, that this very house had belonged to his father. But that was impossible. The house was brand new. The exposed beams overhead were machine milled, though painted black. The floorboards were regular, the floor was flat, the doors fitted very well. Even the latches and catches were made of blackened steel.

'This actual house?'

'Yes.'

There was no more to be said. We wandered down the road through the old quarter, and saw in amazement that every small old building was being demolished and rebuilt. Levoca's restoration was pretty crass, but this was off the register. The levelling of real old buildings and their replacement with fakes – for the replacements were going up, exactly like the old houses, but straighter, neater, smarter – was so extreme as to be almost visionary. Modern Bulgarians so desperately wanted future generations to understand how deeply they felt about the past. They loved the National Revival so much that they were almost jealous, and wanted a part in it themselves.

*

The Shipka Pass was the pinnacle of Bulgarian self-congratulation, and an agony for us that drove home the significance of the battle that had raged here in 1878. Once the Turks had lost control of Shipka, there was nothing to stop them rolling back to Istanbul: in other words, when we reached the summit, the way to Istanbul was clear. We reminded ourselves of this on every switchback, staggering upwards through a forest that kept us out of the worst of the sun but obscured the view back to the Danube. It wasn't a quiet climb, for the Shipka road gathered all the scattered traffic heading north or south, and funnelled it upwards in a grind of smoky gears and down in a solid braking scream.

The notorious saddle of the mountain was forlorn, binding the bleakness of a high pass with the sadness that lingers over battle-fields. I was reminded of the Serbian soldiers who in 1913 had spontaneously stooped to remove their shoes before they crossed the battlefield at Kosovo, where 600 years before their forefathers had been massacred by the Turks.

There was a grotty hotel infested with Bulgarian children who sniggered at our appearance and played loud rock music in their rooms until the small hours. The pass was cluttered with rival tourist kiosks selling coffee at high-altitude prices. At the side of the road was a lorry with Polish plates; we talked routes with the driver, feeling great affection for him because he was Polish and had come our way: but he had taken three days, and had driven through Yugoslavia, and he was too depressed by the Shipka Pass to respond. He was stuck because his brakes had failed in some way, and he had to wait until his company could send spare parts. Perhaps he had to wait until they could afford to buy them. He'd been here five days, and Shipka had become his prison.

In the hotel the waiter had already plotted an escape. He questioned me closely about Aston Martin, and then produced a road map of Germany from his pocket, spreading it out with such finality and pride that it might have been a magic carpet that would whisk him to a plum job with Deutschmarks in Dusseldorf or Bremen.

We climbed the steps to the beacon behind a girl who cheerfully sang out each step starting from one, until she reached three hundred and saw '300' stamped on the tread in front of her, which seemed to depress even her. We had barely reached the top when the haze turned into clouds that rolled towards us on all sides; we had just time to glimpse a plain beneath us, towns like crop circles, and a lower range of hills in the distance before mists and clouds began to creep towards us like Turks encircling a Bulgarian hero. Fissures of mist began to smoke out of valleys, defining wooded hills that had been indistinguishably blue, one against the other, and in the sudden chill we pelted down the steps to the sound of thunder that never brought rain.

The Pole was asleep in his cab. A Turkish couple alighted from a grey Mercedes and had coffee in a ruinous little bar. He wore a shirt and tie and a granite grey suit with tiny stripes, and wrap-around dark glasses, but his trouser bottoms were rolled up against the heat, revealing hairy brown calves and black socks. His wife wore a white suit and pink lipstick and had her sunglasses pushed up against her black bun. Shipka was like a pivot, around which Poles and Turks tilted like children on a seesaw; but we threw our weight onto the Turkish side, and started down the mountain.

Walking manuals will tell you, with a sort of relish, that it is quite as hard work going downhill as up. The books are written by the people who dress up in the African-parrot costumes we'd seen in London in order to blight the gentle green slopes of the Lake District, or lend their sparkle to forbidding Welsh mountains. Perhaps downhill is hard for them, bounding from scree patch to teetering rock; perhaps, if they didn't tell themselves how hard it was, they wouldn't enjoy it very much. It is a piece of gross deception, and we had a much lighter run of it to the bottom. We could smell the ragged thyme that grew across the plain; and the air had cleared electrically just the night before.

There was a monastery in the trees near the bottom, set up to give thanks for Bulgaria's deliverance: the usual mug shots, a few snippets of uniform, a piece of shrapnel the size of my thumb. We were more interested in the restaurant in the village, where we had raw pork but creamy yoghurt, followed by cups of thin Nescafé, elegant and novel, and costing twice as much as dull old coffee, which they pretended not to have. The waiter wore a stained three-piece suit and dark glasses; he served with trembling fingers and soon lost interest in us, turning to the bottle when some of his friends dropped by for a drink.

Two yellow carts cantered by; the first flushed two menacing curs from a factory compound up ahead. We commandeered a ride on the second as a result; sure enough, the dogs came rushing out and tried to snap at the wheels until they got exhausted and slunk back to their den. The carter jogged along happily in silence; he seemed to be going a long way.

On the way into Khazanlak we stopped off at a small factory to ask the way, and found the place deserted except for a fat girl with black ringlets who sat in a basement flicking herself with rose water and learning English from a book.

'What means, long greasy locks,' she said.

We thought her rude under the circumstances, neither of us having washed our hair for four months. But the question was genuine: I looked at her book, and while everything else seemed to be in order there it was, this bizarre phrase, sticking out from a host of adjectival clusters (cold, dark night; happy, laughing boy). The girl ran a very small museum of roses: roses seemed to have nothing to do with the National Revival, for once. Before we left she doused us liberally in the refreshing rose water, and generously gave Kate a bottle of the stuff. We tried to find our way into Khazanlak according to her instructions.

It took a long time; they were vague instructions and the sub-urbs were big and almost completely empty; once, completely lost and exhausted, we sat in a park and watched a children's party through a window in a block of flats. For Khazanlak, also, was not a city: just an agglomeration of dwellings where rose perfumes were traded. Thriving off roses, it should have been much sweeter than it was.

There was no real centre to the town; we placed it at the doors of the big hotel, though a Khazanlaki would probably suggest the market place, for the town had grown around its rose market, where it sold perfumes for the Ottoman aristocracy.

Close to the big hotel was a café where we stopped for breakfast. Diana stopped there too, a few minutes later.

'I'm sorry, I'm sorry, but I heard you talking in English and I have to say something to you. I must. I know it's very boring for you because wherever you go people want to practise their English. Please say if it is too boring. No, ask me a question. You see, I can't help it. I am just a very boring person who wants to practise their English.'

She delivered this speech in less time than it takes to read. She was only eighteen. I would have voted her in as Bulgaria's president. Politics, in fact, attracted her; but she left them to the future.

'This party, that party. I know it's very important, we must start understanding democracy immediately, but the position of the country is just too serious for politics.

'There's nothing around to buy. Around, you say it like that? Well, you must have noticed. One kind of economy has just, ah, collapsed; the other one works well but always the bad people who become rich. People in the old economy do not afford – sorry cannot – to buy anything from the others. So everything become a little grey, become not quite legal, become not quite capitalist. Become. Becomes? We have Vietnamese who were sent here to work in factories. Now they have no jobs so they run the black market.'

Diana had a delicious, plummy accent and worked her face expressively when she spoke, throwing the emphasis on strange words. *Black* market, *kind* of economy. Her movements followed the speed with which she held two separate conversations at once – one which worked in apologetic counterpoint to her main topic.

'Now the government wants private farmers again. But for years people have been leaving the countryside to have jobs in the cities, working in factories that are no good any more. But they won't go back to the villages, because that work is very hard, and there is nothing for them to do. No cinema or café or anything. Bulgarians are very lazy people.'

She moved her fingers as she spoke. I'd read that the ancient Bulgars, before they moved into the Balkans, had the odd practice of hanging people who had earned a reputation for intelligence. I told Diana she should be careful.

'I am not intelligent, I am very stupid,' she replied, smiling. 'It must be true because intelligent people do not stay in Bulgaria.'

We parted, hours later. 'In Stara Zagora you will stay with me,' she said.

We spent a day crossing the valley that separates the two ranges of the Stara Zagora, the old mountains. We stayed with Diana, and met her friends, off to Sofia to study diplomacy and statistics and the law so that Bulgaria would cease to be the elderly womble they felt it had become. They were an encouraging sight. But we did not stay long: we wanted to be off, as well, snowballing to the south, like sprinters at the end of the race spurting to the tape. To Szilengrad; a succession of cheap hotels, flyblown gypsy villages, and a landscape that was drier than anything I could have imagined.

Near the border we took a room in a seedy motel. Someone argued with the receptionist, shouting angrily in a language she couldn't understand: I was surprised to hear it was Polish. There was a man with an eye patch who watched us fixedly, then turned into his room and closed the door. We felt that we'd fallen like fluff in a bag into the bottom corner of Europe. Outside by the road there were gypsy stallholders, flogging the tat of nations: electronic key rings, disposable lighters, Bulgarian flags, shoddy toys, Chinese razors, bootleg tapes, film, boxes of tissues, hand-cream. Anything that wasn't much use, or wouldn't last, was up for sale: all the fluff in the seams.

Some Romanians sat with their frugal picnic, a moth-eaten yellow dog slunk around the motel, showing its ribs. In the morning we set out with the dawn, when the poverty and shoddiness didn't show; only pockets of shadow behind the rocks, and a haze that quickly lifted from the orchards, and an hour or so of quiet before the traffic fired up.

And before noon, in the first fold of the hills from where you can see across the valley into Greece, and ahead to Turkey, we had the ludicrous misfortune of taking a lift that we simply could not refuse.

A Turkish lorry was pulled up at the roadside, and the driver was heaving and straining at a thick, coated cable, trying to slip the end over a battery electrode. A burnt-out wire lay beside him: somehow he had cannibalised a replacement but it was just too short, and he explained, with great seriousness, that he wanted me to hammer the end home with a wrench while he held it as close to the electrode as he could. We did it; the wire was screwed home; and the driver knew that he was under an obligation. So he offered us a lift.

A casual offer is easily refused without offence, particularly if you can explain the reason. We had no Turkish, and it became obvious that this was not a casual offer. We had done him a favour, and he had to pay it back. It was pathetic. We mopped and grinned and slapped our legs and pointed to the border, and said 'good, good' in a dozen languages, while the driver's face clouded. It was as if, by refusing his offer, we were abusing his generosity, belittling his friendship, doubting his word. I had performed a tiny act of kindness, and now the man was getting angry. Before the situation could develop beyond mere awkwardness we climbed aboard. The driver evidently thought we'd strained politeness a little extravagantly, but he was immensely relieved.

We reached the border in twenty minutes. The Bulgarian woman in the booth refused to change our leva back into hard currency. I couldn't be bothered to press the issue – it was about £5 – but Kate suddenly lost her temper. I had tendered the money on the tray in the window; the woman had pushed it back; Kate now pushed it at the woman again. The woman crumbled, shook her head in craven agreement, and counted out $8 I had not even imagined she possessed.

'Visa?' asked the Turkish guard.

My stomach knotted itself suddenly: I'd never thought of getting a visa for Turkey.

'It is five pounds for each person,' he explained. In relief I asked for the rate in dollars.

'No dollar,' he said. 'British passport, five pounds.'

I couldn't believe he was serious. We had spent months in countries whose notorious bureaucracy was meant to smother you like ivy, but not once had we been smothered quite like we were smothered now by a Turkish regulation that stipulated that a British national leaving home should remember that in six months he would need a £5 note.

'Please, take the dollars.'

'No, no. You must to bank.'

It took a moment to realise that he was pointing with a pencil. We looked round. He was pointing not at one bank but at eight or nine banks in a row.

'Yessir, how can I help you?'

'Excuse me, do you want Turkish lira?'

'Change dollars, sir?'

'Pounds, my friends?'

'Deutschmarks?'

'Excuse me, would you like a cold drink?'

'A Turkish coffee?'

'We offer competitive rates, look. Please accept these maps. You are a tourist? These tickets will bring you great reductions in some fine places. Ten English pounds? Of course, from dollars . . .'

Turkey? Capitalism? It was the bearded lady and the Niagara Falls and the rabbit in the hat rolled into one. Half-a-dozen smiling, friendly faces. A shower of little gifts. It was a trick, but where was the catch?

Indecision was the catch. For months we'd changed our money at the bank, when we found one; stayed in the hotel, when there was a hotel; bought food or meals or drinks wherever we found a shop or restaurant or bar. And what struck us when we crossed the border into Turkey, and had slogged up the main road into Edirne, was not the sight of minarets or the new language but the havering paralysis of indecision we were thrown into.

Everying was profuse. The traffic was thick and you had to judge your moment. There were hundreds of hotels, with practically nothing to distinguish each from the next. There were more goods for sale in a single narrow street than we'd seen in the whole of Bulgaria. Where should we eat? We gazed in stupefaction and admiration at reams of people who were making decisions and mental calculations and nice judgments and arranging things just the way they liked, and tried to be firm about finding a hotel. But it was exhausting because you could never be sure that the next place wouldn't be better, or less expensive, or more expensive but also more of a treat: in fact, there seemed no reason beyond

physical collapse why we shouldn't go on peering into Edirne's
hotel bedrooms through the night.

We plumped for a room in an airy old hotel whose owner spent
the evening in a courtyard hosing his roses and drinking coffee
with an elderly friend.

A slim tiara of sparkling blue crowned the dusty hills below us.
They were playing the Lambada in a restaurant on the beach. We
stopped and rested in the shadow of a minaret, where the muezzin
had already begun to call. *All – ah akhbar!* A fat man rolled onto
his stomach and for a moment I thought he was going to pray,
but he had only been disturbed. He nuzzled the crook of his arm
and dozed off.

We lay on our backs and stared upwards, still with nothing to
say, following the slender line of the minaret that touched the
blue sky, brushing the birds. I hadn't noticed them before.

In the morning, when we'd reached the beach again from the
same hotel, they were there still: millions of birds, coming our
way.

The walls of the city were not visible from afar at all. The view
was blocked by the ranks of concrete holiday homes, cranes, dust
clouds billowing away from the back axles of lorries. It looked
like an enormous penitentiary.

We sat together on the beach. We felt crushed and out of place.
A needling smell of exhaust fumes, salt and suntan lotion had
settled on the beach. A drill echoed behind a wall of scaffolding
and the tiny waves prodded a soft mound of brown foam on the
sand.

We lay back. What were they? Gulls? But gulls were wheeling
and diving over the water; the gulls were screaming. The birds
overhead were all going in the same direction, thousands of them,
beating their wings slowly. They were much higher and much
bigger than I had first thought. They beat their great wings, and
passed by, and still more were beating up from the west, filling
the air, sailing along the coast, utterly silent, astonishingly intent.

I sat up. Storks! Thousands and thousands, beating at our backs
and heading east along the Marmara shore – storks out of Poland,
like the family we'd seen that first morning on a village clock

tower; and the pair we'd glimpsed beating their great wings upriver at Biala Gora, when we left Leon Lis – perhaps they were some-where overhead. The storks who had thrown back their heads and clattered their bills – where? beyond Eger, filling the valley as we descended to Csik Sereda – they, of course, were skimming overhead, high in the air, skimming to Hagia Sophia (we saw them, later, perched on its roof).

And we stood up at last, kicking the sand, and walked into Istanbul.